ROGUES IN THE POSTCOLONY

Histories of Capitalism and the Environment
Bart Elmore, Series Editor

Rogues in the Postcolony

NARRATING EXTRACTION
AND ITINERANCY IN INDIA

Stacey Balkan

WEST VIRGINIA UNIVERSITY PRESS / MORGANTOWN

Copyright © 2022 by West Virginia University Press
All rights reserved
First edition published 2022 by West Virginia University Press
Printed in the United States of America

ISBN 978-1-952271-35-9 (cloth) / 978-1-952271-36-6 (paperback) / 978-1-952271-37-3 (ebook)

Library of Congress Control Number: 2021947908

Book and cover design by Than Saffel / WVU Press
Cover image by Artelka_Lucky / Shutterstock

For Karlo

Happy are those ages when the starry sky is the map of all possible paths.

—Georg Lukács, *Theory of the Novel*

Contents

	Acknowledgments	ix
	Abbreviations	xiii
	Introduction:	1
	Why Can't a Rogue Be a Hero?	
1	Revisiting the Environmental Picaresque:	37
	Plantationocene Aesthetics and the Origins of Cheap Nature in Amitav Ghosh's *Ibis Trilogy*	
2	A *Memento Mori* Tale:	77
	Indra Sinha's *Animal's People* and the Politics of Global Toxicity	
3	Slum Ecologies:	107
	Figuring (Energy) Waste in Aravind Adiga's *The White Tiger*	
	Conclusion:	139
	Beyond Extraction: Imagining Solarity in India's Mineral Belt	
	Notes	165
	References	175
	Index	195

Acknowledgments

My first trip to John Pennekamp Coral Reef State Park in the Florida Keys was in December of 2018. Chris and I kayaked through the mangroves, and I recall thinking about a passage from Amitav Ghosh's 2004 novel *The Hungry Tide* in which the author describes the crab population in the Sundarbans—those little janitors of the sea, whose critical ecological role is often overlooked. Floridian crabs live a similar life.

I often think about this same passage when I go fishing—in the mangroves, in the salt, alongside the dunes of my adoptive state; and I also think about the material conditions that shape the lives of fisherfolk throughout the world—whether in the mangroves of Florida or Bengal (home to the Sundarbans). Their lifeworlds are at turns exceedingly local, and yet inevitably framed by the uneven material conditions that shape our contemporary petrosphere. Casting my line, I think too about what Ramachandra Guha and Juan Aliers have famously termed "varieties of environmentalism," and the forms of conservation imperialism too often practiced in South Florida—a place where the majestic sea turtle is a seemingly more valuable neighbor than the scores of laborers toiling in the state's vast agricultural interior.

Ultimately, my mind then turns to those silly Anthropocene fictions that render the human species as a violent, undifferentiated mass bent on destruction; and I wonder how such fictions might be countered in the popular imagination—how indeed such fictions were countered in my own imagination. I conclude that it is in the stories that we tell, that we read, that we share, and that it matters "what stories we tell to tell other stories with . . . what thoughts [to] think thoughts." Thank you, Donna Haraway. I conclude that it is through the indomitable world of stories, and of narrative, that we come to learn new worlds—that we might engage in radical forms of world-making, if only we listened to those stories that are not hemmed in by apocalypse, nor framed by the neoliberal myths of competition, or greed, or scarcity.

I have spent most of my adult life agitating for political change, specifically in the area of alternative transportation infrastructures and mobility (in)justice. But I came to think more centrally about petrocultures and the material impacts of development through the stories that I encountered during the spring semester of 2015 when I first read Chris Abani's *GraceLand* in Ashley Dawson's seminar at the CUNY Graduate Center. Following Ashley's lead, we explored such postcolonial ecologies as are illustrated in Abani's storyworld, or Aravind Adiga's novel *The White Tiger*. It is to Ashley Dawson that I owe my deepest gratitude: the seed of *Rogues in the Postcolony* was sown in that seminar in an essay, later an article, entitled "Rogues in the Postcolony: Chris Abani's *GraceLand* and the Petro-Picaresque" for a special issue of *The Global South* carefully curated by Leigh Anne Hunt and Sabine Haenni. It was in another of Ashley's seminars—"Postcolonial Ecologies" the following year—where I would further cultivate this project, working with Micheal Angelo Rumore, Sean M. Kennedy, Patrick Abatiell, Morgan Buck, Elizabeth Sibilia, and Rafael Mutis.

Rogues in the Postcolony: Narrating Extraction and Itinerancy in India began as a dissertation for the CUNY Graduate Center under the thoughtful and patient guidance of Ashley, then my advisor, who taught me to be a scholar-activist in every sense of that term. I am deeply grateful for the spirited discussions with Ashley, Robert Reid-Pharr, Alan Vardy, and Siraj Ahmed that culminated in the first version of this monograph—for Robert's consistent support, for his commitment to being a true mentor and teacher, and for his uncompromising faith in my picaresque adventures; for Alan's introduction to John Clare, to commoning economies, and mostly for his encouragement in the pursuit of rich connections across time and space; and for Siraj, whose comments on each draft demonstrate a commitment to teaching and scholarship to which I aspire deeply.

My thinking about the stakes of postcolonial representation began in earnest with Fawzia Afzal-Khan at Montclair State University with whom I would write for the first time about the enabling fictions of neoliberalism and liberal capitalism—among them, Salman Rushdie's *Midnight's Children*. More importantly, Fawzia taught me how to be a teacher.

I am indebted to my indispensable writing circle, in particular: Kelly Keane, a gifted scholar and friend, who traveled this road with me from the beginning; Wendy Tronrud, who carefully listened to the many talks that would culminate here; and Micheal Angelo Rumore, whose generosity is truly boundless, reading draft after draft after draft. Thank you, Mikey, thank you.

I would be remiss in not thanking the faculty union at Bergen Community College who fought every day so that this overburdened teacher could have the opportunity to attend CUNY and to begin what would become a rather picaresque adventure in its own right. Thank you Tobyn De Marco, Alan Kaufman, Michael Echols, Brant Chapman, and Jennifer Lyden for your truly heroic work.

I am deeply grateful for my friends, colleagues, and students at FAU who have continued to support this project in its myriad forms—from our colloquia in CU321 to the less formal climes of the Black Rose. Thank you, Eric Berlatsky, for bringing on the first hire in Environmental Humanities and consistently supporting my work. Thank you, Andy Furman, for being a friend and a mentor in countless ways. Thanks especially to Devin Garofalo, Jake Henson, and Ashvin Kini for reading and reading and reading and listening—and for the laughter and the joy. Jake would also (and painstakingly) pore over much of my writing in our little corner of the English department, most recently the conclusion on environmental justice and "solarity."

Sections of this manuscript have benefited from a vast sea of colleagues, and some have appeared in various forms elsewhere. Brent Ryan Bellamy generously read through my introduction, offering vital criticism and wonderful new avenues for intellectual discovery. I thank Gary Rothbard for poring over the second chapter as it made its way to *ISLE: Interdisciplinary Studies in Literature and Environment*. So too, my dear friend Iemanja Brown who organized a panel for the annual SLSA (Society for Literature, Science, and the Arts) conference where I first presented my work on the postcolonial *memento mori*.

The present version of the third chapter on Aravind Adiga's *The White Tiger* began as a conference paper for a panel at ACLA organized by Jennifer Wenzel entitled "Heat, Light, Motion" which featured the brilliant and inspiring work of Jennifer, Graeme Macdonald, Jeff Diamanti, Corbin Hiday, Mark Simpson, Devin Griffiths, Jamie Jones, Joya John, Michael Rubinstein, Olivia Chen, and Monica Mohseni. It was at that ACLA conference in Washington, DC, where I found a group of spirited friends and colleagues with whom I would continue to work—first at the second After Oil school that same year in Montreal where I would finally meet Imre Szeman, and which was funded by a generous grant from the Peace, Justice, and Human Rights Initiative at FAU for whom I proudly serve as a faculty associate. Imre has been a true beacon, and the invitation to participate in "solarity"—extended by Imre and Darin Barney—proved a watershed in my scholarly life. The After Oil school was a whirlwind of ideas, glimpses of possibility, and hope; and as I worked with my subgroup on "Revolutionary Solarities"—led by the inimitable Dominic Boyer and Jamie Cross—I came to embrace the very real possibility of life after extraction. Imre would also author the afterward to our forthcoming essay collection *Oil Fictions: World Literature and our Contemporary Petrosphere*—here too, acting as both a colleague and a mentor. The collection, which I produced with my dear friend and colleague Swaralipi Nandi, a tireless thinker and wonderful teacher, was deeply transformative—introducing me to a myriad of approaches to petrocultural critique that I have marshaled in my work here.

In the five years that this project spans, my family and friends have been a consistent source of support. It is to them that I am most profoundly thankful: my mother, whose unrelenting devotion is truly unparalleled; my dear sister Jennifer to whom I owe everything—my greatest inspiration, my first teacher, and a constant source of light and beauty; my father, who often reminds me of the fruits of my labor and whose pride fills me with joy; my brother Jeff to whom I owe this new life—thank you for believing in me and for pushing me when I thought I wasn't ready; and to my sweet nephew Karlo, whose laughter is a constant source of hope. I love you Karlo, and I promise to do all that I can to leave you a world that you deserve. And to Christopher: I returned to this project in the fall of 2018 when I first met you, and when you opened up a world that I did not know existed. Thank you for sharing this journey with me, thank you for your kindness and generosity, and thank you for my dear (nonhuman) research assistant Asbury . . . I love you.

Abbreviations

AP	Sinha, Indra. *Animal's People*. New York: Simon and Schuster, 2007.
FF	Ghosh, Amitav. *Flood of Fire*. New York: Picador, 2015.
GP	Ghosh, Amitav. *The Glass Palace*. New York: Random House, 2002.
HT	Ghosh, Amitav. *The Hungry Tide*. New York: Houghton Mifflin, 2005.
RS	Ghosh, Amitav. *River of Smoke*. New York: Picador, 2011.
SP	Ghosh, Amitav. *Sea of Poppies*. New York: Picador, 2008.
WT	Adiga, Aravind. *The White Tiger*. New York: The Free Press, 2008.

Introduction

Why Can't a Rogue Be a Hero?

"How Can a Rogue be a Hero?" Able-to-do countered. "In your small town or dis one, eh? Impossible. Anyway, John Wayne Always Wins."

—Chris Abani, *GraceLand*

Early on in Chris Abani's 2004 novel *GraceLand*, the reader is transported to the city of Afikpo in the years immediately following the Nigerian civil war. Years before the protagonist, Elvis Oke, would have to migrate to "the urban anonymity of Lagos," he spent his childhood there amongst three generations of his family—generations that reflect the shifting political landscape of the nation's interior (Abani 2004, 25). The Afikpo basin, which is one of many sites of petroleum speculation, offers a logical starting point for the novel: some 650 km from Lagos, Afikpo is located in the outer regions of the Niger Delta. The narrative arc traces the forced migration of the Okes from a no longer viable interior economy to the slum communities adjacent to Lagos in order to critique the false promises of fossil capitalism and the global cities that are its hallmark (Sassen 2005).[1]

A concise figuration of the postcolonial *pícaro*, forced itinerancy and, eventually, criminality mark Elvis's character. This rogue in the postcolony, like his early modern progenitors—the itinerant "Lazarillo de Tormes" (1554), for example, scraping by in the shadows of imperial Spain—must vie for survival in the gritty landscape of the late-capitalist city.[2] As such, Elvis's tale offers a prescient glimpse into the sorts of internal displacement and mass migration produced by extractive capitalism, and which have lately figured as narrative signatures in an emergent genre of postcolonial fiction writing: the postcolonial picaresque. Replacing mobility with itinerancy, and adapting the picaresque form popularized in early modern Spain to our contemporary moment, novels such as *GraceLand* lay bare the exigencies of daily life in places like Lagos.[3] The genre serves as a viable counter to the spectacular invisibility of such sites of capital accumulation as the Niger Delta, and the countless mines where precious metals and assorted forms of fossil capital—namely coal and petrol—have galvanized global speculation.

Unsurprisingly, literary critiques of extractive capitalism now occupy a central place in postcolonial artistic production; although it must be said that while the Niger Delta—more specifically, the blasted landscapes of Ogoniland popularized in works by Abani or writer-activist Ken Saro-Wiwa—immediately conjures the violence of extractivism in the popular imagination, it is only recently that the lens of industry critics, including Energy Humanists, has turned to the broader terrain of extractivist violence across the Global South.[4] This shift marks a recognition of the robust corpus of works that similarly antagonize global petroculture and the imperial roots of contemporary regimes of resource colonization. Aligned with such a perspective, the present study turns to India where the aforementioned invisibility of extractivist violence is amplified owing to the proliferation of economies—including opium and coal—that are far less remarked than those attendant to the extraction of petroleum. Even beyond the relative invisibility of India's notoriously violent bauxite industry, and similarly rapacious development programs throughout the nation's mineral belt—invisible, that is, to the end consumer—coal, for example, remains king on the subcontinent despite the false perception of its waning imperium.

India's fossil economy, with its roots in occupied Bengal, instantiates the ways in which extractive economies more broadly are linked through the material and ideological legacies of settler-colonial practices such as obtained in the East India Company's opium program: there is no bauxite, for example, without opium, and there is no opium without coal. So too, no means of extracting minerals without an ideological commitment to an early modern system of taxonomy that would render potential laborers as biologically suited (or not) to the backbreaking work of planting, mining, and extracting. I refer, of course, to works like Carl Linnaeus's 1735 *Systema Naturae* in which the famed botanist would endeavor to taxonomize persons and plants in accordance with newly conceived notions of race (and species), thereby auguring new forms of capital accumulation vis-à-vis the perceived fungibility of the dehumanized laborer. Accordingly, works like Amitav Ghosh's 2000 novel *The Glass Palace*—set in colonial-era Burma, but attendant to the transnational community of Indian migrant laborers working there—trace the genealogy of the modern petro-state illuminating the "imbricated phenomena of colonialist improvement projects, fossil capitalism, and the violent abstractions that gave rise to plantation monocultures and indentured labor" (Balkan 2021a, 1). Ghosh's 2004 *The Hungry Tide* is similarly attentive to extractivism and ecological violence, but shifts the narrative terrain to India's littoral landscape: here the author foregrounds the denuded mangrove systems of the Sundarbans (an archipelago in the Bay of Bengal) tracing the ascendancy of imperial-era monocultures like rice, which began a process of forced displacement that continues today through similar mechanisms of removal. Indeed, while novels like *GraceLand*, or more explicit oil narratives like Saro-Wiwa's *Forest of Flowers* or Helon Habila's *Oil on Water*, track the material impacts of petrocapitalism, works like *The Hungry Tide* and Ghosh's more recent *Ibis Trilogy* chart the *longue durée* of extractive capitalism by illustrating the intersecting phenomena of imperial liberalism, modern taxonomy, and colonial dispossession.[5] Arguably, the trilogy—in its attention to the broader terrain of extractivist violence, and in its consideration of other forms of violence, namely taxonomic—allows for a more potent critique of imperial liberalism than might emerge from the more explicit oil novel.

The case of India also provides a concise praxis for examining new technologies of displacement such as we see in the corporate enclosures that Arundhati Roy documents in the Indian state of Andhra Pradesh—the premier site of bauxite extraction and the basis of her stunning documentary *Walking with the Comrades* (2011). Not unlike the notoriously rapacious petroleum industry centered in *GraceLand*, which is similarly implicated across the subcontinent where former farmers have increasingly become migrant oil workers in the gulf and elsewhere, mining and agricultural companies have ostensibly enclosed the whole of the nation. Such programs of enclosure and dispossession—sanctioned, in Rob Nixon's terms, by "the appropriative ambitions of capitalist and colonialist private-property regimes"—are resulting in unprecedented numbers of internally displaced persons, often from the nation's rural interior through marginally legal land grabs (2011, 596). Corporations like Vedanta Resources or Tata Steel, given license by the federal government under the auspices of economic development, have decimated Indigenous (or *Adivasi*) communities, most notably in Andhra Pradesh where Roy has documented a veritable genocide. Prose writer Mahasweta Devi has famously chronicled these same communities through such characteristically anticorporate works as the 1993 *Imaginary Maps*. As regards the nation's spectacularly successful coal economy, novelist Aravind Adiga charts the forced itinerancy of peasant laborers from the interior city of Laxmangarh (in Rajasthan) to the "coal capital" at Dhanbad, and ultimately to the transient housing communities in New Delhi. Perhaps most famously, similar critiques of extractivism and exploitation have been directed at the nation's cotton belt—primarily in Vidarbha, in the state of Maharashtra—where agricultural companies, sanctioned by the gospel of the "Green Revolution," have produced what scholar-activist Vandana

Shiva has named a "suicide economy" (2005). Demonstrating the suitability of Shiva's moniker, Ghosh's *Ibis Trilogy* traces the history of India's farmer crisis, chronicling precarity and itinerancy through its principal characters.

Departing from post-independence satires like Salman Rushdie's *Midnight's Children* (1981), Indian novelists such as Ghosh dramatize the material impacts of modern improvement schemes on the lives of local farmers—characters made less *magical* by the incisive critiques of imperial liberalism that accompany Ghosh's rich prose style. Notably, Ghosh would critique magical realism explicitly in his recent lectures on climate change, noting that magic "robs" such narratives as Partition (or climate change) of that which is excruciatingly *real* (2016, 27). Deeti, the picaresque protagonist of his 2008 novel *Sea of Poppies*, is a case in point: she is a stunning reminder of the human costs of Britain's improving schemes. So too, a concise instantiation of Rob Nixon's characterization of the displaced commoner cum rogue: a "commons-dependent, wandering pastoralist [who] can be dismissed as an unanchored, rogue anachronism" and "someone who, in Lockean terms, refuses to take root in a private-property regime of purported individual (and thereby collective) self-improvement" (2012, 596).

Joining a mass migration of tenant farmers forced out of British-occupied Bengal, Deeti's story illustrates the impact of colonial-era development models that hinged on privatization and the enclosure of the commons. In novels by Indra Sinha and Aravind Adiga, set in late-capitalist Bhopal and Dhanbad, and also New Delhi, the protagonists inhabit similar worlds; and both must also rely on the conventional wile of the *pícaro* figure to survive. Such novels register imperial violence by replacing the magical exploits of Rushdie's postmodern *pícaro* with a palpable corporeality marked by extreme deprivation and forced itinerancy—two signature tropes of the picaresque genre that can be traced to the sixteenth-century Spanish tradition, and which I shall explore as a possible template for narrating life in the shifting topographies of late capitalism.[6]

Rogues in the Postcolony attends to the contemporary Indian picaresque tradition in order to highlight the form's utility for conjuring displacement and precarity—conditions that are significantly worsened in an era of climate chaos. Against the more laudatory narratives attendant to colonial improvement schemes or similar economic programs under neoliberalism, I examine Anglophone Indian picaresque novels—colloquially termed rogue tales—that respond to and productively complicate dominant historical narratives of Indian development. Critiquing economic policies in colonial and postcolonial India, the present study foregrounds the intersections between landscape ideology, agricultural improvement, extractive capitalism, and aesthetic expression as each obtains in British-occupied Bengal, late-capitalist Bhopal, and the coal-soaked terrain of contemporary Dhanbad. From the transformation of commonly held land for agriculture—primarily poppy and cotton plantations in the nation's interior during British occupation and now under various multinationals—to the establishment of India's spectacularly successful coal industry and the construction of premier urban enclaves made possible by successive forms of extractive capitalism, modern improvement schemes have hinged on the removal of figures, who have lately found expression in novels that replace the enabling myths of developmentalism with the itinerant narratives of the postcolonial *pícaro*. These stories constitute what I read as an "aesthetics of indigence," which brings into sharp focus what picaresque enthusiasts have long characterized as *la vida buscóna*, translated loosely as the "low life" of the working-class protagonist.

The postcolonial rogue figure is a *pícaro* in the literary sense, while it is also an instantiation of the internally displaced persons too often left out of popular globalization narratives. Such narratives include colonial-era paeans to steam-powered industry such as we see critiqued in the *Ibis Trilogy*—a series of picaresque novels set in Victorian India where East India Company officials likened the economic impact of the opium trade to Christian salvation; Manmohan Singh's promise of a "Delhi-cious" new city, or putative "new India" forged in the era of neoliberalism; and, more recently, calls for *Swachh Bharat*, or "Clean India," an initiative championed by current Prime Minister Narendra Modi and a grotesque means of "beautification" that harkens back to Indira Gandhi's Emergency-era slum clearances.[7] Characters like Adiga's fictional Balram (*The White Tiger* 2008) expose the shadows of this "new" or "clean India," whose many problems are "unlikely to be solved as long as the wealthy, both inside and outside the country, choose to believe their own complacent myths" (Mishra 2006).

Rogues in the Postcolony proposes a counter history of the subcontinent through the study of representative picaresque novels including Ghosh's *Ibis Trilogy* (*Sea of Poppies* [2008], *River of Smoke* [2011], and *Flood of Fire* [2015]), Indra Sinha's *Animal's People* (2007), and Adiga's *The White Tiger* (2008). Each foregrounds precarity while dramatizing the material impacts of development programs on local communities and their respective landscapes, whether the denuded poppy fields of Bihar in Ghosh's *Sea of Poppies*, or the toxic slum ecologies produced by the lethal combination of industrial sewage flowing from the nation's coal mines coupled with the soaring population of migrant workers forced to live in the detritus of Delhi's feckless development schemes. The latter is featured in *The White Tiger*. I read such works as presenting a materialist history that unsettles the conventionally teleological trajectories of imperial liberalism, shifting the perspective from what Donna Haraway characterizes as "sky-gazing Anthropos" to the earth-dwelling humans excluded from such "grotesque" euphemisms as "development" (Ghosh 2015c, 53).

Accordingly, more than offering a narrow focus on the aesthetic conventions of the novels, I consider the deployment of particular picaresque tropes as productive means of illustrating the impacts of waves of dispossession on the subcontinent—that is, the impacts on farmers like Deeti, or figures like Sinha's titular protagonist "Animal," whose community inhabits a toxic slum on the outskirts of a fictional Bhopal, its walls constructed out of the detritus of the crumbling pesticide factory. I read such figures as rogues—a more capacious category to indicate a substantive departure from the narrower figuration of the *pícaro*. Additionally, and along with Nixon and other theorists, I trace emergent forms of itinerancy produced by historical shifts in land tenure: the enclosure of common land in rural and coastal India or more recent instantiations of forced relocation as the proliferation of cataclysmic weather events dovetails with militarized immigration policies.

The rogue figure, of course, has a long history. In what follows, I consider its genealogy in light of both its economic and aesthetic registers. The rogue has been defined as a "wandering pastoralist" or displaced farmer or tradesman (Nixon 2012, 596); an "unsteady proletariat" made so by a shifting agrarian economy (Linebaugh and Rediker 2012, 20); a "half-outsider," whose position conjures the strange geographies of late capitalism—described also in terms of states or zones of "exception" (Guillén 1971, Stoler 2002, Agamben 2005); and an unreliable narrator, whose pseudo-autobiographical tale functions as an apologia for a criminal underclass, and whose signature hucksterism once produced beloved figures like Lazarillo de Tormes.[8]

Owing to Lazarillo's tale, and its affordances for thinking about contemporary forms of displacement, I locate the aesthetic roots of the contemporary rogue figure in what Stephen Greenblatt (2012, 25) has characterized as Europe's "Machiavellian moment . . . with its subordination of transcendent values to capitalist values," when the rise of rogue pamphlets coincided with London's poor laws, and when the emergence of the Spanish *picarescos* coincided with like attempts to criminalize its own burgeoning underclass. Such postcolonial picaresque novels as Sinha's *Animal's People* serve a similar end to the early modern rogue tales, be they the English "cony-catching" tales, which were ostensibly dime-store crime novels, the anonymously written *Lazarillo de Tormes*, or Francisco de Quevedo's (1626) *Él Buscón*. Thus, in what follows I move between aesthetic and economic histories of roguery in order to highlight their imbricated, which is to say mutually constitutive, chronologies. I consider how, for example, the criminalization of the poor is characterized by the same rhetoric in both the early pamphlets and in England's Poor Laws; or in a contemporary context, the fabricated accounts of trespassing and similar crimes being ascribed to evicted farmers in India and elsewhere.

La Vida Buscóna

In his 1907 *The Literature of Roguery*, Frank Wadleigh Chandler comments on the peculiar nature of the picaresque form—a genre that would centralize images of low life (or "la vida buscóna") in the face of literary traditions that generally favored more heroic protagonists. Literary humanism had no place for the vagaries of the everyday. In highlighting this aesthetic enigma, Chandler's project anticipates a rich discussion of roguery that has continued to focus on such figures—called alternatively rogues, or *pícaros*, by extant critics. Also taking up this discussion, Claudio Guillén, in *Literature as System* (1971), would introduce the concept of the "half-outsider"—a formulation of internal displacement that he used to categorize the liminal position of figures like Lazarillo and which I argue is evocative of persons in Ghosh's Bengal, Adiga's Delhi, and certainly in Sinha's Bhopal.

But while the figuration of the "half-outsider" is germane to both the Spanish and Indian traditions, other oft-cited picaresque tropes, namely "wandering and adventure," often take center stage in discussions of the form. Robert Alter's definition in his much remarked on *The Rogue's Progress* (1965) is exemplary of this distinction. In his study of the European and British traditions, Alter defines the picaresque novel thus: "It is the adventurous story of a rogue's life, usually told in the first person . . . an episodic account of wanderings, adversity, and ingenious role-playing [which] incorporates a satiric view of society" (1965, viii). Less interested in "adventure" than Alter, Guillén also emphasizes the first-person perspective. Guillén reads the device as a means of establishing what he calls a "pseudo-autobiography"—one of eight criteria that he argues is central to our understanding of the form and a productive means, I argue, of antagonizing such "enabling fictions" as the autobiography.[9] Notably, in Lisa Lowe's (2015b) remarkable study of the "intimacies of four continents"—which is to say the immiscible histories of liberalism, indenture, and plantation slavery—she characterizes the genre of the modern autobiography in similar terms, citing Olaudah Equiano's 1789 narrative, a conversion tale notable for its alignment with an emergent narrative of uplift. We might also think of Martin Delaney's picaresque novel *Blake* (1861–62) as a parody of contemporaneous tales of uplift and conversion that, like *Blake*, were narrated from the perspective of "history's outcast burdens" (Delaney 1971, 101). The latter is perhaps more to the point.

In Rob Nixon's account of the picaresque form, he augments Alter's definition with an explicitly economic dimension arguing, "questions that have powered the picaresque from its beginning [include] what . . . it means to be reduced to living in subhuman bestial conditions" (2011, 67). He continues, for "the indigent masses for whom life [is] an hourly scramble . . . the *pícaro* achieves a particular potency as a marginal literary figure, a seldom-heard voice, who nonetheless belongs to the statistical majority" (56). Giancarlo Maiorino makes a similar claim in the context of sixteenth-century Spain: "Like the great navigators of this era," he argues, "picaresque writers charted journeys through the vast geography of poverty, giving literary form to the indigent humanity that nobody wanted to discover" (2003, 7). Significantly, though, Nixon is speaking about a contemporary Indian novel—Sinha's *Animal's People*. It is worthwhile to note that such recent critics, in acknowledging the "subhuman conditions" of this particular rogue, likewise complicate earlier definitions of the *pícaro* in the context of the European and British traditions. Specifically, Alter notes that the *pícaro* often "volunteers to serve" his many masters, but in the colonial (and putatively postcolonial) context this is clearly not the case.

In working toward a stable definition of the picaresque as a "genre," "narrative," or "novel type," generations of critics have bemoaned what might seem problematic slippages between the rogue figure more broadly and the *pícaro* specifically. As a means of solving this problem, I look to the Spanish novels as a prototype, not because they are originary in the sense that they produced what I (and others) read as picaresque conventions, but because they deploy them in a way that I see as generative for postcolonial critique. That is, I look to particular conventions that are often aligned with the Spanish tradition in my consideration of the aesthetic and political nature of the Indian novels under study: the unreliable first-person narration, or the pseudo-autobiography; the nonlinear or episodic form; the persistent leitmotif of hunger, which is often illustrated using grotesque tableaus of privation; and the *pícaro*, whose itinerant journey is set into motion not by any random event, but by forced displacement, if simply the material exigencies of daily life.[10] These particular conventions are quite useful in critiquing both the economic conditions that produce "half-outsiders" over and again as well as those enabling fictions that sanction them either explicitly or implicitly under the pretense of popular economic ideology. Instantiating the former, the 1793 permanent settlement in Bengal, the 1969 enclosure of Bhopal, and the 1995 GATT agreements would privatize much of the corporate, industrial, and agricultural sectors. Each relied, in various ways, on European economic doctrines predicated on theories of private property and free markets, whose mechanisms perpetually reproduce similar instances of displacement and dispossession. To build on

Raymond Williams's (1973) prescient remarks, what we see in colonial Bengal or in late-capitalist New Delhi, where poor communities are criminalized in the service of contemporary improvement schemes, is quite similar to what occurs in eighteenth-century Northampton.

I knowingly rely on Raymond Williams's famous formulation in *The Country and the City* (1973), although I do not easily accept the figure of the country as always already peripheral to an imperial center. I also recognize that Williams's particular focus on place is problematic for a postcolonial praxis, as was made evident in arguments by Paul Gilroy and Stuart Hall in the 1980s. The parochialism immanent to Williams's critique—namely the archive itself—surely belies a myopic sense of Britishness. So too, the modern factory system which is generally considered symbolic of the pivot to industrial capitalism, and thus from a discrete rural imaginary to an urban one, finds it roots centuries earlier in the plantation system in the Americas—imperial networks forged through the nascent Columbian exchange and underwritten by the Spanish crown—as well as the broader trans-Atlantic and Indian Ocean economies. Hence arguments by Donna Haraway (2016) and Anna Tsing (2015) (and countless others) for the recognition of a different genealogy for the Anthropocene, or "age of humans," which has been much contested owing to its elision of the very histories that the novels collected herein seek to map. Without belaboring the point, and as I shall explore in the context of the *Ibis Trilogy*, such formulations as Tsing and Haraway's "Plantationocene," for example, offer critical departures from the normative eschatology of Anthropocene narratives that consistently ignore the apocalypse of the long sixteenth-century in favor of the hubristic fantasies of colonial man.

But all of this notwithstanding, I do find much of Williams's project to be quite useful—particularly his argument for the rhetorical greenwashing of peasant labor and the enclosure of the commons, which surely resonates here and is taken up by Vandana Shiva (2005) in a similar vein to characterize India's "new" enclosures. Each is sanctioned by an economic model that privileges the accumulation of capital, and which thrives on dispossession and the criminalization of the (largely) rural poor. Following successive acts of "enclosure," "all customary relations of the poor to the land (including what was defined as 'trespassing') were prohibited and seen as transgressions against the monopoly of the forest owners over the land" (Foster 2000, 67). A common image of colonial dispossession is concisely illustrated in Ghosh's *River of Smoke*, the second installment of the *Ibis Trilogy*, in which one character describes the effective sacrifice of Indian and Chinese peasants: "This is indeed the cruelest aspect of this trade," Ghosh's Barry muses, "that a few rich men, in order to grow richer, are willing to sacrifice millions of lives" (435).

This particular form of "accumulation by dispossession" is also realized formally through the picaresque genre's common deployment of a kind of transversality—that is, the way that figures like the peasant farmer function in dialectical relation to the emerging bourgeois subject (Harvey 2005). Pace Elvis's friend's remarks in *GraceLand*, a "rogue [can't] be a hero," because his alterity serves a genuine economic function. Figures like Ghosh's Deeti—an illiterate peasant farmer, whose land is allocated for poppy cultivation—are, according to Maiorino, necessarily "sacrificed to the 'better' society . . . celebrated in 'great men' historical narratives" (Abani 2004, 113). Echoing Maiorino, Bruce Robbins would also contend that "it is only by virtue of these monstrous others that 'narrative becomes possible' " (2007, 254). Such persons are often read as evincing a transversal (or parallel) quality: as figures of "radical alterity," they bolster an emergent bourgeois subjectivity (Dionne 2006). To wit, "the true crime of a vagabond was to remind everyone of the ephemeral nature of the social order, his presence an unpleasant symbol to those newly 'stalled' men in the legitimate corridors of power that their own identity was a sham" (Dionne 2006, 55). This is surely the case in novels like Adiga's *The White Tiger*, wherein the tenuous nature of a new middle class is thrown into relief by the roguish Balram—a slum dweller turned chauffeur who ultimately murders the coal speculator who employs him.

However, as we know from the voluminous work by scholars within critical race studies like Sylvia Wynter, Denise Ferreira da Silva, Alexander Weheliye and others on the figure of the human and the specter of Blackness, such a transversal model might unwittingly reproduce a neat binary that ought to be unsettled in our thinking about the category of the human qua subject, and surely the category of citizen. Alterity ought not be deemed a stable category: as I discuss throughout the present study, such notions of a "subaltern" have long been indicted, and rightfully so, for glossing a heterogeneous subaltern as a uniform underclass.[11] As we shall see in our discussion of the Ghosh novels especially, the reduction of the subaltern to an amorphous class—ever silent in Gayatri Chakravorty Spivak's (1988) famous formulation—is a form of epistemic violence that makes possible the technologies of material dispossession that the *Ibis Trilogy* expressly critiques (see Wynter 2003). Pace Wynter, the human ought really to be considered as a praxis for a particular mode of subject formation against which the *inhuman*—the slave, the colonial subject, the miner—is perpetually rendered a fungible object, inert and without agency. It is worth mentioning too that such a "creative ontology"—that is, one that recognizes the dynamism of human subject formation—is particularly critical in our consideration of Indian Ocean identities in the age of sail, such as we also see demonstrated in the Ghosh novels.[12]

So why indulge in such a seemingly outmoded intellectual paradigm? Transversality is a useful model for thinking through the ways that the early modern rogue tales (and their postcolonial analogues) functioned in contradistinction to the heroic tales of an emergent bourgeoisie.[13] That is, the rogue tales served as robust critiques of emergent formulations of personhood tied to Lockean notions of improvement of both self and property. Like the late-capitalist rogue figure eking out a living in the makeshift slums of Delhi, and who is caricatured in popular comics as we see in Adiga's novel, the workers of early modern London were subject to similar political and *aesthetic* representation. The figures of Europe's underclass, who find themselves caricatured in the "cony-catching" pamphlets of the day, engendered an aesthetic tradition of roguery, which I argue augmented contemporaneous political sentiment (in Britain and its colonies) through the medium of a criminalized underclass. In fact, " 'rogue literature' (the tabloids of its day) *influenced* statutes" such that "the word 'rogue' itself seems to have migrated from rogue literature into the Poor Laws" (Woodbridge 2001, 3). It is my contention that the rogues in the postcolony—the protagonists in the novels of Ghosh, Adiga and Sinha—have much in common with such figures, including vagabonds like "Lazarillo." Thus, throughout this study I remain alert to the onto-epistemological violence attendant to the figuration of the human within Enlightenment-era imperial discourse and its attendant fictions, while also considering the persistence of certain formal elements of the picaresque genre (inclusive of the trope of transversality) and their political import. Additionally, and given the slippery historiography of the picaresque—a form of literature that Peter Dunn characterizes as a "virus . . . invading the genres of travel literature, of satiric poetry, of romance, of soldierly adventure, of autobiography, of ingenious swindlers (male and female)," and which literary historians have sought to "encode in identical devices and homologous patterns" despite its inherent resistance—I craft a theory of the genre that makes claims to both its economic and aesthetic registers, while avoiding the trap of a generic model that privileges literary codes over the material exigencies that produce so-called rogues at multiple moments in the long and violent history of capital (11, 8). It is to this history that I now turn.

Enclosing the Commons

Transformations in property relations in the period marked by new mechanisms for "improvement," celebrated in Adam Smith's (1776) *An Inquiry into the Nature and Causes of the Wealth of Nations* and based in part upon John

Locke's (1689) new theory of property—that is, land as capital—tended to produce the conditions for the emergence of rogues. In their study of the revolutionary Atlantic, Peter Linebaugh and Marcus Rediker note what they call the "statutory meaning of 'sturdy rogue' and beggar": "all those outside of organized wage labor, as well as those whose activities comprised the culture, tradition, and autonomous self-understanding of this volatile, questioning, and unsteady proletariat" (2013, 20). "Organized wage labor" is here shorthand for a new system of agriculture (and consequently trade) that would replace the social and economic fabric of the commons in England, its American colonies, and its "permanent settlement" in Bengal. That is, beginning in the fifteenth century, and accelerated greatly during the eighteenth century, land was enclosed by acts of parliament whose philosophical and economic justification may be located in works like Locke's 1689 *Second Treatise of Government*.[14] In his essay on property, Locke (2002, 17) would make his now infamous argument for enclosure and privatization:

> He who appropriates land to himself by his labour does not lessen but increase the common stock of mankind. For the provisions serving to the support of human life produced by one acre of enclosed and cultivated land are . . . ten times more than those which are yielded by an acre of land of equal richness lying waste in common.[15]

Thus, and following Linebaugh and Rediker's definition, the rogue figure can be understood as the commoner, who by dint of his new legal status was rendered an "anachronism," if not an aberration, when read against the new citizen-subject whose mode of husbandry relies on a presumed ability to reason—to be, per Locke (2002, 15), "industrious and rational":

> God gave the world to men in common, but since He gave it them for their benefit and the greatest conveniences of life they were capable to draw from it, it cannot be supposed He meant it should always remain common and uncultivated. He gave it to the use of the industrious and rational (and labour was to be his title to it); not to the fancy or covetousness of the quarrelsome and contentious.[16]

As conceptions of citizenship and statehood were being cultivated in the popular imagination (and in political doctrine) in accordance with economic theories that professed a new understanding of property and agriculture, the idle rogue was necessarily cast as both an anachronism and an impediment to state-building—"quarrelsome and contentious" as he presumably was. That is, the citizen-subject would be defined in contradistinction to this idle and savage figure both in the colonies—Virginia, Massachusetts, or Bengal—where traditional modes of husbandry would be displaced by new forms of systematized agriculture and land tenure, and also in England where agricultural enclosures over an approximately 300-year period would account for the seizure of some six million acres of formerly common land. It is precisely this conception of the citizen-subject and their putative counterpart—the aforementioned rogue anachronism—that would account for such literary figurations as the abovementioned cony-catching tales and picaresque novels of the day. Soon thereafter, these "little, dirty subjects" would become fodder for landscape artist Thomas Gainsborough's imagination; and in a literary context, Romantic poets William Wordsworth and Samuel Taylor Coleridge would similarly render what they would characterize as "rustic" subjects in the famous 1798 *Lyrical Ballads*—the latter formulation the premise for Raymond Williams's (1973) argument regarding the poetic greenwashing of enclosure and dispossession.

Although, and as we know from the satirical tales of C16 London, the rogue who features so prominently in Marxist discourse—the dispossessed farmer for whom enclosure can be read as the original sin of primitive accumulation—was not only to be found in Williams's Arcadian countryside. As common areas—both for pasturage and for wastes—were enclosed, and laborers were rendered without work and without means of subsistence, they joined an existing class of so-called vagabonds who had, in the early modern period, been established as a sort of criminal class. These are the figures of London's underclass—the swindlers and knaves that feature in the early literature of roguery as well as in its correlative visual traditions. The surfeit of cony-catching pamphlets in London, along with similarly popular images in Spanish Baroque paintings like Diego Velázquez's "Aguador," or instantiated by *pícaros* like "Lazarillo," attest to the popular sentiment regarding the underclass in the sixteenth and seventeenth centuries.[17] The eighteenth-century rogue in the countryside (not to mention in Locke's "vacant" American Eden, or colonial Bengal circa 1765) would join this teeming underclass both in terms of their economic position and also in such popular images. If, in the eighteenth century, these figures would find their way into the picturesque works of Gainsborough, then in the sixteenth century, spectators were amused by Velázquez's impoverished street urchins.[18]

Critics read the rogue figure not merely as a fictional scoundrel, but as an illustration of a newly itinerant laborer who finds literary representation in what was less a series of actual criminal accounts than a fetishized genre—that is, the cony-catching pamphlets whose questionable purchase on fact is the focus of much discussion. Painting the new peddler, who ekes out a living in London's murky shadows as a rogue or vagabond, served the purpose of criminalizing persons who were read as impediments to economic progress. Linda Woodbridge (2001) remarks accordingly:

> Fear of disorder . . . was deliberately fueled by authorities, especially the Crown, to justify the growth in power of a centralized state—subversion generated in order to be contained. Marx held that it was in exactly this period and exactly this nation, England, that the preconditions for capitalism came together and that the existence of a vagrant class was one of those preconditions. (5)

She further comments on the many "myths" of roguery by reminding her readers that the food riots were incited "not by vagrants but by settled tradesmen—a cutler, several clothmakers, a shoemaker, a smith; the leader of Kett's Rebellion in Norfolk in 1549 was a tanner" (7).

The literature of roguery (both the pamphlets and the "rogue novels" like *Lazarillo*) of the sixteenth and seventeenth centuries served to "restructure a civic urban identity important for the materialization of an emergent bourgeois culture" (Dionne 2006, 35). As Anna Bayman further observes, works like Robert Greene's and Thomas Dekker's "highlight the tension between titillation and moralizing that many pamphlet writers, including those of the earlier rogue texts, sought to disguise" (2007, 7). Bayman continues: "Delight and edification, they insisted, could operate together; as Greenblatt notes of Harman's work, subversions are contained within the texts' 'affirmations of order' " (7). In this sense, the rogue figure was clearly a manifestation of sixteenth- and seventeenth-century social anxieties.[19] The prolific publication of their tales is explained by Woodbridge (and others) as a projection of such bourgeois anxiety. I argue, following Woodbridge and Dionne, that we might consider the role of both the cony-catching pamphlets and the rogue novels, in their capacity to simultaneously establish a bourgeois class while necessarily criminalizing the underclass other or subaltern, as an early instantiation of similarly problematic representations in the colonies. Such examples include what Ranajit Guha calls, in the context of colonial India, the "prose of counterinsurgency"—that is, colonial registers which spectacularized encounters with putative insurgents (usually just local peasants) in the service of reinforcing British moral and political hegemony. We see this too in the "false encounters" that Roy (2011) documents in the context of twenty-first century Andhra Pradesh—this time, the Indian government similarly constructing fantasies of a criminal rogue to secure their own power. All of these examples are instances in which the genre of counter-insurgency lauds the forces of social control that effectively police a subaltern class with little recourse to truth. In the latter example, the "false encounters" serve to further government programs that are but thinly veiled proxies for private corporations looking to foment a bourgeois class whose anxieties about the "teeming countryside" are assuaged when the insurgent qua farmer is killed (Fanon 1995).

While recognizing the vastly different material contexts of these moments in the history of capital, I suggest that the rogue figure—as itinerant laborer and literary trope—persists in serving a generative "discursive function" (Dionne 2006).[20] Although, and as Dionne also observes: "It is impossible to ignore (if materialist history is to mean anything) what makes rogues and vagabonds of the sixteenth centuries distinctly different, especially when we situate these texts in the context of a fractured, culturally diverse social space of early modern metropolitan London," not to mention colonial and postcolonial India (2006, 38). Of course, we might also consider that the speculative potential of fiction—as world-making apparatus and praxis for crafting new political imaginaries—suggests that we might still look to the picaresque form despite markedly different contexts. Its formally subversive timescales—nonlinear and nonteleological—allow for a potentially radical unsettling of dominant literary forms that align with the sorts of developmentalism that I critique here and which Joya John characterizes in terms of a "developmental temporality."[21] I thus maintain that the rogue then and now is a "dark mirror" of the becoming bourgeois subject in early modern London or colonial and late-capitalist India despite clear differences in structures of power.

A Taxonomy of Roguery

In a column for the *New Left Review* some thirty years ago, Immanuel Wallerstein remarked: "In the mythology of the modern world, the quintessential protagonist is the bourgeois. Hero for some, villain for others, the inspiration or lure for most, he has been the shaper of the present and the destroyer of the past" (1988, 91). Following Wallerstein, I read the *pícaro* as the quintessential *antagonist* in this "mythology." Denied the means of social mobility that are the myth's hallmark, the rogue's presence mocks the triumphalist narrative of uplift that functions indeed as "inspiration or lure for most." Defying narratives in which "expanded production and resource extraction serve to generate shared improvement, these novels highlight the imbricated relationship between accumulation and dispossession by foregrounding the damage caused by such endeavors and by flouting ideas of linear chronological progress" (Balkan 2015, 22). Despite the contention by critics like Alter and Stuart Miller that the picaresque form presages that of the *Bildungsroman*, or popular "coming of age" tale, the sorts of self-realization and social incorporation upon which the *Bildungsheld's* progress hinges are notoriously absent from such novels as *Lazarillo*, if not especially in Sinha's *Animal's People*. The Sinha novel expressly critiques the possibility of normative subject formation—i.e., the aforementioned self-realization and/or social incorporation—by explicitly rejecting its protagonist's development.

To be fair, though, there are different strands of roguery. Despite the enduring political resonance of the abovementioned *pícaro*, the picaresque novel is one species of rogue literature. This is an important distinction, because the sixteenth-century Spanish form departs ideologically from the cony-catching tradition. That is, while "rogue literature was pan-European," the picaresque novel is rightfully the product of such rogue pamphlets as Robert Greene's *The Defense of Cony-Catching* (1592) rather than, for example, Thomas Harman's indictment of this mythical figure in his scathing 1566 *A Caveat for Common Cursitors Vulgarly Called Vagabonds*. Like Greene's *Defense*, *Lazarillo* is also a defense, not an indictment, of the vagabond. He tells his readers as much in his prologue. For this reason, the convention of the unreliable first-person narrator—or Guillén's "pseudo-autobiography"—becomes a distinguishing criterion of what is taken for granted as a stock signature of the picaresque novel.

There are other critical differences as well: the Spanish *picarescos* centralized not a displaced tradesman but a wanton criminal. They were parodies of Spain's inequitable caste system—a system that favored the landed gentry, who were the sole beneficiaries of Spain's exploits in the Americas. One did not ascend in sixteenth-century Spain. Thus, rather than critique farcical narratives about social mobility, here criminality is foregrounded—be it of the vagabond, the corrupt clergy, or the fallen aristocrat who we meet in the third *tratado* of *Lazarillo*.[22] Given that Spanish wealth hinged on the accumulation of capital in its American colonies by way of the dispossession of Indigenous persons (and at home by way of the extermination of its own, largely non-Christian, peasantry), I see the Spanish picaresque tradition as particularly germane to a discussion of accumulation by dispossession in India. While novels like *The White Tiger* and *Animal's People* give primacy to the farce of economic mobility, they likewise centralize criminally mischievous protagonists who know that the sorts of hucksterism made famous in *Lazarillo* is the only plausible means of getting along. *The White Tiger*, perhaps especially, excoriates conventional progress narratives through its foregrounding of the waste of empire and the manifold ways in which formerly colonized communities become, in Ashley Dawson's (2011) terms, so much "excremental" humanity or surplus.

Lazarillo as a Prototype for the Rogue in the Postcolony

In Mikhail Bakhtin's (1937) foundational essay on the chronotope, or "timespace," of the novel, he described the *pícaro* as analogous to what he called the "third man"—a figure who was generally positioned not in the central narrative frame, but instead along the "roadside." Less an articulation of center and periphery, Bakhtin offered a model for imagining the sort of transversality described above and which marks the formation of what Ghosh has elsewhere described as the "bourgeois regularity" of modernity—materially constituted by the dialectical relationship between productive labor and its excrement, and bolstered by contemporaneous pleas to the rational along with the literary forms that augmented their imaginative and political impacts.

Bakhtin would also offer that this "third man" was a figure of synthetic critique owing both to his parodic nature as well as to the often-performative quality of his character. Historically, the *pícaro* was also a sort of jester—literally performing in troupes as in the 1626 *El Buscón*, and more recently in Abani's *GraceLand* and Peruvian author Daniel Alarcón's *City of Clowns* (2006). Quite fittingly then, in their formulation of the *pícaro* qua rogue, Linebaugh and Rediker offer the figure of Shakespeare's "Trinculo" from *The Tempest* who ultimately foments a sort of alternative "hydrarchy" with Caliban at the helm as the prototypical rogue—a *pícaro* of sorts who is duplicated over and again in much postcolonial discourse. I would, however, and as so many have before me, simply offer up the figure of Caliban.

Roberto Fernández Retamar once asked that we recognize in Caliban the foil of the world. In *Rogues in the Postcolony*, I read figures like Caliban as a member of a sort of postcolonial rogue's gallery (despite his early publication) comprised of the surplus populations necessarily produced by global capital shifts and correlative enclosures of Native land. As Silvia Federici notes in *Caliban and the Witch: Women, the Body and Primitive Accumulation* (2004, 11): "Caliban [is] a symbol for the world proletariat and, more specifically, for the proletarian body as a terrain and instrument of resistance to the logic of capitalism." But more than simply an "instrument of resistance," Caliban—as the "proletarian body," and thus ostensibly capitalism's fundamental other—enacts the prototypical position of the rogue. Prospero's lament that "this thing of darkness is mine" precisely mimics the sentiment of what I have argued is the transversal nature of the rogue in the postcolony.

If Shakespeare's "Caliban" offers a prototype for the "proletarian body," "Lazarillo" offers a prototype for what Patrick Chamoiseau (1997, 314) would later read as a "proletariat without factories and without work"—those new proletarians, who continue to exist "outside of organized labor." Understood in this way, we can trace a genealogy of the rogue figure—as other, as proletarian body, as site of resistance and struggle, as "excremental" subject—from Lazarillo to Don Pablos (*El Buscón*), and eventually across the Indian Ocean to Animal (*Animal's People*), to Balram (*The White Tiger*), to Deeti and her many "ship-siblings" (in *Sea of Poppies*), and also to Salman Rushdie's Saleem Sinai (*Midnight's Children*), however much critics have neglected the picaresque qualities of his explicitly pseudo-autobiographical tale.[23]

Owing to the tenuous nature of his existence—a *converso* who, as "half-outsider" must survive on his wits—the *pícaro* who we meet in *Lazarillo* is a logical literary and political progenitor in our thinking about similar persons for whom the notion of ascent and social mobility are also absurd.[24] This (unfinished) episodic novella, takes the form of seven satirical vignettes; each *tratado* is exceedingly brutal in its conspicuous illustration of privation and hunger. The vignettes chronicle the life of "Lazarillo" (his name, the diminutive of the more famous Lázaro—itself a means of satire and caricature). "Lazarillo" was also born on a river, but was the son of a millworker (who was later imprisoned for theft), and a prostitute made so by her husband's conviction and untimely exit.

Centralizing such a rogue had again been popularized in visual works, but *Lazarillo de Tormes* was unique in its deployment of new narrative conventions such as its unreliable (first-person) narrator, and its episodic format. If Srinivas Aravamudan (2011) recognized in his category of "Enlightenment Orientalism" the "pseudoethnographic" or "pseudobiographical" nature of what was ostensibly Orientalist agitprop, in the anonymously published *Lazarillo de Tormes* we have an intentionally satirical, and overtly critical, portrait of a rogue who now purports to tell his own story. Notably, in Aravamudan's earlier *Tropicopolitans* (1999), he would also remark on the preference for first-person narration as an "emancipatory trope"—along with what he called the autobiography's implicit "ideology of progress." The latter is also brilliantly mocked by the picaresque form.

The rogue, or *pícaro*, tells you that he is not be trusted, and he then proceeds to offer caricatures of actual moments whose violent effects we know all too well. The *conversos* were not so many wily outcasts; they were exiles—violently displaced and forcibly moved into such positions. Thus the early caricature, like its postcolonial descendants, has an evident material substrate. This is precisely the case in *Animal's People*, which is narrated by an exceedingly roguish figure—perverse and often quite offensive—who we know often lies, but who we also know is the product of a new form of enclosure that has directly produced his deformed state. Walking on "all-fours," his namesake ("Animal") is fitting—itself an antihumanist caricature that serves his tale quite well.

The Sinha novel is the central focus of Rob Nixon's (2011) "Slow Violence,

Neoliberalism, and the Environmental Picaresque"—the seed of his popular monograph *Slow Violence and the Environmentalism of the Poor*—because it offers a perfect critique of both the inadequacy of narrative formats that neatly "bracket" incidents of environmental violence and thus eschew their prolonged effects, and it is also a postcolonial instantiation of the sixteenth-century *Lazarillo*. In the novel, "Animal" is a grotesque *pícaro* made so by the "subhuman . . . conditions" produced by the 1984 chemical explosion in Bhopal (Nixon 67). This environmental disaster presages two decades of court hearings in which persons like "Animal," whose spine has been irrevocably twisted by the accident, vie for justice. Sinha contests the neoliberal narrative that companies like Union Carbide ultimately do more good than harm—that "progress" somehow requires an ostensible genocide which, in the words of the "poison minister" and his many nonfictional analogues, would have happened anyway.

Animal is also a grotesque reminder of Ghosh's argument regarding the "disinherited ones to whom neither the past nor the future belongs" (*HT*, 137). With no means of "getting on better," persons like Animal instead offer a tangible parody of the principles of development and "human rights" that institutions like Union Carbide preach and which don't seem to apply to persons like Animal (Alpert 1969). If, as Bakhtin suggested back in 1937, Lazarillo was a prototype for the "third man"—that is, the servant alongside the grand road toward modernity—"Animal" is surely a prototype for the erstwhile hands of empire, who are likewise occluded in such visions of progress as those touted by the Union Carbide Corporation, or the Vedanta Resources corporation, whose copper plant in Tamil Nadu has closed following widespread protests after toxic runoff rendered local water supplies lethal.

An Anatomy of Postcolonial Roguery

The "postcolony" is here acknowledged as a geographically amorphous site, which exists in various stages of autonomy and which has spawned a discourse that has been largely emptied of meaning as it becomes clear that conventional periodizations eschew any meaningful understanding of the economic consistencies among precolonial, colonial, and postcolonial epochs. Indeed, and per Pablo Mukherjee's (2010, 3) argument regarding postcolonial environments, "the material registers of the flows between the past and the present, the colonial and the postcolonial periods, form a core cultural sensibility of contemporary India." I use the term, despite its geographic and political insufficiencies, because "the term continues to have explanatory power when it sheds light on shared discursive strategies among writers situated in similar historical circumstances" (Esty 1999, 34). The "postcolony" in the context of this project refers both to the traditional critical discourse, but also to the "Global South"—the latter encompassing the often strange geographies of global capital, specifically those postcolonial states that suffer disproportionately under corporate globalization.[25]

As such, and against an evangelical adherence to "development" and "progress" in the popular imagination, the rogue persists as both a parody and a remonstrance. That is, if we are wont to read the "Global South" as a laboratory for the project of liberal democracy and free market initiatives—both of which will presumably play a sort of messianic role for those "slumdogs" in, for example, Mumbai—picaresque novels such as Adiga's and Sinha's tell a very different tale (Boyle 2008). They remind us that the poor can't be "removed like laundry stains"—that, while these "encumbrances" often mar the landscape of our persistently Orientalist imaginations, they are the grist of the system (as workers—formal and informal); and their poverty is a necessary means of sustaining the uneven topographies of global capitalism (Roy 2011, x). The rogue in the postcolony functions, in this sense, as a *memento mori* figure reminding the well-heeled of the tenuous nature of their existence: he is both the antithesis of bourgeois comfort, and a chilling reminder of the material substrate of its possibility. Perhaps this is why their communities are so often bulldozed in "beautification" schemes the world over.

As is made evident by such schemes, the alienated *pícaro* is not and cannot be incorporated into the system; their exclusion is a necessary condition of imperial liberalism. In fact, the rogue figure is a precise index of combined unevenness—instantiating the constitutive outside that has long forged the colonial elsewheres of our imperial imaginary. As well, the process through which "capitalist globalization incorporates peoples outside the European world-system by violently destroying their worlds"—"maintain[ing] a place of habitation in the face of the leveling violence of global technologies of temporal calculation" (Cheah 2016, 12). As such, rogue figures like Ghosh's Deeti or Abani's Elvis materialize sites of production and extraction all too often invisible to those within this "world-system." As I shall discuss in the context of the Adiga novel, the "structural absence" that Energy Humanists ascribe to such sites of extraction—what is often regarded as the *spectral* presence of carbon despite the numerous, and noxious, coal mines that dot India's interior and account for the lethal atmosphere in adjacent cities—is materialized in such novels. As such, the narrative terrain of novels like *GraceLand* or *The White Tiger* foreclose any reading that might rely on idealist (read normative) tropes of *Bildung*, or those which imagine the sort of ideal *telos* afforded to those fortunate enough to live in places with sufficient stores of clean air and water.

To be sure, the sort of alienation that presages the liberal narrative of upward mobility and ascent is starkly absent from the *pícaro's* tale. Notably, the liberal (and later neoliberal) narrative of ascension and/or incorporation into what Paul Gilroy (1993) terms the "fatal" conjunction of capitalism and democracy is marked by a teleology that is more appropriately ascribed to the abovementioned *Bildungsroman*. The *pícaro* cannot be incorporated; their tale subverts the arc of the *Bildungsroman* in which "human personality development is a process of socialization, a process of enfranchisement" (Slaughter 2006, 20). As the above discussion around transversality makes clear: the rogue's alterity is a necessary/logical condition for the *Bildung* of Wallerstein's (1988) "quintessential protagonist." Against such optimistic narratives, the *pícaro* figures "an unequivocal failure of self-formation and socialization" (Dawson 2011, 19–20).

This is precisely why I see the earlier rogue—a Swiftian portrait of destitution and exploitation—as an early instantiation of the rogue in the postcolony living in what Ann Laura Stoler describes as "new zones of exclusion" (2006, 128). She further remarks: "Critical features of imperial formations include harboring and building on territorial ambiguity, redefining legal categories of belonging . . . [they] thrive on turbid taxonomies that produce shadow populations and ever-improved coercive measures to protect the common good against those deemed threats to it" (128). In noting that such "imperial formations" determine "who was outside and who within at any particular time," Stoler's argument (also aligned with Giorgio Agamben [2005]) for a state of exception follows the same logic as Guillén's "half-outsider," Maiorino's notion of "outsiderism," or the abovementioned "constitutive outside" that makes possible the ongoing accumulation of global capital (139). Such "shadow populations" are again instantiated by figures like Animal, who remarks in reference to the fictional representatives of the Union Carbide Corporation: "They will build factories above our graves and use our ashes as cement" (*AP* 275). Comments such as these account for why I read the novel as a late-capitalist *memento mori*—testament to the necessarily uneven model of development that sustains global capitalism.

Without denying the material specificity of individual postcolonial states, *Rogues in the Postcolony* considers how a new *pícaro* is produced by similar modes of colonial and corporate violence, and how their representation in both fictional and journalistic accounts works to either upend or support such economic programs. More specifically, I scrutinize those forms whose *telos* is not "incorporation," but resistance. *Rogues in the Postcolony* studies picaresque novels that illuminate the zones of exception—also described herein as "sacrificial zones," or by Macarena Gómez-Barris (2017) as "extractive zones"—in colonial and postcolonial India, and which push back against triumphalist accounts that would deny the necessity of such forms of systemic (or "slow") violence as the dumping of toxic effluvia on poor communities according to what Pablo Mukherjee reads as the "horrendous logic" of corporate capitalism.[26] We might recall that such a logic was once referred to as "impeccable" by former World Bank president Larry Summers (Vallette 1999). It is precisely this sort of systematized violence that is critiqued in the novels under study.

The New Picaresque and the Making of Modern India

In his 2013 *Crossing the Bay of Bengal: The Furies of Nature and the Fortunes of Migrants*, Sunil Amrith describes what he calls the "El Dorado of the Bay of Bengal"—Bihar with its fields of poppy, Malaya with its stores of rubber, and Ceylon (now Sri Lanka) with its reserves of cinnamon. All three were sites of imperial plunder—poppy and cotton especially, which functioned as the bedrock of Britain's imperial economy. If we consider the role that cotton continues to play (along with copper, bauxite, and especially coal), we can certainly argue that the British presence in the region in the seventeenth century onward (and the introduction of state-sanctioned monopoly trade on poppy and later coal) marks the beginning (in India that is) of a process of enclosure, extraction, emigration, and dispossession that has been justified in each instance under the banner of empire building, state formation, and various forms of globalization.

Surely, though, to reduce this story to the purely economic—the amorphous and abstract categories of subaltern, colonial, or capitalist consciousness—is to reproduce the same historical elisions that proffered Gayatri Spivak's (1988) foundational question, "can the subaltern speak?" Consequently, the thrust of *Rogues in the Postcolony* is a focus on those aesthetic interventions which at least gesture toward a more productive representation of subaltern subjectivity, if only a satirical one. Neither Ghosh nor Adiga are *speaking* for the subaltern; but the *pícaro* figure is, nonetheless, a useful counter to Wallerstein's "quintessential protagonist." Furthermore, at least in the *Ibis Trilogy*, the emphasis on local knowledge and local environments makes clear the virtue of such materialist critiques of empire as Ghosh's picaresque novels.

Likewise, the form itself—in its episodic structure and its persistent emphasis on the corporeality of survival—is a generative counter to the anesthetizing propaganda of global capitalism that continually eschews mention of its ever-growing "fringe." Avoiding such normative tropes as the "transition to capital" as the defining moment of a broadly modern consciousness, the nonteleological (because episodic and occasionally recursive) format of the novels allows the reader to envision a more complicated story—what Sugata Bose describes as "a hundred horizons" over and against the single horizon of a narrowly imperialist history (2009). The novels' privileging of a subaltern voice also allows for a very different historical perspective. In what I am calling a "new picaresque," the convention of the pseudo-autobiography—in Ghosh's novels rendered through a rich panoply of historically occluded voices—calls attention to, and perhaps in some ways assuages, perennial questions concerning subaltern representation.

Although, economic questions—particularly those posed recently in response to new development initiatives and climate change—ought to remain central in our thinking about both subaltern representation as well as the material exigencies of survival in the Global South for those "ecosystem people" who are being displaced in ever-increasing numbers (Guha and Alier 1997). The "capital fringe" where the *pícaro* lives is in fact the product of a new round of legal and illegal land grabs and corporate enclosures, be it for explicitly agricultural initiatives or a host of other improvement projects—a practice that will only increase in the face of cataclysmic shifts to global climate and the consequential displacement of massive swaths of the global populace living in areas vulnerable to impacts like sea-level rise.[27] Arguably, here too the picaresque novel—in its emphasis on the tactile and the real, as opposed to ideal types or hypothetical figures—is again quite effective.

A Note on the Globalization of Form

While recognizing arguments regarding the globalization of generic forms (e.g., the modern novel, presumably also including the picaresque novel), I read the picaresque novels in the present study as attending to transnational geopolitical phenomena while still rendering what Raymond Williams would call the "close living substance" of the local. Further, while Peter Hitchcock (2003, 323) rightfully argues that "genre [is] too often . . . an alibi of cultural integration, a mode in which the African novel, for instance, is celebrated precisely because its 'local color' is rendered in a recognizable form," we might also consider that there is a "shared topography of labor"—and per Lowe (2015), an intimacy across global labor regimes cultivated through transnational trade networks—that constitutes both the "postmodern geography" of late capital and which produces a similar narrative terrain (Pereira 2014). So too, and pace Pablo Mukherjee, the promise of a heterotemporal worldview that would recognize the simultaneity of multiple histories and thus the necessarily pluralized forms of postcolonial literary production—what he describes in his discussion of postcolonial environments as the way in which the local interpolates the global such that normative (read linear) models of temporality are collapsed.[28] Such a nonlinear, nonteleological timescale as is employed by the picaresque form might afford a productive departure from such short-sighted temporal configurations, allowing for a more robust depiction of life in the informal sectors of late capitalism where intimacies continue to be forged amongst otherwise disparate communities of laborers—those forced into the sorts of slum ecologies that we see in *The White Tiger*.

Significantly, I am borrowing the concept of a "shared topography of labor" from Sonali Perera's (2014) critique of Mulk Raj Anand's 1936 picaresque novel *Coolie*—a novel that also foregrounds waste (both literal and figurative in the form of Anand's "excremental surplus") and makes clear those very same "turbid taxonomies" that we see in, for example, Ghosh, Adiga, and Sinha. In Perera's treatment of the novel, she considers the "shared sociology of form" that "working-class writing" employs while foregrounding what she sees as a common narrative trope: the "interruption" (5, 10). The interruption, she argues, accounts for the slippages between dominant forms and "emergent practices"; and it illustrates the "discontinuous nature" of a dynamic working class. The interruption disrupts normative models of literary temporality and subject formation and is thus a generative trope with which to cultivate an ethics wholly absent in what Perera terms an "incommensurable aporia."

We might read the picaresque novel similarly in so far as it subverts normative modes of *Bildung*. Although these are not interruptions; they are recursive vignettes. But more than this, its form attests to a different mode of *Bildung*—or what has been called over and again, its "protean form" (Blackburn 1979). As we struggle to keep in mind the mutable nature of class—as, in Marxian terms, always contingent—such a protean form seems quite fitting as a means of representation. This is precisely the case in Ghosh's novels wherein he "avoids linear, teleological representation of time, favouring instead cyclical, anachronistic patterns" (Mukherjee 2010, 127).

We must, however, take seriously arguments like Graham Huggan's (1995) regarding the potential for literary forms to exoticize and thus domesticate the Other. Not to mention recent work on the uneven and combined development of the literary market, which ensures that particular texts are read, and that those same texts are read in a particular way. The notion of "combined and uneven world literature" that the Warwick School advances in their recent book on the topic is significant: world literature, as the argument goes, is indistinguishable from world markets (Deckard 2015). The present study demonstrates how select picaresque tropes attempt to unsettle certain normative genre categories; but I remain vigilant in my awareness of facile arguments for any form's liberative nature when embedded in the very same market it seeks to critique (see also Levine 2015). This is all to say, following Mukherjee's argument, that we must look for moments of, or gestures toward, singularity that allow for particular texts to cultivate a space of resistance within an always already domesticated global literary market. We must also, however, recognize the limitations of any form, if also the impact of other, more local, forms on cultural production—themselves indices of uneven and combined literary development. I thus make a plea for the generative nature of the postcolonial picaresque without assigning it undue political merit.

A New Literature of Roguery

In Chandler's 1907 *The Literature of Roguery*, he opens with the following: "The literature of roguery occupies a peculiar place in the history of letters. Determined by subject-matter rather than form, and depending upon observed actuality rather than ideals, it presents low life in lieu of heroic, and manners rather than conscience and emotion" (1). A century later, the term "peculiar" still resonates as the daily homages to such neoliberal fictions as "free trade" continue to extol the virtues of development and to mourn those wretched figures "left behind" by capitalist progress. Accordingly, the assemblage of a new "literature of roguery" is an important intervention that takes up issues both narratological and explicitly economic, and which moves beyond the established (albeit productive and useful) arguments against the *Bildungsroman*—celebrating, as it does, the outcast's "incorporation" into the system of global fossil capital.

Book-length studies of the picaresque genre have been mostly concerned with early modern roguery and, later, British and American roguery. While rich connections have been made in their prefatory remarks regarding the continued role of the margin in contemporary state-building, *Rogues in the Postcolony* looks to bring the various strands of this discussion into conversation with postcolonial literary studies, but primarily with questions about degraded environments and the nonhuman (and inhuman) costs of corporate tyranny. *Rogues in the Postcolony* is a materialist history, and one attentive to local landscapes and the communities who inhabit them. By looking at the material substrate of Mukherjee's (2010) "postcolonial environment," for example, I make the case for the picaresque novel as a useful genre in the context of Global South studies, if also in discussions of the Anthropocene more broadly. I also extend Rob Nixon's argument for the temporal virtues of the form to read the rogue as a *memento mori* figure and thus a means of contesting the spectacular invisibility of such figures at various moments in the history of fossil capitalism. The story of expropriation, accumulation, and enslavement is an old one. And the gospel of development that goes along with it continues to sound the death knell of Indigenous communities the world over, who are read as the refuse of global capital—those inhuman subjects, or fungible objects, living in the sacrificial zones of a global petrosphere. Their tales are harder and harder to narrate, because they are less and less spectacular, and less and less visible, obscured over and again by apologists for economic development within ever new regimes of enclosure and dispossession.

India, Old and "New"

Obscured indeed, in the case of India, the triumphalist narratives of the "world's largest democracy" (or "India Shining," and more recently "*Swachh Bharat*") tend to ignore the real lived experiences of the nation's vast (still rural) majority. Cast against the backdrop of the "new" India is a growing number of internally displaced persons, whose communities have been ravaged by market-oriented policies that render arable land naught but a sea of commodities—agricultural policies conceived in the nation's colonial period by trading companies along its eastern shoreline. As is still the case in development schemes that privilege markets over sustenance, the introduction of speculative modes of land tenure in the eighteenth century would benefit a small property-owning class (comprised of Indian *zamindars* and English East India Company officials) at the cost of tens of thousands of peasant farmers. The latter form a central focus of Ghosh's *Sea of Poppies*, which opens in rural Bihar in 1838 when the extension of *zamindari* rights (under British rule) to *raiyati* areas had already produced endemic debt and, consequently, mass displacement.[29] This usurious program required peasant poppy farmers to pay punitive fines for either a refusal to grow the commodity or an inability to produce desired amounts. As I argue in the context of the Ghosh trilogy, the economic period from approximately 1720 to 1857—marked as it was by mass privatization schemes and the capitalization of agriculture—illustrates a specific shift in political ideology and economic practice that disproportionately affected the nation's peasantry.

The philosophical shift from a commoning economy to what Gyan Prakash (1990a) describes as "land as an object" is, in part, a legacy of Locke's abovementioned thesis and a precursor to current private-property regimes now working under the guise of economic development. Also commenting on the capitalization of agriculture as well as its human costs, Manpreet Sethi (2006, 77) argues that the neoliberal transformation of "land tenure into a market-oriented system of exchange" works to exacerbate trenchant forms of inequitable land distribution—that is, colonial-era programs that forged the semi-feudal system now in place. He further remarks that such practices persistently contribute to the erosion (and also salinization) of soil and water sources. The destabilization of the soil and water would likewise contribute to the precarious slum ecologies that we see represented in novels like Sinha's and Adiga's.

It is precisely this despoliation of the native landscape—both through violent economic reforms and also through agricultural technologies that replace life-sustaining crops with commodities such as poppy and cotton—that also ushers in the sorts of mass urbanization too often celebrated as a hallmark of modernity. As we know, several of the new urban settlements in the putatively "new" India take the form of transient slum communities. This is surely not the sort of urban migration that one associates with the promise of economic development. The proliferation of urban slums that have cropped up in the wake of economic liberalization schemes stand as a relief to the glittering lights of Mumbai, not to mention such weird "off-worlds" as Delhi's flourishing Gurgaon. In *The White Tiger*, we learn that the neoliberal utopia envisaged by the new elite—Gurgaon especially, where the novel is partially set—thrives on a similarly rapacious economic model to that of the East India Company before it. As the novel also illustrates quite presciently, the new multinational elite exists only by virtue of the nation's burgeoning underclass. The Faustian presence of the rogue in *The White Tiger*, for example, is a stunning remonstrance to those who continue to boast of Delhi's grandeur. Adiga's is perhaps also the most pristine example of the strangely parallel role that the rogue figure plays in relation to an emergent Indian bourgeoisie. In *The White Tiger*, we have portraits of an urban India that looks radically different than those celebrated by the exponents of economic liberalization. Such scenes will remind readers of Salman Rushdie's portrayal of Delhi's "magician's ghetto" in *Midnight's Children*, although Adiga substitutes a palpable corporeality for magic.

Of course Rushdie's novel, and perhaps more memorably, also broaches another important topic—that of Partition and the imaginative construct of the modern nation-state, including also an incisive critique of the oppressive monoculture of the ruling elite.[30] The partitions of the continent—first Pakistan in 1947, and later East Pakistan (now Bangladesh) in 1971—were responsible for massive displacements of local communities. Not only were these "diseased limbs" populated by Muslim communities, as we also see in Rushdie's rendition of the Sundarbans, they were often dispossessed farmers as well (Ahmad). What Rushdie fails to mention in his novel (among other things for which he has been rightfully criticized) is the Bengali famine of 1943–44, which was produced by a similar economic model to that which caused the 1770 famine. As Janam Mukherjee describes in *Hungry Bengal* (2015), independence would be delayed by more than Churchill's interests in a WWII victory. Just as the English had sacrificed Indian and Chinese peasants for poppy cultivation a century prior, in 1943 Britain would once again sacrifice Indian farmers in their fight to secure Burma from a Japanese encroachment. The British in fact instituted a policy of "Denial," which demanded that rice stocks be burned or exported—any surplus destroyed before it could benefit Japanese soldiers. It was, unsurprisingly, only Bengali citizens who suffered.

I mention this episode, because the narrative around independence often obscures not only the violence of Partition, but, and even more egregiously, the endemic hunger wrought from such imperialist tactics as Britain's "Denial" program—a hunger that in 1770, 1943, or 2020 surely complicates more palatable notions of "progress." Thus, before turning to the novels themselves, I first want to consider the enduring resonance of figures like Ghosh's farmers for thinking about contemporary political struggles—those of persons who, like the uprooted citizens of Bihar, must also vie with the dangerous consequences of political and economic interests that subordinate the welfare of local populations to the sorts of narrow visions of a Churchill, or any of a number of multinational corporations currently *denying* Bengali farmers the right to basic sustenance. Ghosh's novels in fact constitute a radical politico-aesthetic intervention—his portraits of farmers resonating deeply as the mechanisms of agricultural enclosure and free trade continually produce vast numbers of internally displaced persons whose recourse has lately been suicide. The epidemic of suicide in the cotton belt is a stark reminder of a long history of imperial liberalism that has systematically sacrificed local populations to capital gain.[31] What better illustration of accumulation by dispossession than forcing wheat and rice farmers to grow cotton? The tragic reality of the suicide epidemic reminds us that the new India exists in name only—a grotesque fiction indeed, and one that never applied to farmers and rural laborers.

Rogues in the Postcolony: Narrating Extraction and Itinerancy in India

The novels under study in *Rogues in the Postcolony* foreground such figures while offering substantive critiques of almost three centuries of Indian development—colonial-era plantation economies, the post-independence "Green Revolution," and late-capitalist modes of extractivism fostered by neoliberal-era economic reforms. The first chapter closely scrutinizes shifting modes of land tenure that occurred primarily between 1765 and 1838 during which the English East India Company, working initially as a proxy for the British government, acquired trading rights on the Coromandel Coast of Bengal. Interested in taxing peasant farmers directly and allocating more land for the cultivation of poppy—the cash crop that both replaced subsistence farming and which provided for their spectacularly successful opium trade—East India Company tradesmen transformed the local economy into a speculative one that quickly produced intractable debt and an unprecedented internal diaspora. Farmers from upland Bihar, who were forced to grow the crop and to manufacture opium in the factories at Ghazipur and elsewhere, constituted the bulk of migrant labor that ended up on Indian Ocean slavers at the turn of the century.

In Ghosh's picaresque *Ibis Trilogy*, the reader is presented with a fictional version of the razing of Bihar and the consequent diaspora in the Bay of Bengal. Ghosh offers a haunting portrait of the real consequences of resource extraction for farmers like his *pícara* Deeti, who figures as a fictional analogue for farmers in eighteenth- and nineteenth-century Bengal. The novel foregrounds the impact of the opium trade on local peasant economies, including poppy farmers and also migrant lascars. Both are rendered, in Jason Moore's (2017, 600) terms, "cheap nature"—a term he coins to describe "capitalism's ontological praxis," which is to say the gross abstraction of human and nonhuman communities by way of free market ideology. Cheap nature refers to the cheapening of work in which the labor of "many humans—but also of animals, soils, forests, and all manner of extra-human nature—[is rendered] invisible or nearly so." Contra Marx, who privileges a rift between human and nonhuman subjects, Moore explains such modes of cheapening as the process through which capitalism must "[convert] the living, multi-species connections of humanity-in-nature and the web of life into dead abstractions" (598). As Ghosh's fictional prospector in the 2000 novel *The Glass Palace* would also come to learn: "Land and labour were what a planter needed most" (183).

By virtue of such a cheapening, the local peasantry would be subjected to colonial-era taxonomies that posited the Bihari peasant within a capacious category of unimproved "Nature"—their labor imaginatively coupled with that of the putatively uncultivated landscape. Poppy farmers would be thrust into a mode of production reliant on the reduction of complex ecosystems into impoverished but exchangeable forms—so many dead abstractions, and thus concise instantiations of cheap nature. Indeed, "before the colonial project could prosper, it had to render territories and peoples extractible, and it did so through a matrix of symbolic, physical, and representational violence"—that is, through the sorts of taxonomic violence that I document below (Gómez-Barris 2017, 5). In this chapter, I consider Ghosh's trilogy of picaresque novels as a documentary of the cheapening of the Bengali landscape through the imperialist taxonomies of René Descartes, John Locke, John Stuart Mill, and Carl Linnaeus. While Locke and Mill would provide the philosophical justification for colonial improvement schemes—whether Locke's 1689 thesis on property or Mill's 1861 mandate to civilize the Company's aforementioned "rude" subjects—Linnaeus's 1735 classificatory framework would make possible the monoculture of poppy, cotton, tea, and persons. Each was predicated upon the Cartesian partitioning of the cognizant subject (*res cogitans*) and observable object (*res extensa*) that would form the central dynamic upon which the colonial *episteme* was based. The inhuman figures of the slave or indentured farmer would be rendered, logically, as *res extensa*—indistinguishable from the commodities that they produce, if also the brute matter that they extracted from the earth.

Out of the trilogy, *River of Smoke* is perhaps especially attuned to emergent discussions around the relationship between colonial-era plant taxonomies and the ontological simplification and thus indenture of local communities; although all three novels demonstrate the sort of onto-epistemological violence at stake in the cheapening of life in colonial Bengal. To be sure, more than a subaltern archive, or a contestation of the region's "elite historiography" to take a term from Ranajit Guha's (1996) magisterial history of the region, the novels make flesh otherwise abstract instantiations of cheap nature while dramatizing the complicated cartographies of the poppy trade—both its oft-neglected riverine topographies as well as the intersections of the Atlantic and Indian Ocean networks.

In the second chapter, I examine Indra Sinha's 2007 novel *Animal's People*, which I read as a *memento mori* tale: more than an "environmental picaresque" as Rob Nixon has argued, Sinha's novel forces the economic logic of neoliberalism into sharp focus. The novel is set in contemporary Bhopal where the economic, political, and, especially, biological/ecological legacy of Union Carbide's 1984 chemical explosion is illustrated through characters like Sinha's titular *pícaro* "Animal"—so named for the injuries that he incurred on the night of the disaster. Sinha uses his grotesque form to critique both the company's malfeasance as well as the developmentalist ethos that implicitly sanctioned such business practices—the promise of mobility a rhetorical veil for the human cost of India's economic gains.

Sinha's deformed protagonist is a "ghoulish parody" of economic liberalization, and also a haunting remonstrance (Dionne 2006, 54). As such, I read him as a late-capitalist instantiation of the seventeenth-century *memento mori* tradition, an artistic movement in which pastoral landscapes were interrupted by spectral tombstones and the occasional skull—otherwise Arcadian spaces shrouded by the casualties of early modern enclosures in Europe. Animal, I argue, serves a similar aesthetic and political function to works like Nicholas Poussin's 1637 painting "Et in Arcadia Ego." I further suggest that Sinha adopts the historically antihumanist genre of the picaresque novel to critique both the tradition of liberal humanism from which the colonial (and corporate) subject was necessarily excluded, and to parody what have been called the "enabling fictions" of classical and neoliberalism—whether the eighteenth-century autobiography, the nineteenth-century *Bildungsroman*, or the "twentieth-century development dreams" that undergirded programs like India's "Green Revolution" (Tsing 2015, 4).

While Animal's tale alternates with that of his city and his "people"—mostly fellow citizens who bear the brunt of MIC's long-term (if also teratogenic) effects, be they asthmatic children or lactating mothers producing poison—the novel is primarily a documentary of his survival and one that is both ruthless in its telling and in its form. Throughout, Sinha relies on the picaresque tropes of unreliable narration, an episodic structure, and the use of abjection to foreground what Pablo Mukherjee (2010) has called the "politics of global toxicity": the juridical gymnastics of company shareholders and their government proxies, and the corresponding narratives that sanction these institutions whether explicitly or implicitly. The novel parodies representational strategies that augment the project of global capitalism—specifically, the liberal narrative of development—through its episodic form, and with a narrator whose mutilated body illustrates the toxic underside of industrial progress.

The dialectic that emerges here also serves as a generative praxis for thinking through figurations of the human—as onto-epistemological category, reasoning modern subject, and protagonist of the Anthropocene. Animal questions such categories throughout, recalling work by Wynter (2003) on the human as praxis for imperial liberalism, as well as Weheliye (2014) on the human as a conceptual limit for the figuration of Blackness. Animal's body serves as an ontological limit for such theorizations, while his persistent questioning of his nature serves similarly to critique the sorts of epistemic violence inherent to, for example, Wynter's argument regarding the subordination of most humans to the category of the inhuman vis-à-vis Enlightenment discourses of rationalism and reason.

The novel also engages with theories of transcorporeality—or the porosity of the human body and/in its respective ecology—as well as critiques of geontopower that recognize the short-sightedness of any theory of life (or "bios" and thus "biopower") that eschews consideration of the political history of human subject formation, not to mention the role of the nonhuman.[32] Thus, in this chapter I also attend to the centrality of the "biocentric subject of late liberalism" as a legatee of "colonial Man" living in the extractive zones of late (global) capitalism—the latter represented through the interlocking narratives of pesticide production in Bhopal and also the toxic steel mills of Coatesville, PA, where one of the liberal "Amrikans" in the novel is born and where her parents suffer the impacts and indignities of deregulation (Yusoff 2018, 11). The example of Coatseville, PA, also enables Sinha to critique extractive capitalism in the Global North and the vast tendrils of accumulation that enable new forms of entangled intimacy across a broader topography of labor.

Following my discussion of post-independence development initiatives in the agricultural sector, in the final chapter I turn to coal and forms of extractivism newly emboldened by neoliberal-era economic reforms that enable the continued exploitation of local communities through financial speculation and electoral dispossession. So too, the persistent figuration of workers as the refuse of late capitalism. In this chapter, I read Aravind Adiga's *The White Tiger* as a parody in which images of waste—whether industrial sewage or persons—displace the conventionally optimistic visual rhetoric of the "new India," or "India Shining," the latter by far the most popular reading. In this way, I perform a materialist intervention that foregrounds the slum ecologies of (in this case) the cities of Dhanbad, New Delhi, and Bangalore, and in so doing consider slow violence in the context of urban ruin.

Work on what Mike Davis (2006) has called a "slum ecology" abounds in postcolonial discourse as the locus of discussion increasingly moves from the country to the city. This is particularly true of India where the Gandhian emphasis on rural virtue has been displaced by development models focused on the "new" city: intentional cities from Chandigargh in the nation's capital region to the city of Gurgaon where the Adiga novel is partially set, and whose description eerily recalls the fictions of J. G. Ballard. As in Rana Dasgupta's (2015) *Capital: The Eruption of Delhi* and recent work on Indian waste economies like Assa Doron and Robin Jeffrey's (2018) *Waste of a Nation: Garbage and Growth in India*, Adiga is interested to expose the lie of economic mobility in places like Dhanbad.

Owing to the imbrications of extractive capitalism, electoral politics, and the proliferation of new modes of removal and forced apartheid—the latter grounded in theories of the inhuman, human, and nonhuman—in this chapter, I pursue three discrete questions in order to identify the intersections between global capital, waste, and the skeins of imperial ideology that produce figures like Adiga's Balram Halwai. Balram is a concise instantiation of the *pícaro* figure, if also earlier literary critiques of local waste economies such as were illustrated in works like Mulk Raj Anand's (1935) *Untouchable*. Both instantiate that "primordial urban contradiction" (Davis 2006, 137)—that is, "generations of human beings, out of whose lives the wealth of [the nation's elites are] produced [and who are] compelled to live in wealth's symbolic negative counterpart" (Marcus qtd. in Davis 137–38).

Beginning with a discussion around *bios* and the taxonomies of imperial liberalism, I ask how colonial regimes operating through technologies of exclusion are reinstantiated in new modes of accumulation that produce new forms of excremental humanity. Furthermore, I ask: how do *particular* forms of fossil capital produce new forms of sacrificial communities such that the forms of "wastelanding" that we see in India are necessary technologies of accumulation?[33] Thus I trace the production of excremental surplus, here understood as the laboring poor who are excluded from the productive forms of labor that are ascribed to figures like Balram's employer "Ashok" and the cast of improving landlords under whom Balram and his community must vie for survival. But I remain alert to Black Anthropocene histories that remind us that contemporary forms of wastelanding—of the inhuman *and* nonhuman—are but the material legacies of the Black Anthropocene's ongoing story.

Moving from the inhuman to the nonhuman, I then consider the material waste born of extraction, specifically coal but also of petrol. This is illustrated throughout in images such as the irradiated river that snakes through Balram's hometown as well as the thick descriptions of a thoroughly toxic Ganges and its many tributaries; so too, the noxious atmosphere of Delhi, saturated as it is with diesel dust. Here I attend to India's fossil economy, tracing the production of coal as well as surplus labor. Last, I turn to the novel as a carbon fiction, taking up questions of representation that underscore petrocultural studies and broader concerns about what have been called severally petro-fictions or oil fictions, but which might in fact more productively be termed carbon fictions.[34] That is, I consider how the Adiga novel focuses on the immiscible histories of coal and petrol, making clear the complicated genealogy of the nation as both a prominent coal producer and nascent petro-state to the extent that a great deal of petro-labor is in fact extracted from the nation's southern states in addition to how its urban economies are increasingly dependent on the importation of automobiles. The interpolation of automobile culture in intentional cities like Gurgaon is described in the novel in terms that evoke a sort of techno-sublime. A case in point is Adiga's description of Balram's oil-soaked baptism: "Late every evening, I emerged from under a taxi like a hog from sewage, my face black with grease, my hands shiny with engine oil. I dipped into a Ganga of black—came out a driver" (*WT* 48). In reading such passages, I also engage a speculative methodology that seeks to eschew convention and to *read* energy. In lieu of a conservative positioning of the coal mine or the oil field as mere backdrop, I read the novel through the lens of its detritus. Here I am also careful to attend to the network of relationships that constitute the carbon economy in an effort to recognize what Energy Humanists describe as the inseparability of energy and culture.

Rogues in the Postcolony concludes with the possibility of imagining just alternatives to conventional extractive economies. Concluding as such, I extend arguments forwarded by Rebecca Solnit (2009), Shelley Streeby (2018), and others, in offering robust portraits of world-making movements that are galvanizing support across India and the Global South more broadly. I follow Macarena Gómez-Barris's argument that "if we only track the purview of power's destruction and death force, we are forever analytically imprisoned to reproducing a totalizing viewpoint that ignores life that is unbridled and finds forms of resisting and living alternatively" (2017, 3).

Resistance to environmental tyranny has a long history in India: we might recall Ramachandra Guha's *Unquiet Woods*, which documents the Chipko, or tree-hugging movement—now mirrored by sanitation workers agitating for pay equity by hugging dumpsters. So too, the prose of Mahasweta Devi, whose *Imaginary Maps* (1995) critiqued the rapacity of extractive capitalism in the nation's interior. But beyond the widely acknowledged prose of Guha and Devi are local communities like the Dongria Kondh in Odisha fighting to reclaim the commons from companies like the abovementioned Vedanta Resources. Yes, resistance to the forces of extractive capitalism takes many forms.

The Indigenous futurisms articulated in the protests of the Dongria Kondh are but a part of the robust effort to transition away from conventional extractive economies—to imagine just futures that rely on alternative energy sources like solar power. Considering, however, that solar projects across the subcontinent have been bitterly contested by local farmers, in the conclusion, I consider the possibility of "solarity" over against mere solar. That is, and following the pioneering work of Darin Barney and Imre Szeman (2019), I imagine what energy might look like if untethered from the extraction of rare metals, and the development *ethos* that continues to justify such forms of violence. I also consider how new forms of solidarity—hence "solarity"—might productively depart from the settler-colonial rhetoric motivating Modi's development projects, and how new energy regimes might instead employ Native, which is to say *Adivasi*, knowledge systems in building just futures. This is precisely what activists like C. K. Janu are working toward in their demands to resist the "logic of land as property" and instead promote "regenerative" Indigenous practices of land stewardship (Boyer 2019, 69). This too is what historian Dipesh Chakrabarty (2019) argues for when making a plea for the planetary—as opposed to the global, or that which generally refers to the transnational map of interconnected sites of capital accumulation—as a category concerned not with the "sustainability" of destructive forms of development, but instead the "habitability" of such sites as Kerala. It is here where Janu has now established a viable political platform constituted by *Adivasis* (or Indigenous persons) and *Dalits* (or those within the so-called "scheduled castes," i.e., untouchables) who are collectively agitating for land justice.

Relying in part on anthropologist Jamie Cross's (2019) work on the rural poor, and electricity as an index of modernity, in the conclusion I attempt to imagine otherwise. That is, and pace Gómez-Barris, I consider how such communities imagine anew and how we too, as activists and scholars, might engage the speculative over and against the prison-house of conventional critiques of power, and of literature. Specifically, I counterpoise the work of figures like Janu against the greenwashing of liberal capitalist ventures such as we see in Modi's commitment to solar power. It is in the spirit of such imaginings that I now turn to the *Ibis Trilogy*—an example, I would argue, of world-making in the era we have come to call the Anthropocene, and a vibrant project that demonstrates the virtue of the speculative in these times.

Chapter 1

Revisiting the Environmental Picaresque: Plantationocene Aesthetics and the Origins of Cheap Nature in Amitav Ghosh's *Ibis Trilogy*

> We have become so accustomed to national histories and nationalist maps that it is difficult to put the Bay of Bengal, with its traffic of people, ideas, and things, at the heart of our story. But to do so opens new perspectives on the past and the present.
>
> —Sunil Amrith, *Crossing the Bay of Bengal: The Furies of Nature and the Fortunes of Migrants*

Subaltern Studies scholars have long examined what Partha Chatterjee has called "the fruits of Macaulay's poison tree"—the successive means of securing political hegemony on the Indian subcontinent by "setting the valorized culture over the Other" (*Present History* 6, Said 12). The phrase, of course, is a specific reference to the infamous *Minute on Indian Education*, which was penned by British Statesman T. B. Macaulay in 1835 and which would ultimately frame the official educational policy of the occupying forces of the English East India Company (Cutts). In the *Minute*, the aging Briton would advocate for English-language education by citing the inadequacies of the Sanskrit language, if also "Hindu learning" more broadly (Cutts 824). Utilitarian in approach, Macaulay, like James Mill and other contemporary apologists for occupation, favored the creation of an elite Indian class educated with the "useful knowledge" (to cite Mill) that only an English education could afford (Cutt 825).

Critiques of such colonial logics are legion and include foundational works like Gauri Viswanathan's 1989 *Masks of Conquest* along with recent studies on Anglophone world literatures (and the persistent centrality of the Anglophone academy) penned by practitioners such as Gayatri Chakravorty Spivak, Emily Apter, Pheng Cheah, and others. So too, Chatterjee's own vast body of work on the colonial and postcolonial state, inclusive of biopolitical modes of civil governance and education. By contrast, and despite the expansive field of Indian Ocean Studies in which the traffic in "people, ideas, and things" across the Bay of Bengal figures centrally, Amitav Ghosh's recent *Ibis Trilogy* is the first materialist reckoning with the Bay's history (foregrounding, as it does, the opium trade) which makes clear the intimacies between such *taxa* as "people, ideas, and things" (Amrith 5–6).

The transnational economy attendant to opium production had previously received surprisingly little attention despite claims by many critics that there would in fact "be no empire without it," not to mention the conspicuous presence of opium use in Victorian-era cultural production.[1] It might even be argued that the most notorious "fruit" was the cooptation—through the corporate campaigns of Britain's premier trading company—of India's poppy economy. This would also depend upon colonial racism in the form of liberal development schemes—that is, the cultivation and "improvement" of local persons and plants so central to the ascendant (and transnational) plantation economies of the Indian and Atlantic Oceans. The plantation, as C. L. R. James and others have long argued, was both the condition of possibility for modern capitalism and was only possible through a burgeoning system of imperial taxonomy that would understand Indian persons within the same rubric as poppy or tea.

At the risk of overstating the role of poppy cultivation, especially given the formidable role that cotton played in the imperial project, Ghosh contends that opium—the popular narcotic manufactured from poppy—was *the* keystone commodity in the creation and maintenance of Britain's largest colony. He further argues that there has been insufficient critical attention to the plight of laborers working in the opium trade: most of the literature on poppy cultivation and trade hinges on abstract economic questions or narrowly moral ones—the latter, a central focus of the Royal Opium Commission, who were more interested in temperance than justice for opium farmers, not to mention the myriad of itinerant labor regimes employed by the Company.[2] Consequently, the novelist's recent trilogy, which focuses on the plight of the farmer, the lascar (or local sailor), and the factory worker—marshaling a host of local language systems in the service of rendering these otherwise abstract communities—has been hailed as the first subaltern history of poppy cultivation.[3]

While Macaulay and generations of Anglo-American scholars after him indulge a fantasy of British superiority (including also an unsubstantiated economic and political acumen), British rule in the region was achieved through the co-optation of an existing system of land tenure, whose legacy would reverberate in a semi-feudal agrarian economy governed first by the English East India Company and today by its corporate legatees—companies like Monsanto "only the latest instance of a transformation in relations between bodies, capital, and land that has its roots in the 16th century" (Moore, Allewaert, Goméz, and Mitman 2019). Coinciding with the construction of their settler colony in Bengal, East India Company agents would ostensibly hijack the local opium trade through the implementation of a new tariff system, and thus an unprecedented monopoly that Adam Smith would notably indict in his treatment of Bengal in the 1776 *An Inquiry into the Nature and Causes of the Wealth of Nations*. The notoriously corrupt antics of Company officers would also come under fire, and would ultimately lead to the lengthy impeachment trials of the first governor of Bengal's permanent settlement—Warren Hastings, who despite the tireless efforts of Edmund Burke was eventually acquitted, but whose trial laid the foundation for the revocation of the Company's charter.[4]

Of course, any sanctions on the EIC notwithstanding, the British would retain their stronghold on the subcontinent for another century. It was in fact Hastings's impeachment trials (and the attendant fanfare) that allowed Britain to simultaneously retain their power in Bengal while "mask[ing] the scandalous origins of empire" (206). As Nicholas Dirks and others have observed, Burke's public indictment of EIC practices paved the way for a popular embrace of empire: Britain would come off as morally sound, committed as they were to improving the putatively "rude" culture of the subcontinent, while they maintained the plantation system begun by Hastings and Charles Cornwallis (Mill 1861). To wit, Hastings's 1772 edict imposing a state monopoly on opium persisted well into the nineteenth century—this rapacious business model creating the conditions for the Opium Wars.

It is precisely this version of company and imperial rule that frames Ghosh's picaresque novels. *Sea of Poppies* (2008), *River of Smoke* (2011), and *Flood of Fire* (2015) offer a protracted commentary on East India Company trade practices, inclusive of damning caricatures of EIC officials. The novels give primacy to the ecological substrate of British imperialism—that is, the cultivation of its most profitable commodity (opium), and the subsequent movement of opium and indentured laborers (usually former farmers) across the bay. Deploying a picaresque, which is to say a nonlinear, timescale, the novels track the itinerant movement of Indian Ocean communities, and the goods that they tarried, in lieu of promoting a normative (read colonial) *Bildung*. In fact, such a narrative arc is expressly critiqued in the final novel *Flood of Fire* through the ultimate enfranchisement of freedman Zachary Reid—a sailor from Baltimore who passes on the *Ibis*, and whose narrative is a clear satire of similar stories of uplift that would have been impossible for figures like Zachary. Zachary, who begins his journey as a ship hand, enjoys what we might call a typically liberal *Bildung*: he becomes a Company man, and a free agent.

Through their subversive narrative structures and explicit indictments of eighteenth-century theories of political economy and the paeans to industrial progress that they sanctioned—that is, the emergence of imperial liberalism and such fictions as "free trade," which Ghosh's fictional company official "Benjamin Burnham" likens to Christian salvation—the novels effectively expose Britain's imperial program as, to quote Ghosh's "Paulette," naught but "so much duperie" (*SP* 487). Theirs was an illegal drug trade that served to shore up their wartime economy, and which thrived on the blood of Indian farmers along with other (often informal) labor regimes conscripted to move such commodities as opium and "coolies" across the Bay—the latter term, per Lisa Lowe, a "shifting, historically contingent designation for an intermediary form of Asian labor, used both to define and to obscure the boundary between slavery and freedom, and to normalize both" (*Intimacies* 25). I shall turn to Ghosh's rendition of indentured and informal labor regimes below in the context of "cheap nature." Sufficed to say here that the figure of the "coolie," and also of such informal labor communities as lascars, instantiates a sort of rogue figure in so far as both are routinely criminalized and pathologized—existing as the constitutive outside of networks of accumulation, and reducible to the excremental surplus of the Indian Ocean trading community.

As fungible objects, the human and nonhuman cargo on Ghosh's ships—the titular *Ibis* among others—constitute what world ecologist Jason W. Moore has termed "cheap nature," or in Marx's terms the impoverished commodity forms produced by the abstraction of labor. For Marx, this would refer primarily to human labor; against such anthropocentrism, the agentic qualities of the nonhuman are exquisitely rendered in Ghosh's vibrant landscape. I use the term cheap nature following Moore to characterize the cheapening, through taxonomic simplification, of the Bengali landscape—the human, inhuman, and nonhuman actors that constitute Ghosh's multispecies lifeworlds. As such, cheap nature constitutes "capitalism's ontological praxis"—that is, the abstraction of work in which the labor of "many humans—but also of animals, soils, forests, and all manner of extra-human nature—[is rendered] invisible or nearly so" ("Capitalocene" 600).

Lifeless and inert matter, the commodity as such replaces—ontologically—the poppy flower and the farmer. Moore explains such modes of cheapening as the process through which capitalism must "[convert] the living, multi-species connections of humanity-in-nature and the web of life into dead abstractions" ("Capitalocene" 598). Marx would characterize this process similarly, although significantly replacing "humanity-in-nature" with humanity *and* nature. The production of a sort of cheap nature/labor in *Capital* is rendered as "a degraded and almost servile condition of the mass of the people . . . and the transformation of their means of labour into capital," with "means" here referring to an abstract "nature" (1990, 881). The dissolution of "the unity of living and active humanity with the natural, inorganic conditions of their metabolic exchange with nature, and hence their appropriation of nature," which Marx also outlines in the *Grundrisse*, similarly privileges such a rift; for Ghosh (as for Moore) this relationship is somewhat more complicated (1973, 489).

Departing from the normative Cartesianism that characterizes popular ecological and political thought, and which is instantiated in discussions around the putative Anthropocene epoch, Ghosh's lifeworlds conjure the vibrant materiality imagined by thinkers like Donna Haraway or Jane Bennett, both of whom eschew the tired authoritarianism of conventionally anthropocentric worldviews. Such critics make clear that "sky-gazing" *Anthropos* is of a particular type—an agent of capital, and of empire (Haraway 53). As such, *Anthropos* instantiates Sylvia Wynter's notion of "colonial man" and thus fails to represent his many subjects. Moore's theory is aligned with such readings to the extent that he favors a capitalogenic understanding of the planetary transformations of the last five centuries, which potentially reinforces the singularity of *Anthropos* as a geological agent—capital being the purview and the product of "colonial man's" improving labor. The shift, however, from *Anthropos* to capital in Moore's formulation might be read more generously— that is, through the lens of what he describes as a "world ecology" connected through networks of capital, but attendant to the human and nonhuman actors long excluded from such narratives of improvement as might be implied by an Anthropocene.

Within the alternative formulation of a Capitalocene, or "age of capital"— a term originally coined by Andreas Malm—Moore and others foreground the accumulation of capital as the principal actor in the radical transformations of a world ecology forged through a planetary network of plantations that begin (for Moore) in Madeira, or the island of wood, in the sixteenth century. Aligned with historians Christophe Bonneuil and Jean-Baptiste Fressoz, who are also interested to trouble dominant Anthropocene narratives, Moore clarifies that the "long historical process of economic exploitation" begins well before the emergence of steam, and surely before any correlative industrial "revolution"—a term largely emptied of its meaning if we take even a cursory look at successive models of uneven and combined development characteristic of global capitalism in the long sixteenth century if not before (*Shock* 229). As we discussed in the introduction, the steam-powered factory system may be understood as an outgrowth of plantation economies throughout Britain's colonies—thus a continuation of extant industrial practice and not an innovation or revolution in any sense. For this reason, and amidst a flurry of neologisms, Anna Tsing and Donna Haraway have spurned even Capitalocene in favor of something like a Plantationocene. In a similar vein, François Vergès uses an even more succinct gloss to refer to a world ecology organized by global networks of human and nonhuman capital: the racial Capitalocene. Both models usefully examine plantation logics that "organize economies, environments, bodies, and social relations" within the rubric of cheap nature or cheap *labor* (Moore, Allewaert, Goméz, and Mitman 2019). This also affords a more robust historical understanding of what historian Dipesh Chakrabarty has described in terms of the "immiscible chronologies" of the accumulation of capital and the continued degradation of Earth systems ("Climate" 220).

The Plantationocene model relies precisely on the sort of cheapening that Moore and Vergès take up; and the burgeoning study of plantation logics—a platform for asking what "environmentalism [might] look like if we began, not from wilderness, but the plantation"—gives space to alternative formulations of geologic history interested in the intersecting phenomena of ecological degradation and enslavement, both of which depended upon the sorts of scalar logic (and requisite ontological cheapening) that Tsing and Moore critique in their formulations of cheap nature (Moore, Allewaert, Goméz, and Mitman 2019). Indeed, "the plantation [is] an important site to consider the ways in which land, labor, and capital have been ordered to profit some, while imperiling the lives and livelihoods of others, across the globe" (Moore, Allewaert, Goméz, and Mitman 2019). As such, I substitute the term Plantationocene for Anthropocene in what I read as an instantiation of Plantationocene aesthetics; and I thus acknowledge the racialized histories of capital embedded in the plantation economies that form the heart of Ghosh's novels.

In what follows, I explore the implications of the aforementioned plantation logics, in the form of ontological cheapening, in colonial Bengal where the local peasantry would be subjected to colonial-era taxonomies that posited the Bihari peasant within a capacious category of unimproved "Nature." As such, the plantation economies foregrounded in Ghosh's novels—poppy and also tea—operated under the contemporaneous principle of improvement, or cultivation "in the fullest etymological sense," which is to say the Lockean mandate discussed above (Nixon 2012). The coupling of the colonial peasant with commodity crops like poppy, or tea as Ghosh dramatizes in the context of *River of Smoke* (the second novel in the trilogy), was a necessary taxonomic condition for plantation capitalism: "Only as constituent parts of such a system, could the otherwise variegated category of unimproved nature—human and nonhuman—be subordinated to a universalizing scalability" ("Documenting Cheap Nature" 5). This scaling, of course, was critical to the domestication of such an unruly landscape as eighteenth-century Bengal where John Stuart Mill's "rude Hindoo" served as a literal illustration of the "state of nature" from which the bourgeois subject would logically emerge.[5] Ostensibly no more than "waste," the landscape and all who dwelled within it would have to be cultivated.[6] Thus, we read the human, nonhuman, and inhuman actors in Bengal (and ultimately across the Indian Ocean into China) as cultivars, and as "cheap nature."

In the remainder of this chapter, I trace the legacy of the long sixteenth century and the correlative emergence of cheap nature within a particular moment of accumulation in late eighteenth-century Bengal: the poppy plantations cultivated during the English East India Company's occupation between 1765 and 1838—"cheap nature" here taking the form of an un/underpaid rural peasantry, a vast sea of poppy monocultures, and emergent modes of circulatory labor including lascars, an amorphous term for any number of East and South Asian sailors.[7] I read Ghosh's trilogy as a historic chronicle of the opium trade and its economic, ecological, and geopolitical preconditions; as a documentary of local farmers and lascars forced into the employ of the company to cultivate, manufacture, and ultimately transport poppy *cum* opium on Company-owned steamships across the Indian Ocean; and as an instantiation of the picaresque tradition in its reliance on such tropes as itinerancy and survival, and in its evocation of other maritime picaresque novels like Martin Delany's 1859–61 *Blake, or The Huts of America*.

Sea of Poppies, for example, elaborates how the accumulation and movement of global capital—enmeshed in an intricate web of human and nonhuman life—makes possible an Anthropocene, while bodying forth the communities too often elided in triumphalist globalization narratives, conventional Marxian critiques that eschew nonhuman agency, and postcolonial realist fictions that continue to tend toward the Naipaulian or Orwellian.[8] Additionally, and as I shall demonstrate here, in animating an otherwise abstract instantiation of cheap nature, the novel exhibits the usefulness of fiction over and against other rhetorical mediums, potentially mitigating the aforementioned tendencies of capitalogenic theories to reify the inhuman as fungible object. While the rich histories penned by Moore and others—including also Carl Trocki as well as noted environmental historians Alfred Crosby and Ramachandra Guha—offer robust portraits of capital's embeddedness in the "web of life," novels like *Sea of Poppies* conjure something rather different. Exploring the opium trade through the lens of farmers, Ghosh's novel intervenes radically in a historic discourse long framed by the developmentalist *ethos* undergirding colonial expansion; the archives of the Royal Opium Commission, whose vast elisions testify to Spivak's foundational arguments regarding epistemic violence; and by liberal economists concerned with the origins and impacts of free trade in the region—among them Smith who, as aforementioned, cites the 1770 Bengali famine as evidence of the Company's failures, but maintains his ideological commitment to improvement in the Lockean sense.

Until recently, few historians had taken up the material impact of the trade on local populations and local environments. Trocki's 1999 *Opium and Empire* is emblematic of this shift, and it serves as a useful companion to *Sea of Poppies*, and to the trilogy more broadly. But Trocki's, like Ranajit Guha's landmark indictment of the East India Company's Bengal settlement—the 1963 *Rule of Property for Bengal*—is primarily concerned with the appropriation of land titles and the usurpation of common right. Ghosh's novels take this on, but shift the locus of discussion from the accumulation of capital to the impact of the trade on local communities. This is accomplished to a great extent through its adaptation of the picaresque form—that is, and more than its dizzyingly atemporal structure, its haunting depictions of scarcity and precarity, which are also signatures of the genre. Thus, in what follows I begin with a discussion of the picaresque mode, and Ghosh's deployment thereof, to underline its significance for transmitting stories like those of Deeti, a poppy farmer in Bihar. I then consider the construction of "cheap nature" in the context of human and nonhuman labor—that of the farmers and lascars at a moment prior to their formal subsumption into networks of global capital, and also poppies which were the dominant agricultural product of Bengal in 1838 when the novel opens. Here I employ a radical materialist critique, acknowledging the agentic qualities of the in/non/more-than human, in order to trace the epistemological and material conditions necessary for the production of the categories of nature and of the human. In particular, I follow scholars like Tsing and Elizabeth Povinelli as I explore systems of colonial taxonomy that were predicated upon contemporaneous theories of biology and phylogenesis.

In order to situate this discussion within the broader context of an emergent Indian Ocean discourse—one committed to exploring the myriad of colonial-era maritime communities located throughout the Bay and its littorals—I also place Ghosh's novel in conversation with similarly attuned works by historian Sunil Amrith and others, who are interested also to "open up new perspectives on the past and present" that might further unsettle the sorts of historically impoverished rhetoric associated with popular formulations of an Anthropocene—that is, as a category designating an "age of Anthropos" and thus reproducing a particular understanding of the human subject, and one rooted in the *ethos* of imperial liberalism to which I shall turn later in this discussion (Sunith 8). Against such an *ethos*, which envisaged the Indian Ocean world as *terra nullius*—an empty landscape rife for conquest—I read Ghosh's terraqueous landscape as a heterogenous, heterotopic space that affords such radical imaginings as might be glimpsed in characters like his *pícara* Deeti. Deeti offers a precise model of postcolonial roguery, and a deft figuration of the precarity produced by agricultural enclosures then and now.

Although more than a focus on precarity, in its polylingual prose style, which is to say that the novels are flush with numerous languages, the trilogy dramatizes a heterotemporal world. The simultaneity of histories—of lascar communities or the littorals of Canton—forecloses any reading of the period reliant on the sorts of imperial teleologies attendant to the Anthropocene, if also to Indian Ocean histories that privilege what Micheal Rumore reads as a "cosmopolitical imaginary," and one shot through with a settler-colonial subjectivity aligned with the liberal capitalist *ethos* that the novel expressly critiques (2021a). Ghosh's more nuanced portrait of the Indian Ocean trading world during the height of the Opium Wars helps to shatter such spatiotemporal coordinates as obtain in conventional Indian Ocean methodologies, if also in the normative worldings sustained through popular Anthropocene discourse. This again is a virtue of the picaresque mode in so far as such worldings rely, per Pheng Cheah, on a temporal logic that understands colonial conquest as the birth of South Asian history, if also the Global South more broadly (2015).

The Ibis Trilogy as Environmental Picaresque

In Rob Nixon's 2011 *Slow Violence and the Environmentalism of the Poor*, he makes a case for the picaresque form as particularly well-suited to representing the sorts of environmental violence that he refers to as "slow violence"—a violence that cannot be easily bracketed and thus resists representation in more teleological narrative forms like the *Bildungsroman*. He likewise notes that its central character—the rogue, or *pícaro*—succinctly illustrates the plight of persons, not unlike Ghosh's farmers, whose lives are most directly affected by ecological tyranny. Such "ecosystem people," to take a term from Ramachandra Guha and Juan Aliers, are, generally speaking, amongst the poorest and most marginalized of our global ecology (1994).

In foregrounding such figures as peasant farmers and itinerant lascars within a sweeping historic narrative that moves constantly between historical moments and thus consistently unsettles normative colonial histories—both their temporal configurations and the onto-epistemological assumptions inherent to their figurations of persons, who are necessarily stripped of subjecthood and thus any formative narrative arc—*Sea of Poppies* (and the trilogy more broadly) is in many ways characteristic of the form. The novel, pace its sixteenth-century forebears, makes legible itinerancy, precarity, and displacement through such picaresque conventions as nonlinear timescales, forced displacement, relocation, and deprivation. But *Sea of Poppies* also departs formally from the novels that we shall consider elsewhere in this study: less neopicaresque novel than a postcolonial rogue tale, Deeti's narrative is one of forced itinerancy, but duly one that eschews particular conventions that picaresque enthusiasts too often privilege in their allegiance to Lazarillo—most notably the first-person narration that we discussed in the introduction, and surely the trope of adventure.

Unlike the clearer instantiations of the *pícaro* figure who we encounter in the pages of *The White Tiger* and *Animal's People*, Ghosh's rogues register a different historico-material sensibility. Additionally, and as elsewhere in his *oeuvre*, here the anthropologist offers documentary over and against satire. That is, in lieu of the tightly circumscribed, pseudo-autobiographical narrative of the typical *pícaro's* tale, the novels constitute a comprehensive history—one told through a myriad of local languages and with a rich tableau of images and landscapes so often ascribed to the author's work. As in earlier novels like *The Glass Palace* (2000), Ghosh expands the lens of realist fiction to encompass sprawling landscapes and histories—in this case moving across continents, in and through the ever-shifting littorals of India and China.

Responding to what he sees as a dearth of literature on the Indian side of the trade, Ghosh purports to shift the historical emphasis from Canton's infamous entrepôt to the littoral communities adjacent to Bengal.[9] This is the thrust of *Sea of Poppies*, which begins on the banks of the Ganges River in Bihar where Ghosh's *pícara* Deeti first glimpses the titular "Ibis." The novel then traces her journey and that of several other farmers from Bihar, who join a maritime community of similarly displaced persons en route to Canton. In *River of Smoke*, the author then moves the locus to China, but in the latter novel much of the action takes place not on land—that is the "floating city" of Canton—but instead in the water; or more accurately aboard ship, be it a slave ship, a "floating greenhouse," or any of a number of makeshift vessels that populate the many maritime highways of the two novels. The burden of *Flood of Fire*, to which I shall turn later, is, in part, a battleship.

Significantly, while one might argue that Ghosh's portrait of Canton at times echoes earlier chronicles of the trade, we might pause to consider the many and varied descriptions of the city as a sort of flotilla, itself a portrait of what Margaret Cohen (2006) would describe as the "chronotope of the shore"—one of "six waterside chronotopes" that she poses in contradistinction to Bakhtin's road, which is to say a reconfiguration of the normative time-space of the modern novel because Cohen (like Ghosh) is interested in what occurs off shore.[10] Ghosh's Canton, in which we learn that the European "factories" were both situated along the shore and cordoned off from the mainland illustrates her argument succinctly:

> On the shore, the scope of [the] social world expands from one society or even several societies to include people from all over the globe, and, indeed, all who take human form, even if they have no place to call home, or traffic in the supernatural: pirates, renegades and castaways, demigods, and magicians. In promoting the contact between different members of the same social world, the shore offers a good example of what Pratt calls a "contact zone," a liminal space of meeting that has its own identity even as it is shaped by the distinctive cultures it brings together. (Cohen 2006, 661)

Pace scholars like Sugata Bose, Isabel Hofmeyr, and Antoinette Burton, Ghosh is interested to populate this otherwise liminal space and does so through the privileging of local language systems that make palpable the region's heterogeneity. In this sense, the novel constructs an alternate imaginative schema for envisioning not only the many communities entangled in the India and China trades, but the geography of the trade itself. While "most scholars . . . see the oceans of the world as anti-spaces, as blanks that lie in between, which are somehow unreal in comparison to the landed, national spaces that surround them," Ghosh's novels reveal the populations who in fact lived in these putative "anti-spaces"—animated through a rich polyphony of language (Frykman et al. 2013, 5). This applies to the docks of Canton as much as to the putative *terra nullius* of the nineteenth-century Indian Ocean imaginary.

Aligned with Paul Gilroy's formulation of the chronotope of the sea, Ghosh's focus on the sea and also the ship—in this case the *Ibis*, in order to privilege the trope of crossing, but also of the aforementioned polyphony—stands as a rejoinder to normative conceptions of globality, if also to the terracentrism of popular postcolonial discourse. Commenting on the rich plurality of the sailing ship and its affordances for envisaging new Indian Ocean imaginaries, Ghosh notes:

> The sailing ship is perhaps the most beautiful, most environmentally benign machine the world has ever known. But what really sets a sailship apart from other machines is that its functioning is critically dependent on language: underlying the intricate web of its rigging, is an unseen net of words without which the articulation of the whole would not be possible. (2008a, 58)

The fidelity with which Ghosh then illustrates this linguistic diversity is both a testament to this oft-forgotten community as well as a means of repositioning discussions of the opium trade and of the broader lineaments of Indian Ocean trade within postcolonial and Global South studies. The ship, in its perpetual motion, is agentic, dynamic, and ultimately transformative. The *Ibis* is not merely a container for the movement of dead objects—a reductive reading that has come under fire in discussions of the Atlantic as well. The titular ship is described as a "vehicle of transformation" and a means of fomenting a family:

> And there she was, in the distance, with her two masts and her great beak of a bowsprit. It was now that Deeti understood why the image of the vessel had been revealed to her that day, when she stood immersed in the Ganga: it was because her new self, her new life, had been gestating all this while in the belly of this creature, this vessel that was the Mother-Father of her new family, a great wooden *mái-báp*, an adoptive ancestor and parent of dynasties yet to come: here she was, the *Ibis*. (SP 348)

The *Ibis*'s constant movement mimics that of the "discontinuous histories" of diaspora—a picaresque adventure of sorts, but more so a means of unsettling paradigmatic figurations of colonial time and space.[11] If the Oriental Tale gives primacy to the trope of adventure that Robert Alter outlines, Ghosh's itinerant stories work quite differently—reminiscent indeed of Lazarillo's persistent and *necessary* wandering.

The sorts of forced "wanderings . . . adversity, and ingenious role-playing" that are often attributed to the 1554 *La Vida de Lazarillo de Tormes de sus fortunas y adversidades* are realized in figures like Deeti, or his unlikely sailor Zachary—both of whom must engage in the transient transformation of masquerade to conceal their identities. Deeti, as we know, is a displaced poppy farmer (and an escaped *sati*) being transported as a migrant laborer; and Zachary is a freedman from Baltimore passing along board the *Ibis* as a second-mate. Despite being catalogued as "Black" in the ship's manifest, his light complexion secures him safe passage. Thus, Ghosh transforms the picaresque trope of masquerade in the service of postcolonial critique. So too, the author deploys the form's signature corporeality in order to critique normative maritime histories that eschew what Meena Alexander has called the "phenomenology of passage"—the "corporeal ecology" materialized in the ship's hulls, the opium factories, and the penal colony at Mareech.[12] Against Cartesian observations of inert bodies in motion, the phenomenal also emerges as the reader is offered glimpses of the landscape through the folds of Deeti's sari—her visions made palpable in the strange aperture that Ghosh creates through varied descriptions of the tattered cloth falling against her translucent eyes: "Deeti drew the ghungta of her sari over her face, but the old cotton, cheap and thin to begin with, was now so worn that she would see right through it: the faded fabric blurred the outlines of everything in view, tinting the edges of the plump poppy pods with a faintly crimson halo" (*SP* 27).

Throughout the trilogy, Deeti's perspective is consistently employed as the lens through which to understand the world of the opium trade. Such observations take on a hauntingly tactile hue aboard the *Ibis*: images of extreme deprivation and its impacts are showcased here in lieu of the otherwise inert objects that generally populate such spaces. Deeti is quite literally assaulted by the presence of bodies. In the novels we are faced with the hull (or *dabusa*) of the slave ship: "The leaden gloom, combined with the midday heat and the fetid stench of hundreds of enclosed bodies, gave the unstirred air a weight like that of sewage: it took an effort even to draw breath" (*SP* 361).

In considering the function of the corporeal as a means of both refuting more popular (or palatable) visions of British rule, as well as departing from dominant modes of satire (Salman Rushdie's signature magical realism especially), Ghosh remarks that he was "interested [in] the absolute unbelievableness of what is true." "If you look back on *The Sea of Poppies*," says Ghosh, "what these people endure is unbelievable, nothing magical could equal it" (qtd. in Reddy 2008). That is, while much can be said about the problem of representation evinced by Orientalist images of the opium den, we should also consider narratological arguments that question the efficacy of magic—that magic which potentially "robs" such tales of "precisely the quality that makes them so urgently compelling—which is that they are actually happening on this earth" (Ghosh 2016, 27).

Ghosh's picaresque retelling of the cultivation, manufacture, and ultimately trade of opium qua poppy evinces the "unbelievableness of what was true" though satirical critiques of more popular narratives of opium and addiction. Here we have a parody of the violent Orientalism of Romantic-era writers like Thomas De Quincey. His notorious opium dreams haunt such portraits of abjection as we see inside the Sudder opium factory (in Ghazipur) where Deeti's husband worked before collapsing early on in the novel.[13] When she enters the factory to claim his body we are assaulted by the haunting miasma of this sublime space. Ghosh describes the air as quite literally permeated by the ash and smoke from the factory:

> A miasma of lethargy seemed always to hang over the factory's surroundings. . . . Ground up for storage, these remains produced a fine dust that hung in the air like a fog of snuff. Rare was the passer-by who could brave this mist without exploding into a paroxysm of sneezes and sniffles—and yet it was a miracle, plain to behold, that the coolies pounding the trash were no more effected by the dust than were their young English overseers. (*SP* 89)

Ghosh's evocation of the sublime terror of passage—his phenomenological accounts of Deeti's journey over the black waters, or *kala pani*—is rivaled only by such images of the factories wherein workers like Deeti's husband are so many "legless torsos" swirling about in a narcotic mass. Their disembodied figures are disturbingly reminiscent (if also parodic) of De Quincey's dreamscapes. If, for De Quincey, the "Nilotic mud" of "Hindoostan" conjures an inconceivable terror that is thrown into sharp relief by the revelatory language with which he characterizes empire, for Deeti that mud resonates rather differently.[14]

After navigating the miasmic air, she must enter the inner chambers of the factory. Here, Ghosh collapses his almost indistinguishable human subjects into the vile effluvia of the opium vats:

> No sooner had [Deeti] steadied herself, than her eyes were met by a startling sight—a host of dark, legless torsos was circling around and around, like some enslaved tribe of demons. . . . Their eyes were vacant, glazed . . . [they] had more the look of ghouls than any living thing she had ever seen. . . . Almost as frightening were the white overseers who were patrolling the walkways—for not only were they coatless and hatless, with their sleeves rolled, but they were also armed with fearsome instruments. (*SP* 92–93)

There is something to these descriptions of porous bodies—human flesh redolent with opium dust—which signals a desire to encapsulate a more capaciously imagined ontology of being. Here we see the collapsing of denuded bodies—human and nonhuman. So too, however, we see the disembodied guards—reducible also to "fearsome instruments." Such abstractions correlate to other critiques of imperial taxonomies to which I shall turn below in the context of the broader "age of flowers" with which the novel is centrally concerned. Sufficed to say here that rather than present Indian bodies as somehow lifeless—the stuff of trade and thus fungible, or surplus, commodities—it is the "instrument" of capital that is brute, dead matter. Of course, such parodic indictments are also the purview of the rogue's tale, but here again Ghosh transforms convention by marshaling the agentic capacity too often denied the *inhuman* colonial laborer.

The transcorporeality of bodies shot through with the detritus of opium—such as we see in the paroxysms caused in Deeti and Kabutri through the "opium trash" as well as through stoned butterflies and monkeys—is also illustrated through addiction. If capital mediates through the mechanisms of the opium trade, bringing together Indian and Chinese workers, Ghosh's rearticulation of this relationship productively foregrounds the corporeal experience of both production and addiction. Surreal images of addiction such that we see when Neel first encounters Ah Fatt map opium onto the body in yet another way. Ah Fatt was a Chinese criminal (really just an addict) with whom Neel must share a jail cell. In the descriptions of his writhing body, the horrors of colonial commerce are mapped onto his very skin. What follows is just one instance of violence that is appropriately unapologetic in its excesses. Ah Fatt was "an *afeemkhor* [addict] who had no opium":

> Gradually, Neel became aware of a whimpering sound, accompanied by a soft clicking, like the chattering of teeth. The sound was so close that its source had to be somewhere inside the cell: he dropped to his knees and looked under the charpoys, to discover an unmoving heap lying beneath one of them. He recoiled, more in fear than revulsion, as he might from an animal that was badly wounded or grievously sick—the creature was making a sound that was more like a whine than a moan, and all he could see of its face was a single glinting eye . . . prodded by the stick, a limb came snaking out from under the bed and Neel saw that it was a man's arm, encrusted with filth . . . as the rest of the body slowly emerged, it showed itself to be so thickly mired in dirt and mud that it was impossible to tell whether the man was naked or clothed. Then suddenly the cell was filled with the smell of ordure and Neel realized that it was not just the mud the man was covered in, but also faeces and vomit. (*SP* 309)

In disgust, this former *zamindar* wants to turn away, but he can't. Neel is suddenly sympathetic to this strange figure. We learn in the second novel that their friendship is forged as a consequence of their shared plight: the British effectively sacrificed two populations for which Neel and Ah Fatt become symbolic. The Indian populace would be subjugated through land seizure and enclosure, and the Chinese one through addiction. And so, both end up in the same jail cell on the same ship. And while Zachary and his mate Jodu would be characterized in terms of a general "confederacy of maleness," from the perspective of the EIC and their Indian proxies, Neel and Ah Fatt were seen as a "filthy foreigner" and a "fallen outcaste" (*SP* 300, 374). Consequently, while Neel previously wouldn't deign to eat from the same plate as such a man as Ah Fatt, he would now clean the filth from his body. As Ah Fatt's "bladder and sphincter [were sent] into uncontrollable spasms" (316). Neel would be there first to clean the mess and later to wean his cellmate from this crippling addiction. This addiction was much less luxurious for the Chinese *afeem-koor* than the English one—the English one (as described by De Quincey), of course, offering precisely the sorts of gross abstractions discussed above: human bodies rendered indistinguishable from the tarry source of his famed hallucinations.

In telling this story, Ghosh's novels surely "expose the limits of imperial archives," but they also serve as a sort of history in their own right (Arora 2015, 23). In an interview shortly after *Sea of Poppies* was released, Ghosh remarked:

> I think we have such a distorted idea of our history of the 19th century. . . . When you actually look at the past, it was so different. From writers like Naipaul and so on, we had a picture of what it was like for the Indian migrants after they arrived in places like Mauritius. But for me what was so hard to imagine, so incredibly poignant, was the moment of departure. What did it mean for them? They were farmers, the most rooted people. The courage it took at that time for a Bihari to set out across the kala pani is something you and I can barely conceive of . . . what was it really like, the actual moment of departure when you see everything you know disappearing behind you. (Reddy 2008)

In *Sea of Poppies*, he describes the farmers' rootlessness thus:

> The hand of destiny had strayed so far inland, away from the busy coastlines, to alight on the people who were, of all, the most stubbornly rooted in the silt of the Ganga, in a soil that had to be sown with suffering to yield its crop of story and song. It was as if fate had thrust its fist

through the living flesh of the land in order to tear away a piece of its stricken breath. (389)

It is precisely then the displacement, departure, and consequent movement of the farmer that is the focus of Ghosh's project. The mosaic of discontinuity, which was the colonial landscape of the Indian Ocean, is achieved in part by the novels' nonlinear form. The novels attest to such discontinuous histories, and also to the non-alignment (temporally and spatially) of the various histories of the Bay that recent scholars such as Sugata Bose and Sunil Amrith have sought to expand.

In this sense, Ghosh helps to reinvent the canvas of the nineteenth-century Bay. He gives primacy to both its littoral communities as well as to the newly forged communities aboard the ships that traversed its waters—his titular *Ibis* for one, which carries the "great stream of silt" that were so many migrants (*SP* 75). Thus, prior to turning to the poppy program and the origins of cheap nature, an excursus into Ghosh's remapping of the Indian Ocean and the ways in which such remappings allow for a productive reorientation of Indian Ocean discourse will be useful, especially for thinking through the material stakes of casting this space as somehow *terra nullius*—among them the erasure of lascar communities of the sort represented in Ghosh's character "Serang Ali."

Re-Mapping the Indian Ocean

In his 2013 *Crossing the Bay of Bengal: The Furies of Nature and the Fortunes of Migrants*, Sunil Amrith notes that "the littorals of the Eastern Indian Ocean were linked [in a global imagination] by British imperialism—the movement of soldiers, the posting of garrisons, the exchange of legal codes, and the circulation of officials" (2). But in the *Ibis Trilogy* movement between these ports is reinscribed with a very different story. The maritime communities of the novels are "composed of diverse worldly currents that dispute contemporary Euro-centric notions of modernity and globalization" (Mukherjee 2010, 124). Ghosh's novels "unsettle normative understandings of belonging and displacement" both through the movement of their protagonists and, in Ghosh's case, with the presence of a topography that is itself "ever-shifting" (Mukherjee 2010, 116). On its strange topographies, Amrith also comments that the Indian Ocean "archive lies . . . in the shape of the landscape as much as in the writings of poets and visionaries" (2013, 29).

The chronotopic and heterotopic qualities of Ghosh's titular sea and river are particularly effective in unsettling both the more dominant histories of the region as well as colonialist spatial ontologies that understand "displacement" in rather limited ways. Following recent movements in Global South scholarship—specifically South Asian histories that increasingly dispute the primacy of the nation-state in narratives of colonial and postcolonial identity (Bose, Amrith and others)—projects like Ghosh's "keep in play an Indian Ocean interregional arena of economic and cultural interaction as an analytical unit" (Bose 2009, 21). I would further argue that through their episodic narrative arcs, the novels masterfully "avoid the pitfalls of assuming any uncomplicated and unsustainable thesis about continuity" (Bose 2009, 21). Like Sugata Bose's spatial heuristic—his "one hundred horizons" as a counter to singular understandings of Indian colonial and postcolonial identity—the narrative terrain of the novel reaches across multiple nations as well as regions within the ever-shifting topography of British India's cartography: "The Indian Ocean is a palimpsest for Ghosh, and in his evocative mapping of this place and time, it becomes a rich archive where he reads layers upon layers of stories of power and violence, exchange, resistance, and survival" (Arora 2015, 22).

As we know from extant histories of the region, the "Indian Ocean was an important medium of interaction and exchange long before the arrival of the Portuguese at the end of the fifteenth century," not to mention the British (Arnold and Guha 1996, 13). Thus, recent work in the field of Ocean Studies reflects both a means of recasting conceptions of the Global South predicated on an insufficient (if outmoded) understanding of colonial and postcolonial space as well as a means of recuperating the material histories of the sea: "The Indian Ocean in particular has become an important . . . matrix that has allowed scholars to explore archives of connections that exceed the nation-state through tracing histories of slavery and indenture" (Hofmeyr 2019, 12).[15] Accordingly, in arguing for a terraqueous over and against a "terracentric" ontology of space in the age of sail, Cohen (2010a) remarks:

> Literary studies across the twentieth century preferred scales that came from territory and terrestrial existence. In novel studies, for example, these scales included the city, the factory, and the country; the public and the private; and the nation and the colony. The maritime world, in contrast, introduces oceans and continents, islands, archipelagoes, and coasts, as well as the ship. These spatial scales connect different kinds of landmasses and have histories of their own . . . literary scholars are [now] pioneering new paradigms and concepts of critical and cultural analysis scaled to what the early modern period called the *terraqueous globe*. (658)

Surely, the matrix of the Indian Ocean world as represented in *Sea of Poppies* challenges old paradigms; although more than a simple transposition from land to sea, it takes a less dialectical tack: the novel explores the imbrications between the large-scale agricultural enclosures upon which poppy cultivation depended; the consequent displacement of local communities; and finally the maritime trading networks that both moved hundreds of thousands of chests of opium and which provided for British prosperity at home and abroad.

In this way, Ghosh certainly complicates the sorts of terracentrism that Cohen critiques. But more than subverting such dominant discourses—through the abovementioned repositioning of Indian Ocean trading networks and the centrality of his littoral communities—Ghosh also conjures an early modern "cosmopolitanism [that] offers a counterpoint to the narrowness of the modern nation-state system" (Hofmeyr 2010, 723).[16] He does this, Isabel Hofmeyr argues, by "moving us away from the simplicities of the resistant local and the dominating global" (722). The novels instead move us toward a richer understanding of early modern trade networks, not to mention a more sophisticated understanding of their "terraqueous" environments. Of course, it is Hofmeyr who likewise indicts Ghosh's depiction of such trading networks as problematically romantic—works like his 1992 *In an Antique Land* illustrating what Gaurav Desai has also described as a "romance with free markets" (2013). But *Sea of Poppies* (and the trilogy more broadly) in no way conjures such an ideal imaginary. To wit, Ghosh foregrounds the trenchant inequality of early modern trading networks that relied on forced labor—the abovementioned farmers as well as the lascar communities to whom I shall return below. In this way, Ghosh challenges old paradigms, although not merely land-based ones.

The novels complicate Cohen's taxonomy of maritime tropes. Cohen distinguishes between "blue water" (the vast ocean), "brown water" (the river), and "white water" (sites of chaos broadly defined). While Ghosh is also careful to distinguish between different maritime terrains (both literally and metaphorically)—i.e., the many rivers of the first novel that flow from the farms to the sea, which then ultimately lead to the ocean—his figuration of the black water, or *kala pani*, seems to depart from an otherwise generally sublime "blue" space. That is, more than vastness, it is imbued with a particular horror and one meticulously documented in much South Asian fiction. This is also not the horror of the "white water"—illustrated, in Ghosh's novels, with cyclones—but is instead a horror generated by something more ominous. The "black waters" mark the space between freedom and forced indenture as well as the space between forms of oceanic thinking that are non-assimilable to conventionally cosmopolitan notions of trans-oceanic spaces (Rumore 2021b). And the islands situated therein are not the "utopian counterpart to [the] injustices and problems" of the mainland (*a la* Defoe or More) (Cohen 2006, 659). They are sites upon which both prisons and plantations are constructed. In *Sea of Poppies*, the oft-cited utopian island is a penal colony: "It was only to the outside world that Alipore Jail presented the semblance of a unitary realm: to its inmates, it appeared rather as an archipelago of fiefdoms, each with its own rules, rulers, and ruled" (*SP* 306). Thus, Ghosh's manipulation of the maritime chronotopes that we see in earlier novels of the sea is itself a significant departure.

Notably too, the "sea of poppies," which supplants the natural order of the terrain, works on multiple registers. It usurps both the indigenous flora and fauna of the bay as well as the economic and political institutions that functioned within this social ecology. Here Ghosh's maritime landscape again brings to mind earlier picaresque novels penned by Delaney and Herman Melville—works that also centralized the cartography of the Atlantic and Indian Oceans in the age of sail. Their maritime picaresques likewise take to task putatively legitimate economies that were in fact "so much duperie" (*SP* 487). We see this aboard the *Pequod* with Melville's scrutiny of the colonialist substrate of the whaling industry. We might also make the case that "Extracts" and "Etymologies"—the actual first two chapters of the 1851 *Moby Dick*—were a critical departure from normative onto-epistemologies in their positing of an agentic whale as the central narrative figure.

Although, in his emphasis on language and on the social hierarchies of the lascar communities on his ships, Ghosh's is surely a departure from the sorts of Orientalist imaginings that are evinced by figures like Queequeg and Fedallah. Characters like Serang Ali do more than pay lip service to a more pluralized understanding of the Indian Ocean world; this is not a trite homage to some sort of universalizing (read Kantian) cosmopolitanism. Ghosh is meticulous in conveying Ali's "motley tongue":

> That motley tongue, spoken nowhere but on the water, whose words were as varied as the port's traffic, an anarchic medley of Portuguese calaluzes and Kerala pattimars, Arab booms and Bengal paunchways, Malay proas and Tamil catamarans, Hindusthani pulwars and English snows—yet beneath this farrago of sound, meaning flowed as freely as the currents beneath the crowded press of boats. (*SP* 102)

In *River of Smoke*, this "rich farrago of sound" is also given primacy through figures like Neel, who becomes a *munshi* for a local trader, crafting the chrestomathy for which the trilogy has also become notable.

The Chronotope of the Sea

The sea, as a trope in postcolonial fiction, has long registered an imperial history. As well, the rivers of Joseph Conrad and Naipaul, if also T. S. Eliot, have become touchstones for popular perception—the dark sea wending its way through the heart of darkness in novels rife with images of stagnation and horror. Although, we might contrast this against Derek Walcott, whose 1948 poem *The Sea is History* paints a maritime space rich with crossings—persistent movement over and against stasis. Ghosh's sea works similarly. Its constant movement—traveling itself while traveled upon—reorients what we take to be stable conditions of the postcolony: "Its liquidity, its seemingly anonymous materiality, resonates with a postrepresentational understanding, an anchorless image loaded with time" (Chambers 2010, 679). Iain Chambers remarks that "the liquid insistency of the sea can provide ontological criteria with which to reconfigure our theoretical prison house" (679). And he adds: "This fluid matrix interrupts and interrogates the facile evaluations of a linear mapping disciplined by the landlocked desires of unilateral progress and a homogeneous modernity" (681).

Ghosh's sea (and river) interrogate such facile understandings of the geography of empire: in centralizing the terraqueous landscape of the Opium Wars—including also the illegal practices of England's premier trading company, and Chinese resistance to British hegemony—we come away with a very different history. We might also consider how a focus on the Opium Wars complicates our understanding of China's position in current networks of global capital. Surely, any history that begins in the nineteenth century with Lin Zexu paints a very different economic portrait of China. Ghosh reminds us that their economic (and military) might is not a recent phenomenon.[17] But, and more to the point, Ghosh's history does in fact move us away from the abovementioned landlocked discourse to realize the significance of what were surely not "anti-spaces," nor utopian ones, but simply populated and rather heterogeneous ones. Ghosh's maritime topography resonates quite differently. For this reason, we might argue that the river—in its ornery, because always itinerant nature—is an ideal chronotope for representing the uneven topographies of an ascendant imperial imaginary. This is so particularly in the novels wherein the Bay is illustrated as "a world marked more by border-crossing and heterogeneity than the clean divides of imperial rule" (Arora 2015, 39).

We might also pause to consider that the river itself—be it the Ganga or the Rio Tormes in Cervantes's Spain—inheres with a picaresque quality both because of its movement and because of the *literary* history that sediments its banks. Surely, we cannot read of Deeti's rebirth without considering Lazarillo who "was born on the River Tormes" and thus has "that [as a] surname" (Alpert 1969, 5). When Deeti is roused awake amidst the waves of the Ganges, after fleeing her proposed *sati*, Ghosh writes:

> Then, through the whisper of a deep, hoarse voice it was made known to her that she was alive, in the company of Kalua, on the Ganga—and there was no destination or aim to their journey except to escape . . . and she knew that it was with Kalua that this life would be lived, until another death claimed the body that he had torn from the flames . . . she could hear the whispering of the earth and the river, and they were saying to her that she was alive, alive, and suddenly it was as if her body was awake to the world as it had never been before, flowing like the river's waves, and as open and fecund as the reed-covering bank. (*SP* 175–76)

Like Lazarillo, Deeti is also reborn. Although, Deeti's position as an escaped *sati* certainly complicates any neat transposition of genre, particularly in a colonial context where the simultaneous emasculation of Indian men and fetishization of Indian women served to further British interests. Not to mention, the *pícaro* as symbolic register falls short in our consideration of such material/taxonomic conditions as made possible imperial networks of trade. As instantiations of cheap nature and cheap labor, there is something else operating in the world of the novels. Deeti—as colonial subject, as would-be *sati*, and as indentured servant—is less a parody than a robust critique of the gross abstractions that Ghosh will take up in the context of other human and nonhuman actors, also including soldiers who constitute the regime of cheap nature qua labor that enabled British rule and which form the locus of representation in the final novel of the trilogy, *Flood of Fire*.

But it is perhaps the poppy flower and the farmer, who logically figure in the first novel, where we must begin: both are concise indices of the production of cheap nature in the era that ought rightfully be understood as the Plantationocene, and both were subjected to the rudimentary calculus of a Linnaean taxonomy in order to reify the fungibility of human and nonhuman labor. As we shall see in the following chapters on economic liberalization in the neoliberal era, and given the pervasiveness of the Plantation aesthetic in part authored by Linnaeus—that of a system of flora and fauna drawn to immaculate scale wherein such fauna as colonial subjects are fungible indeed—it would be apt to embrace the term Plantationocene as a means of characterizing what has in fact been a "long process" and an ongoing one. Thus I now turn to the origins of such imperial aesthetics.

Imperial Taxonomies: Botanical Gardens and Floating Greenhouses

In her haunting critique of imperial botany, in an essay entitled "The Flowers of Empire," Jamaica Kincaid comments on Carolus Linnaeus: "It was in a glasshouse," Kincaid notes. "The glasshouse of a rich man named George Clifford, that Carolus Linnaeus, Adam-like, invented modern plant nomenclature. He gave names to the things he saw growing before him" (1996, 30). "Adam-like," Linnaeus's work was ground-breaking in so far as his 1735 *Systema Naturae* would provide categorical distinction to the otherwise amorphous mass of brute matter that constituted "nature"—heretofore understood in the terms of René Descartes as *Res Extensa*, or simply the expressions of the thinking subject in the era of Enlightenment. Now, to follow Francis Bacon in "torturing the secrets" out of this feminized space, one had a viable guide. If Locke, in 1689, would follow *Genesis* in arguing for improvement through imperial domination, Linnaeus would augment this project with a useful schematic. Improvement could now be understood taxonomically—through a system that could achieve the requisite scalar coordinates for the plantation, and thus the requisite cheapening required for the creation and accumulation of capital. Through this initiating taxonomy, a new cosmogony of the modern world would be born (Debaise 2017). The Christian narrative of creation is recast in the language of discovery, conquest, and ultimately scientific enlightenment—a process made possible by the systematic ordering of the landscape. If for Locke in 1689, "all the world was America," savage and free for the taking, Linnaean understandings of landscape, coupled with the armies of scientists and artists employed by Britain's imperial project, would enable the domestication of such wild lands—those sublime landscapes of De Quincey's "Hindustan" and alluded to more broadly in colonial discourses whose only inclusion of a putatively developed India would be couched in the rhetoric of miasma and disease.

Critiques of imperial liberalism rightfully begin with the language of enlightenment—inclusive of emergent theories of *bios*—and the ways in which what we might understand as a form of uneven enlightenment was made possible through the "grotesque fictions" of Locke, along with the social contracts of Jean-Jacques Rousseau and John Stuart Mill (Ghosh 2015b). Effacing the material histories of colonial suffering with a narrative of civilizational progress, the contractarians collectively authored a version of the modern whereby the colonial elsewheres that form the constitutive outside of global capitalism could be imaginatively erased. To echo Lowe's vital discussion of the skeins of imperial ideology and its imbrications with contemporaneous systems of indentured labor and the destruction of native landscapes, it is clear that the continued decimation of a global ecology is only possible through the imperial-era abstractions of a Rousseau or Mill. So too, through the Lockean mandate to improve, which could only be made materially possible through the sorts of botanical simplifications crafted by Linnaeus.

This is dramatized, perhaps especially, in *River of Smoke*. Disregarding available Native traditions/epistemologies, Linnaeus would offer: "No natural system of plants, though one or the other approaches it quite closely, has so far been constructed . . . as long as a natural system is lacking, artificial systems will definitely be needed" (qtd. in Engel-Ledeboer and Engel 1964, 23). Linnaeus would, more notoriously, venture to categorize humans in such a way; his categorizations of non-Europeans would engender (materially and politically) the savage "other" at the precise moment when such persons were being stripped of their land: "In his . . . *General System of Nature*, [Linnaeus] offered a typology that put humans in the class of mammals, the order of primates, the genus of *Homo*, the species of *Homo sapiens*. But he also included observations on different kinds of *Homo sapiens*, noting variations in appearance and character" (Patel and Moore 2017, 187). Such categorizations included (qtd. in Patel and Moore, 187):

2. Copper-coloured, choleric, erect. *American* . . .
Hair black, straight, thick; *nostrils* wide; *face* harsh; *beard* scanty; *obstinate*, content, free. *Paints* himself with fine red lines. *Regulated* by custom.

3. Fair, sanguine, brawny. *European*
Hair yellow, brown, flowing; *eyes* blue; *gentle*, acute, inventive. *Covered* with close vestments. *Governed* by laws.

4. Sooty, melancholic, rigid. *Asiatic*
Hair black; *eyes* dark; *severe*, haughty, covetous. *Covered* with loose garments. *Governed* by opinions.

5. Black, phlegmatic, relaxed. *African*
Hair black, frizzled; *skin* silky; *nose* flat; *lips* tumid; *crafty*, indolent, negligent. *Anoints* himself with grease. *Governed* by caprice.

Monstrous. Varying by climate or art.

There is no opium without the sorts of categorical distinctions that we attribute to modern taxonomy as such; and there is no "cheap labor" without the reduction of the human as outlined above—a phenomenon to which I shall turn following my discussion of poppy monoculture.

Documenting Cheap Nature: "The Age of Flowers"

Such a hagiographic means of recasting occupation as Ghosh's "age of flowers"—a term that effectively reconfigures normative colonial timescales—allows for the author to foreground the destructive nature of the trade without necessarily reducing all of the characters' experiences to the economic, or a mere "interruption in capital's logic" (Ahmed 2011, 5). Within the rubric of an "age of flowers" the novels render the fabric of the broader experience of poppy; as well, its imbrications with local custom. The intertwining narratives of the local and the global also instantiate arguments regarding the limitations of genre, such that we discussed in the introduction. As an example, Deeti's comments regarding her tragic fate as being ruled "by a malevolent star" are contrasted against observations of the nuanced position of poppy in the lives of peasant farmers more broadly: "This miniscule orb [was] at once bountiful and all-devouring, merciful and destructive, sustaining and vengeful" (*SP* 439). Here Deeti effectively maps this symbol of imperial commerce onto a more intimate, and very local, narrative. While the reader is ultimately to conclude that poppy is singularly determinant of Deeti's fate, this ambivalence forces a recognition of a more complicated experience than a purely capitalogenic explanation might allow. Of course, this sort of critique has long occupied scholars of Subaltern Studies concerned to avoid reproducing the sorts of economic abstractions that historians Dipesh Chakrabarty (2000a) and Ranajit Guha (1988b) would replace by "provincializing" such narratives.

Owing to such historical work, the hegemonic narrative regarding the singular capacity of British India and its imperial agents has been productively unsettled. And despite the imperial fictions of apologists for empire—from T. B. Macaulay to former World Bank president Larry Summers—the economic history of opium has been well documented by scholars similarly interested to trouble such perspectives. Carl Trocki's meticulous map of opium trade circuits and of the region's history is a notable example; and like Ghosh, Trocki also contends that "without the drug, there probably would have been no British empire" (1999, xiii). His is an economic argument on par with Amrith's (2013) and also John F. Richards's (1981, 2002), both of whom posit opium as the sole explanation for the sudden and, according to some, inexplicable takeover by the English in the eighteenth century. Notably, and as Trocki also points out, India had successfully kept the "strangers at the gate" at bay for centuries (34). This particular network of global capital was well-situated before the British gained the *diwani*, or right to collect taxes, in 1765, but the "strangers at the gate" would now, through the use of increased military might and illegal monopoly, make their way through. Trocki cites Parkinson accordingly:

> As far as one can judge, the British businessmen brought to their affairs neither capital, energy nor ability. They were certainly not in a position to teach the natives anything about business methods. They could introduce nothing novel in the way of banking, but they were white men and therefore able to inspire confidence in other white men . . . with this advantage they were able at least partially to elbow the natives out of ship owning and insurance. (Parkinson qtd. in Trocki 1999, 48)

John F. Richards also remarks:

> The opium cultivation, as a cash export crop grown under uniquely restricted conditions set by a state monopoly, did have considerable importance for the peasant economy of the northern opium producing tracts. . . . The Indian [and later British] Government created a state controlled system which successfully regulated the quantity and quality of production, stabilized prices at a high level, and consistently undercut or assimilated other sources of international competition for the Chinese market. (1981, 61)

The monopoly on poppy cultivation reaped enormous profits for company shareholders, and consequently for the crown. It also served as an economic solution for a hemorrhaging wartime British economy: "If not for opium, the drain of silver from Britain and her colonies would be too great too sustain"; but "if they could sell enough opium to pay for the cost of tea purchase it would eliminate the bullion drain from Europe" (*SP* 109, Trocki 32). Amrith also remarks: "Levies on opium accounted for 20 percent of revenues from India," and were responsible for restoring fiscal health to the empire (2013, 67). To wit, "the British government waged the Napoleonic Wars virtually free from foreign debt, thanks to the enforced tribute levied upon India—and this alone allowed for a sixfold increase in public spending between 1792 and 1815" (Amrith 67). But it is the local impact with which Ghosh, and historians like Amrith, are centrally concerned—its human and ecological costs. If, in his piece for *Blackwoods* in 1840, De Quincey strikes a very different tone—a triumphant plea for "the opium trade [which] contribute[d] upwards of three millions per annum!" (De Quincey 1890c, 167)—Amrith and Ghosh reveal the human cost of Britain's impressive GDP.

The human and ecological costs of the trade were astounding. To be sure, Ghosh's novels effectively expose an economic genocide—genocide, that is, if we consider the human costs of enclosure and resource extraction. The depictions of Deeti both as a *sati* and later in the hull of a slave ship anticipate Vandana Shiva's argument in the context of India's cotton belt regarding the genocidal practices of agribusiness. Not unlike the vast tracts of land in Vidarbha apportioned for cotton production, the land required to cultivate opium on such a scale was also quite vast. The 1793 acquisition of the Bengali coast (following a 1765 free trade agreement with the extant leaders of the Mughal Empire) would be expanded substantively beyond the initial *zamindaries*. Land reaching some 400 miles north (into Bihar) would be annexed for the purpose of cultivating poppy on land that once provided sustenance for local farmers.

Consequently, De Quincey's strangely ephemeral accounts of addiction stand in stark relief against the horrific images of the factories in *Sea of Poppies* and surely of the horrors that we see below deck when those same farmers are being transported to prison camps. Soon after Deeti is entreated to the horrific vision of the opium factory, she muses about the sublime, "sepulchrally quiet" place "as if it were some cavernous shrine in the high Himalayas, chilly, damp and dimly lit" (*SP* 94).[18] Subsequently, on her way home, she passes by the mausoleum of the "Laat Sahib"—that is, Lord Cornwallis, whose memorial haunts the factory. The "Laat Sahib" was in part responsible for a continued mode of imperial rule that simply shifts from rent farming to opium cultivation. The Cornwallis Code named the contract between the East India Company and the *zamindars* across what became the Company's permanent settlement. The East India Company effectively coopted an Indian system that, however inequitable as regards to indentured peasant farmers, practiced a mode of agriculture that at least produced more food than debt.

In Gyan Prakash's (1990a) study of the "genealogies of labor servitude," he notes that local landlords at least furnished farmers with some degree of social welfare. But following the economic agreement between the company and local landlords, rent gained primacy as the central commodity in the region; and corruption soon followed. Significantly, the conditions for famine (in 1770 and after) were induced not by any natural cause, but by the failures of the new administration for whom the accumulation of capital took primacy over the welfare of the Bengali population. In Adam Smith's 1776 *An Inquiry into the Nature and Causes of the Wealth of Nations*, he remarks: "Some improper regulations ... imposed by the servants of the East India Company upon the rice trade, contributed ... to turn that dearth into a famine" (qtd. in Ahmed 2011, 120).[19] Siraj Ahmed also notes that:

> The reports from Bengal claimed that rather than let markets redistribute grain to distressed regions, Company officials and their agents monopolized rice and wheat, closed off supply lines from areas of abundance, and created the famine ... the Company's own directors concluded that "the [peasants] were compelled to sell their rice to ... monopolizing Europeans [who] could be no other than persons of some rank in our service." (120)

The improprieties of Company practices are well documented as is the discontent with their business practices, which eventually led to the dissolution of their charter. Beyond the cooptation of the *zamindari* system, which initiated the now infamous culture of corruption and exploitation in British India, the shift from rent farming to opium cultivation further exacerbated an already volatile situation. Local revenue collectors, who were emboldened by company representatives, were exceedingly dishonest and also quite violent. Deeti describes Ghosh's fictional EIC collectors accordingly: the "English sahibs ... would go from home to home, forcing cash advances on farmers, making them sign *asámi* contracts. It was impossible to say no to them: if you refused they would leave their silver hidden in your house ... it was no use telling the white magistrate that you hadn't accepted the money" (*SP* 29). Richards also observes: "The East India Company officers who bid low for the farms of opium misused their official powers to force the contractors to surrender their crop at less than the cost of production" (1981, 63). This economic model, which produced endemic debt and widespread famine, accounts for my earlier comments regarding the novels' resonance in current discussions around India's cotton economy.

Not surprisingly, the newly taxed farmer is of little concern both in the colonies and certainly still at home: agricultural enclosures in England circa 1793 were similarly catastrophic—also inducing conditions for hunger and widespread poverty. Ironically, 1793 also marks the birth of another Briton whose *Village Minstrel* was published the same year as De Quincey's *Opium Eater*. But John Clare's work—perhaps most famously his 1821 *Village Minstrel*, which stands as a rejoinder to Oliver Goldsmith's 1770 pastoral *The Deserted Village* in its literal population of said village with such "laboring swains" as the poet-farmer himself, and in its explicit indictment of contemporary agricultural enclosures—evinces the sentiment of the displaced farmer who by dint of his new economic condition was rendered a "rogue anachronism" indeed. It is this sentiment that informs *Sea of Poppies*, though here it is the farmer of poppy and not wheat (or rice) who suffers, perhaps doubly insofar as this cash crop consumed the bulk of arable land in the region. Deeti observes accordingly:

> Their hut . . . looked like a tiny raft, floating upon a river of poppies . . . [its] roof was urgently in need of repairs, but in this age of flowers, thatch was not easy to come by: in the old days, the fields would be heavy with wheat in the winter, and after the spring harvest, the straw would be used to repair the damage of the year before. But now, with the sahibs forcing everyone to grow poppy, no one had thatch to spare . . . when Deeti was her daughter's age, things were different: poppies had been a luxury then, grown in small clusters between the fields that bore the main winter crops—wheat, masoor dal and vegetables. (*SP* 28)

"A Rule of [Poppy] for Bengal"

As we see in the novels, the EIC's poppy program was in fact catastrophic for local farmers, particularly given the size of the operation. Ghosh's titular poppies in the first installment of the trilogy refer to the dominant agricultural output of the region of Bengal in the 1830s—some 25,000 acres at the outset; and significantly more as the trade makes its way into the next century:

> The English, following their takeover of Bengal, pushed opium to the forefront as the primary exchange commodity in Asia . . . if we look at the trading world of Asia as a system of interdependent relationships, the role of opium emerges as a pivotal agent of change. For most of the nineteenth century, the drug was the major export from India to China, pushing aside Indian textiles as the most valuable of India's products. (Trocki 1999, 48, 58)

Adding to this, Bihari peasants were often forced to grow the commodity: "Even in years of famine farmers were forced to give up grain cultivation in favor of opium" (Trocki 66).

In Guha's foundational text on colonial land tenure, he recounts the trajectory from the *zamindari* system to that of the EIC's mode of revenue farming— or the extension of *zamindari* rights (under the Mughals) to "areas that may have been *raiyati* earlier" (Prakash 1990a, 87). Gyan Prakash similarly observes:

> By 1720, hitherto undercultivated and unmeasured lands were developed and measured; their responsibility to pay the land revenue to the

Mughal emperors was calculated and fixed; and the *zamindars* holding these *parganas* were charged with collecting the calculated demand. In this process, it is very likely that those villages which at the time of the *Āin's* composition were raiyati, or controlled by non-Hindu groups, were now invaded by *zamindari* rights. (87)

He further remarks that the "settlement . . . [invoked] European economic doctrines and recall[ed] the experience of improving English landlords"; following "permanent settlement . . . land became the fixed property of *zamindars* so long as they paid revenue fixed in perpetuity" (Prakash 100). Significantly, Bihar is one of the foci of Prakash's study in which he uses several anecdotes to trace the evolution of land tenure legislation from land as collectively owned to the "emergence of land as an object" (120).

It is this philosophical understanding of land as an object—subject to abstract speculation and modern market schemes—that accounts for Prakash's comments about English landlords. It is likewise this market-driven orientation to land use that would lay the foundation for the ecocidal poppy program foregrounded in the novels—the storyline beginning in 1838 just before the first opium war and some forty years after Burke's indictment of Bengal's first governor. At this point Lord Cornwallis, the author of the doctrine of "permanent settlement" or Cornwallis Code, is long dead. He died in Ghazipur, the site of the company's premier factory, in 1805—the factory, that is, where we see Deeti witnessing the "vacant ghouls" who render her harvest into a commodifiable drug.

It is worthwhile mentioning that the initial edicts authored by Hastings, Cornwallis, and others would be augmented by an inequitable tax system that favored corporate monopoly—a monopoly of the sort frequently exalted by Ghosh's fictional EIC captains. The Company's monopoly allowed for unprecedented profits both through their exploitation of farmers like Deeti and also through a series of corrupt tax schemes. In 1818, the Company resolved to allow for the transportation of Malwa opium through the British ports, but exercised a heavy tax: "Indian exporters paid an excise fee of Rs 175 per chest [which] immediately added two million rupees per year to the revenues of the Bombay Government" (Richards 1981, 65). Consequently, "by 1828 cultivation had risen to 79,488 acres, by 1838 to 176,745 acres. Just prior to the Opium war, over fifteen thousand 140 lb. chests of Bengal opium were sent to the China market . . . and [from] 1834–39, opium proceeds amounted to an annual average of 6 percent of the total Indian government official revenues (6.8 million rupees to 112.6 million) total income" (Richards 1981, 65–66). To maintain such profits, the Company needed a war—the first "Opium War" commencing in 1839. Ghosh's depiction of the war constitutes the narrative burden of the third novel in the trilogy, *Flood of Fire* (2015). Here the author describes both China's superior military technology as well as Britain's reliance on Indian soldiers (or *sepoys*). The latter occupy the novel's central storyline—Deeti's brother Kesri Singh numbering among them.

The theater of war that Ghosh paints in the third novel offers a sort of dramatic recompense for the horrors that we confront in *Sea of Poppies* and *River of Smoke*—both portraits of a rapacious business model that is hauntingly similar to current imperialist practices. In *Flood of Fire*, Ghosh exposes the EIC's army as parasitic, capitalizing on their colonial subjects, both Indian and Irish. He likewise offers stunning portraits of camaraderie. The reader is momentarily removed from the stark reality of the opium ships, and is offered instead two friends in the form of a *sepoy* and an Irish fife player. But the third novel ultimately ends, perhaps as it must, with a transformed Zachary Reid poised to continue the EIC's economic exploits; and if the reader is wont to read Zachary's new role as an ironic one, we might recall Lowe's argument (discussed in the introduction) regarding the modern autobiography as an enabling fiction. Ghosh is clearly parodying such fictions: that a former slave would aspire toward capital gain is representative of the sorts of liberal narratives that the picaresque genre has historically critiqued—the abovementioned *Blake* a prime example in its skewering of contemporaneous narratives of uplift. Such narratives, we know, have historically lauded the forces of the free market while ignoring a vast underclass who are persistently sacrificed in its name. Deeti is but one example, and her story continues to resonate deeply.

Documenting Cheap Nature, Part II: Other Flowers

Sea of Poppies is, as its namesake implies, concerned primarily with the cultivation of poppy and the consequent production and trade of opium; but the taxonomic and thus economic conditions that govern the trade also obtain in the production of other commodities—inclusive of persons and language as discussed above, and also of tea. Additionally, beyond the putatively singular innovation of botanists like Linnaeus there was an army of painters and artists responsible for the production of a massive archive of *medica materia* of the sort that Paulette will marshal in her work in Mauritius in *River of Smoke*. Such images make possible the "botanical babels" that figure in the second novel and likewise expose Orientalist notions of a "pure" nature—sublime, impenetrable, and productive of the sorts of "melancholic" figures that Linnaeus described—as the necessary epistemological condition for imperial domination (Batra 2013, 322).[20] Also speaking to the taxonomic substrate of the "age of flowers" more broadly, toward the close of the novel, Ghosh's "Robin Chinnery" muses: "It seemed to me exceedingly *peculiar* that a man should love flowers as well as opium—and yet I see now that there is no contradiction in this, for are they not perhaps both a means to a kind of intoxication? Could it not even be said that one might lead inevitably to the other?" (*RS* 470). On these grounds, one could argue that the botanical imperialism at work in the second novel should have come first—perhaps.

Ghosh sets up a clear analogy here between the garden and the poppy field—the garden also described in analogous terms to the slave ship. Such descriptions again recall Kincaid's exquisite argument regarding the "flowers of empire": "This benign way of expressing an extraordinary historical event-'trade being developed,' leaving out the nature of the trade being developed: trade in people and the things that they possessed, plants, animals, and so on-never ceases to amaze me" (1996, 31). The Linnaean cartography that is deployed throughout the subcontinent—rendering the natural world as so many objects to be studied, and thus recalling Prakash's comments about "land as object"—is the first step toward the sorts of cash-cropping that we see practiced in the opium trade. In one prescient scene, we see Paulette dutifully watering the paltry remains of the local flora—the few indigenous plants that she cultivates on the outskirts of Burnham's gardens. Burnham, like the other British dignitaries, lives in a home that boasts magnificent gardens; theirs are called Bethel. If we, following Robin (and later Neel), read the practice of "botanizing" as a substratum of the more overt mode of ecological imperialism that we see at work in the opium trade, then we must surely read Burnham's "Bethel" as a testament to its namesake—a literally demiurgic understanding of the Bay. Here "nature's economy" is replaced by that of the British, and violently so. Zachary even comments at one point: "Bethel loomed in the distance, like the hull of a darkened ship" (*SP* 298).

The elaborate gardens that we see in the second novel "reveal how early modern science and especially natural history, of which botany was a subfield, remained strategically important in global struggles among emerging nation-states for land and resources" (Schiebinger and Swan 3):

> Instead of freely circulating in an idyllic and seamless republic of letters, science in Europe when observed from the vantage point of the Indian Ocean, moved in spaces bounded by national political and economic interests, and shaped by different regimes of performativity within which alone the meaningfulness of knowledge can be determined. (Schiebinger and Swan 68)

We see this most clearly in the character of Fitcher—the cold Englishman whose tears startle him in one particularly comical portrayal—and also in the search for paintings of the *Camellia Sinensis*, or tea plant. Fitcher captures the *Redruth*, a floating greenhouse that offers a strange relief to the *Ibis*. If the former is a "vehicle of truth" that exposes the piracy of the company through explicit images of slave ships, the latter is duly a "vehicle of truth" revealing another sort of piracy. Significantly, the strangely artificial landscape aboard this "floating greenhouse" is mimicked on land: "In Nature there existed no forest where African creepers were at war with Chinese trees, nor one where Indian shrubs and Brazilian vines were locked in a mortal embrace. This was a work of Man, a botanical Babel" (*RS* 35).

In *River of Smoke* Ghosh tells us that Fitcher "looked upon Nature as an assortment of puzzles, many of which, if properly resolved could provide rich sources of profit . . . to him plants were no different from doorknobs, or sausages, or any other object that could be sold for a price on the market" (*RS* 74, 77). Hence Robin's remarks concerning opium and flowers. Sausages indeed, the plants themselves seemed to have no individual (or intrinsic) worth. Notably, in the novel it is the painter of the tea plant who Fitcher (and the unwitting Paulette) pursue.[21] But, that no paintings actually exist of the plant, and that Fitcher's journey is futile, adds comic relief to what is a significant component of the imperial practices in the region:

> The search for the golden camellia in the novel connects directly to the search for tea plants later in the century. Tea, or *Camellia sinensis*, is part of the camellia family but that is not what Fitcher is looking for in the novel. His trade is in flowers as objects of beauty, though he does mention that, following in William Kerr's footsteps, the golden camellia he is hoping to find has medicinal properties that could "reverse the effects of ageing" and be useful in battling "consumption." (Batra 2013, 329)

The search for the simulacrum—not an actual plant, but a mirage—further illustrates Ghosh's critique of colonial knowledge systems that work to supplant local systems with a language of order that transcends and thereby effaces local ecologies, and of course, local cultures. A means, that is, of transcending local difference and imposing a neat critical method not only to "know humans across space and time," but to dominate them (Ahmed 2013, 305).

The genre of *medica materia* that is mostly parodied in the second novel epitomizes the role of such knowledge systems in colonial programs across the Indian Ocean. It also anticipates that other knowledge system—the emergent genre of the dictionary, which is also central to the novel. In the construction of both a set of local dictionaries as well as the cultivation of an encyclopedic *medica materia*, "obstinate clerks" like the unfortunate Neel "were able to reduce Indian society, which they found forbiddingly complex and heterogeneous, to a discrete number of legal and religious texts, which they rendered legible and coherent" (Ahmed 2013, 321). We see this too in the letters between Paulette and Robin, which trace both the genealogy of local plants as well as the history of botanical paintings. We see this perhaps most shockingly in the abstractions of the human qua inhuman such that the "forbiddingly complex" categories that lie outside of "colonial man" are easily rendered surplus, if excremental. I thus turn finally to "cheap labor" and thus "cheap lives," both of which make possible the opium program from the outset.

Documenting Cheap Nature, Part III: Cheap Labor

To understand labor only in Locke's terms—that is, the productive expression of rational man who domesticates an otherwise unimproved space—or through a Marxian lens that similarly operates through a rift between "society" and "nature," is to participate in the same mode of ontological cheapening as obtains in the cultivation of opium or tea. Labor, as a requisite component in the production of capital, is an abstraction, and one long understood through such representations as, e.g., Charles Dickens's "hands" in the 1854 novel *Hard Times*—a novel that dramatizes the dehumanization and commodification of labor in the English factory system. Such a representation is consistent with Marxian renderings of similarly atomized bodies at work. However much such critiques serve to redress liberal notions of improvement, they nonetheless do little to intervene in the sorts of violent abstractions that Ghosh takes to task.

As an index of the abstraction and commodification of labor, we might first look to the lascars in the novels—seamen, who like so many others have taken to the sea in pursuit of freedom, and who epitomize the *pícaro*, or *buscón*: "Most of the lascars were itinerants and vagrants, who did not care to speak too much about their past; some didn't even know where their origins lay, having been sold off as children to the ghat-serangs who supplied lascars to ocean-going vessels" (*SP* 184).[22] In the novels and elsewhere, their lives are the stuff of much romance, and much misconception. And yet "Ghosh's response to colonialist demonization or archival marginalization of these sailors is not necessarily to portray them as romanticized heroic adventurers but rather to paint a fuller picture of their lives in a realistic and sympathetic tone" (Arora

2015, 28). Images of key figures like Serang Ali are neither empty homages, nor are they weirdly Orientalist depictions like those of Melville's Fedallah. They are made flesh in thoughtful portrayals that deploy both local language systems as well as more nuanced geographies. If Fedallah was a sort of mute "celestial"—attributed a noteworthy maritime acumen, but no real agency in the novel—Ghosh's Serang Ali resonates quite differently. Ali is not only the foreman; he is a critical resource to Zachary as well as the architect of their eventual escape at the close of *Sea of Poppies*. Like Fedallah, Ali possesses an unmatched navigational sense—one that also finds them safely in China in the second novel. But rather unlike Fedallah, Ali is a dynamic character upon whom much of the action of the first novel depends.

Sea of Poppies is partitioned into sections entitled "land" and "sea" with the latter often taking center stage. Ghosh makes a point of illustrating the twin points of the company's program—its terrestrial conquest, which is realized in the monocropping of poppy; and its maritime one, which is realized in the network of coolie and opium ships that move back and forth across the bay transporting both commodities. If the farmer is, by dint of an increasingly inequitable system of revenue farming, rendered a "rogue anachronism," the same might be said of the lascar:

> The social history of South Asian steamship workers sits rather uneasily with apologetic "globalization" narratives that celebrate unending beach parties of happy "hybridity" or revel in "the Dance of the Flows and the Fragments" . . . as Sherwood, Tabili, and others have shown, the maritime labour market of the nineteenth and twentieth centuries was structured into a rigidly racist hierarchy with South Asians at its bottom. (Ahuja 2006, 112).

Ahuja also notes: "In the political and economic context of imperialism, the enormous nineteenth-century expansion of shipping within and beyond the Indian Ocean facilitated the development of a new and increasingly transcontinental regime of labour circulation" of the sort we see illustrated in both the opium and coolie trades in the novels (111). Central to this circulation of labor were the lascars who "served under their own petty officers. The most important of these was the serang, whose duties corresponded to those of a boatswain" (Jaffer 2013, 155). Although, and as Ghosh illustrates in such figures as Ali who serves under Zachary, there was a significant disparity in rank:

> Serang Ali's demeanour became suddenly insistent. Picking up the trowsers, he held them up to Zachary. "Mus wear," he said in a voice that was

soft but steely. "Malum Zikri one big piece pukka sahib now. Mus wear propa clothes." Zachary was puzzled by the depth of feeling with which this was said. "Why?" he asked. "Why in the livin hell is it so important to you?" "Malum must be propa pukka sahib," said the serang. "All lascar wanchi Malum be captin-bugger by'm'by." "Eh?" Now, in a sudden, bright flash of illumination, Zachary understood why his transformation meant so much to the serang: he was to become what no lascar could be—a "Free Mariner," the kind of sahib officer they called a malum. (*SP* 49)

The serang's pleadings here signal more than an aspiration for freedom: the relationship between Ali and Zachary to some extent mirrors that of Neel and Ah Fatt—an unlikely alliance. Zachary's past also offers an ironic twist to Ali's pleadings and intimates a shared plight. Zachary's frequent musings about his own past remind the reader of just this: "A memory came to him, of listening to his mother as she told the story of the first time she was summoned by the master—his father—to the cabin in the woods . . . the whims of masters could be, at times, kind as well as cruel, for wasn't it just such an impulse that has caused old Mr. Reid to grant his mother her freedom so that he, Zachary, would not be born a slave?" (*SP* 298).

If new currents in Global South studies are noteworthy for positing a new ontology (and geography) of colonial space within the usual land-based discourse of British India, Ghosh's project is also a nod toward recent efforts to similarly consider "circulatory" modes of labor (like the lascars), whose tales are equally obscured by both an elusive colonial record as well as the "prose of counter-insurgency" that emphasizes the perceived criminality of this figure. As Ian Kerr remarks: "Their imputed criminality, marginality, and poverty—their 'stigmatization'-has preoccupied scholars to the detriment of understanding their important economic functions" (2006, 86). But Ghosh's efforts here too are more complicated. That is, what we might call the trope of the mutiny in maritime literature is not eschewed but amplified. Rather than paint the lascars as "romanticized heroic adventurers" or petty criminals, we are presented with a picture of the serang that again contests the putative progressivism of Melville.

The novels deploy the trope of the mutiny, because there was a surfeit of such mutinies in maritime history, and because far from merely illustrating criminality, the mutiny conveys agency. Like the mutiny featured in maritime picaresque novels like *Blake*, the "minutia of plan" and keen design deployed by Ghosh's sailors effectively refutes yet another racist charge (De Quincey 1890d). That is, in one of his many Orientalist tirades, De Quincey (1890d) would also scoff at the 1857 uprising, noting (in a sort of quizzical tone) that they couldn't possibly have pulled it off—that they surely weren't (couldn't be) communicating with one another without the knowledge of the British. De Quincey's comments on the "childishness and defect of plan" are thrown into relief by the cunning of Ghosh's roguish sailors. The mutiny with which *Sea of Poppies* culminates is a brilliant portrait of *subaltern* agency—devised by Serang Ali, Jodu (a former boatman from Canton), Zachary, Kalua (a former untouchable from Bihar), Neel (the aforementioned *zamindar*), Paulette (the daughter of a fictional Carl Linnaeus), and finally Deeti. Such an ending, it might be argued, is an ideal means of sustaining ambiguity—sequel aside, we are left in the dark—and further parodying a conventional/colonial *Bildung*. Ghosh's novels expose the lie of an archive that denies the humanity of the many seaman who were largely responsible for steering the riotous winds and seas of the Bay of Bengal "with frequent readings of the stars" born not from any "celestial" heritage, but from generations of navigational acumen (*SP* 17).

Of course, this is by no means to undercut the experience of forced labor, and surely not of formal indenture networks in the Indian Ocean trading world. If the *de facto* practices of what is colloquially termed the Indian Ocean slave trade—the abovementioned manacles and the treatment of former farmers on refitted slave ships—resemble the practices of its Atlantic counterpart, it is the *de jure* distinction, or the contract of indenture which instantiates a form of market freedom, which Ghosh masterfully critiques through the vile comments of his fictional Company officer Benjamin Burnham. For Burnham, forced indenture, in so far as it aligns with market interests, is a form of "freedom." Hence also his comments above regarding "Jesus Chris [as] free trade" (*SP* 113). More to the point, per Burnham: "Free trade is a right conferred on Man by God, and its principles apply as much to opium as to any other article of trade"—the latter including farmers, or "coolies" (112). To Zachary's incredulous queries, Burnham would retort: " 'Freedom, yes, exactly' " . . . " 'Isn't that what the mastery of the white man means for the lesser races?' " (77). That human labor (whether farmers or lascars) would be rendered indistinguishable from other commoditized forms concisely instantiates Moore's argument, and mine, for both as a form of "cheap labor" and thus "cheap life"—a denuded category of *bios* easily rendered fungible and thus deployed by the Company accordingly.

Girmitiyas and Indenture

As itinerant laborers, the lascars figure a significant departure from the regime of indenture that is likewise foregrounded in the novels and which constituted the bulk of labor necessary for the production of opium. If there is a charge to be made about romanticizing early modern trading networks, it could possibly apply to the *serang*. Surely, this cannot be said of the descriptions of indenture. While the ship-bound fraternity—the "confederacy of maleness"—that we see between figures like Zach and Jodu and Ali, and even Ah Fatt, offer some recompense for the horrors below deck, and the sorority of women in the hull similarly figure modes of intimacy that might assuage previous images of forced separation, such modes of intimacy clearly represent the "intimacy" to which Lowe refers. This is the intimacy forged through the tendrils of an emergent global plantation economy; and it thrives on the exploitation and ultimate extermination of labor.

Deeti is one of many farmers who are forced into debt because of the poppy program and the system of *asami* contracts described above. She will ultimately become an indentured laborer after losing her land and her livelihood. She ends up on the *Ibis* precisely for this reason; and however much the ship is a "vehicle of transformation" and a site where relationships will be cultivated across caste, it is likewise an ostensible slave ship, and Deeti (and Kalua) are *girmitiyas*:

> They were so called because, in exchange for money, their names were entered on "girmits"—agreements written on pieces of paper. The silver that was paid for them went to their families, and they were taken away, never to be seen again: they vanished, as if into the netherworld. . . . A boat will take them to Patna and then to Calcutta . . . and from there they'll go to a place called Mareech. (*SP* 71)

Mareech is one of several island prisons that, again, contests more popular images of maritime utopias—instantiating, as it does, the carceral geography of the Indian Ocean imaginary.

In their stunning collection of "Coolitude" writing and the Indian labor diaspora, Marina Carter and Khal Torabully (2002) archive a series of poems and folksongs that lay bare the sentiment of the *girmitiya*:

> Born in India, we are prepared to go to Fiji,
> Or, if you please, to Natal to dig in the mines.
> We are prepared to suffer there,
> But brothers! Don't make us labourers here. (31)

So too, the conditions of forced itinerancy and indenture in the Indian Ocean:

> I am a chamar from the plains of the Ganges Pallanm Palli
> Already a slave from Canara

> At Andhra I struggled under the yoke of Misradar Tiourel
> Ready to leave the burnt earth of Meerut. (18)

If the "parched remnants" of earth that comprise the Gangetic plains of Bihar account for Ghosh's disturbing meditations on ecological violence, it is in the dark hull of the *Ibis* where the images of this desecrated landscape alternate with an equally disturbing maritime narrative (*SP* 188).

The "shared topographies of labor" that we see aboard the *Ibis* were forged through such itinerant networks. Accordingly, perhaps another virtue of the novels' polylingualism is their affordances for imagining the transnational qualities of Indian Ocean indenture. Of course, in this vein we might again look to Lowe's work on the intimacies of East and South Asian laborers; or to the tradition(s) of "Coolitude" writing that makes clear the complicated historiography of the Indian labor diaspora. Or we might simply return to *Sea of Poppies* and characters like Deeti and Serang Ali. Both exceed the caricatural representations of the laborer in the age of sail.

Conclusion

In the final novel of the trilogy, *Flood of Fire*, yet another exploited labor source is explored: Indian sepoys, who fought in multiple theaters of war for the British. While the modes of dehumanization characteristic of indenture might seem to afford a unique glimpse into theorizations of the inhuman, the sepoys in the novel, many of whom are former wrestlers, figure similarly. Prized for their strength and agility—not unlike Kalua, who is early on rendered a fetish object owing to his size—sepoys like Kesri Singh were in a sense indentured to the EIC army and valued only for their brute strength:

> I am without value
> Unsuited for field labour
> Sheik is my name, grimacing in the face of grease
> Of pigs in the enemy's cartridges
> A Paria spitting cow's grease into the barrel
> Of an Enfield. (Carter and Torabully 2002, 27)

Characters like Ghosh's fictional Kesri were likewise prized for their ability to subordinate any inclination toward resistance to the towering union jack for which they would fight until 1947. Following the dissolution of the company charter and the installation of the British Raj, Indian soldiers would be deployed over and again—finally in WWII during which the largest number of British casualties would be Indian subjects.²³ As such, *Flood of Fire* offers a logical conclusion to the trilogy in its rendering of the Opium Wars and its resolution of the myriad narrative strands that move the reader through this magisterial critique of the trade.

The novels move from the cultivation of poppy, to its manufacture and distribution as opium, to the wars fought in order to maintain its dominion. As such, the trilogy presents a sweeping history of the region—inclusive of Napoleon at some point, and quite a few other notable historical figures; but, and without belaboring the point, the novels also pivot on the local and the corporeal to testify to the archival violence for which even Chakrabarty's efforts toward "provincializing" fall short. Perhaps this is the virtue of fiction, or more specifically of what we might consider a form of speculative fiction in so far as the novels both manipulate a dystopian past in order to project a possible future—one "not incompatible with happiness" as the second novel demands—and one that allows for the sort of heterotemporal imaginary that might finally displace the hegemony of "colonial man," exposing the material horrors that he has wrought.

Additionally, we are reminded of the stakes of the speculative—or imagining anew as a means of galvanizing political change. *River of Smoke* closes in fact with such a demand, albeit authored by an American advocate for temperance: "The cultivation of poppy, throughout India, should immediately cease. The lands which have been engrossed by this deleterious culture should be returned to uses not incompatible with human life, virtue, and happiness" (504). This plea to speculate on the possibility of "life in capitalist ruins" also works to imagine the impossible (Tsing 2015). Thus, more than a banal critique of empire, the *Ibis Trilogy* is an imaginative praxis for not only understanding heterotemporality and the stakes of monoculture (whether the forced *cultivation* of land or persons); it is a literal means of mapmaking through which readers can grapple with Indian Ocean imaginaries heretofore erased and thus imagine otherwise. It also makes clear the *longue durée* of colonial aggression and ecological imperialism such that when we read a novel like Indra Sinha's *Animal's People* (to which I shall now turn) we might also consider such demands for "happiness." Animal surely does.

Chapter 2

A *Memento Mori* Tale: Indra Sinha's *Animal's People* and the Politics of Global Toxicity

Toxic bodies catalyze narratives that decline disassociation, sequestering, and invulnerability. Instead, these stories inhabit the ethical, political, and theoretical quandaries of the Anthropocene by finding themselves, retroactively perhaps, within sites of enunciation that interlace the scientific, historical, personal, and political.

—Stacy Alaimo, "Afterword: Crossing Time, Space, and Species"

Contra the amorphous hyper-object that Timothy Morton offers as a theoretical paradigm for thinking through environmental collapse, Dominic Boyer offers the "hyper-subject" (2019): Sylvia Wynter's "colonial man" (2003); Donna Haraway's "sky-gazing *Anthropos*" (2016); or put more simply for our purposes in this study, any of a number of protagonists in the story of an ascendant neoliberalism that proliferates in India's post-independence period and is abetted by the sorts of global economic initiatives instantiated by programs like the nation's "Green Revolution." Originating in the cold-war era as fears of "red" revolutions dovetailed with new technocratic development initiatives, this revolution would begin in Mexico and later shift to the "hungry continent" of Asia.[1] It was a revolution in agriculture whereby traditional farming methods—native strains of wheat or rice, which had long provided sustenance to rural Indians—were replaced with large-scale industrial initiatives that relied on monoculture and new forms of pesticide, inclusive of pest-resistant crops. The latter have become notorious in India's cotton belt where the cash crop has replaced life-sustaining grains, and where the multinational agrochemical corporation Monsanto has marketed its pest-resistant Bt (bacillus thurgensis) cotton, which has left much of the landscape in ecological and financial ruin—Monsanto just one in a series of corporations laying claim to the subcontinent, and a clear legatee of the East India Company.

Following centuries of ecological imperialism at the hands of foreign agents of capital, and following independence in 1947, local governments would forge public-private partnerships with multinational corporations that continued to privilege the accumulation of capital over the welfare of local communities, and which thrived on the very same developmentalist rhetoric of imperial liberalism that we discussed in the previous chapter. Pace arguments by literary critic Pablo Mukherjee regarding the "politics of global toxicity" (2010), David Harvey on the material means of "accumulation by dispossession" (2003), and Stacy Alaimo on the "toxic bodies [that] inhabit the ethical, political, and theoretical quandaries of the Anthropocene," in this chapter I turn to a notorious example of environmental toxicity and the comparatively toxic economic policies that allowed for it to occur. So too, the aesthetic expressions that have long sanctioned the "sequestering [and vulnerability]" of such bodies as we see in Indra Sinha's 2007 picaresque novel *Animal's People* (Alaimo 2019).

On the Aesthetic Logic of Global Toxicity

On December 3, 1984, a plume of deadly gas (mostly methyl isocyanate, or MIC) was released from the Union Carbide pesticide factory in Bhopal killing an estimated 5,000 to 10,000 people instantly. The ecological legacy of this disaster—the persistent toxicity of the soil, air, and water in the region—would cause the deaths of tens of thousands of more people over the next thirty years. Regarded as the "worst industrial accident in human history," the catastrophe in Bhopal likewise illustrates the distorted economic logic of Union Carbide's business practices specifically, and of the neoliberal pathologies of free trade more broadly (Guha 2008, 570).

Following the trenchant debt crises of the 1970s, and in compliance with the World Bank, then Prime Minister Indira Gandhi would essentially "hand over the keys to the kingdom to the industrial elite and foreign capital" paving the way for what neoliberal economists have dubbed the "new India"; and corporate agriculture was among the first industries to benefit (Prashad 2007, 216). Under the aegis of "liberalization" and "free trade," the agricultural sector would be transformed; and multinational corporations like Union Carbide would find few legal obstacles to profitable business ventures—lax safety regulations, for example, translating into increased profit.

This rapacious economic model is in part the narrative burden of Sinha's

Animal's People. In the novel "Animal," the titular *pícaro*, is an orphan whose parents were killed the night of the explosion. Owing to his mangled spine—one of many mutagenic effects of MIC in our nervous systems—he is forced to walk on his hands and feet; hence the name "Animal." Sinha uses his grotesque form to critique both the company's malfeasance as well as the developmentalist ethos that implicitly sanctioned such business practices—the promise of mobility a rhetorical veil for the human costs of India's economic gains.

Sinha's deformed protagonist is a "ghoulish parody" of economic liberalization, if also a haunting remonstrance (Dionne 2006, 54). As such, I read him as a late-capitalist instantiation of the seventeenth-century *memento mori* tradition, an artistic movement in which pastoral landscapes were interrupted by spectral tombstones and the occasional skull—otherwise Arcadian spaces shrouded by the casualties of early modern enclosures in Europe. Animal, as I shall argue, serves a similar aesthetic and political function to works like Nicholas Poussin's "Et in Arcadia Ego" (1637–38) which foregrounds a tomb in an otherwise pastoral landscape; an earlier rendition (1618–22) painted by Giovanni Francesco Barbieri (also known as Guercino) showcases a skull peering at rural laborers who appear as conventional picturesque objects—instantiations of the "rural virtue" too often ascribed to the peasant worker, from the wheat thresher to the shepherd to the farmer, whose material experiences have been historically subordinated to aesthetic ideals (see figures 1 and 2).[2] In both compositions, the Arcadian fantasy is disturbed by this macabre specter—an aesthetic precedent for what I shall discuss below in terms of a postcolonial *memento mori* such as we see in *Animal's People*.

In figures 1 and 2, the rustic laborer—memorialized (literally) in the work of Poussin, and also by landscape artists such as Claude Lorrain (1600–1682) and John Constable (1776–1837) whose work also demonstrates the picturesque tradition of petrifying labor as such—is but a European example of the inhuman figure of labor that prefigures characters like Animal. Such images offer imaginative praxes for what Raymond Williams (1973) once described as the "magical erasure" of labor from the English countryside through the mechanism of what Alan Vardy terms "aesthetic enclosure"—that is, the erasure of the working-class subject (rendered as a "picturesque" object or "rustic subject") from the Ancient pastorals to the "green language" of the English Romantics (Vardy 2003). This was accomplished not merely by the marginalization of the worker to the frame, but by an accompanying economic ideology that understood such workers as fungible—vassals in a residual feudal agrarian economy. Arguably, the developmentalist rhetoric of post-independence India, such as we see in the Union Carbide ad (see figure 3) in which the rural Indian laborer is succored by a benevolent white hand, serves a similar end: in

Fig. 1. Nicolas Poussin, *Et in Arcadia Ego*, 1637–38, oil on canvas, 87 x 120 cm (Musée du Louvre, Paris)

both instances, the visual rhetoric that accompanies either aesthetic pleasure or agricultural improvement effaces the materiality of labor, if also the plight of the laborer. In the case of Union Carbide's development campaign we are told:

> Oxen working the fields . . . the eternal river Ganges . . . jeweled elephants on parade. Today these symbols of ancient India exist side by side with a new sight—modern industry. India has developed bold new plans to build its economy and bring the promise of a bright future to its more than 400,000,000 people. But India needs the technical knowledge of the western world. (qtd. in Fortun 2001)

As in the historical context of Guercino's peasant laborers, within the uneven topographies of late capitalism the laboring subject is similarly erased—imaginatively that is. Indeed, and as we shall discuss in the next chapter, the (often itinerant) laborer in our contemporary petrosphere exists largely as a constitutive absence, such that he is in fact invisible—removed spatially through the mechanisms of global capital shifts. However much petrocultural

Fig. 2. Guercino, *Et in Arcadia Ego*, 1618–22, oil on canvas, 82 x 91 cm (Courtesy of the Gallerie Nazionali di Arte Antica, MIBACT—Bibliotheca Hertziana, Istituto Max Planck for the History of Art/ Enrico Fontolan)

critics might contest the putative invisibility of labor regimes in the Global South—invisibility a byproduct of the very same enabling fictions that we have discussed throughout this study—such laborers as were exterminated in Bhopal are surely invisible to consumers in the Global North, who are increasingly anesthetized by the civilizing qua improving campaigns of companies like Union Carbide.

A Postcolonial Picturesque?

Artistic representations of peasant labor within the picturesque tradition aligned with a particular economic ideology—that of a quasi-feudal system in which laborers were understood as inhuman, domesticated objects necessary to fuel a proto-capitalist plantation economy in an era of unprecedented

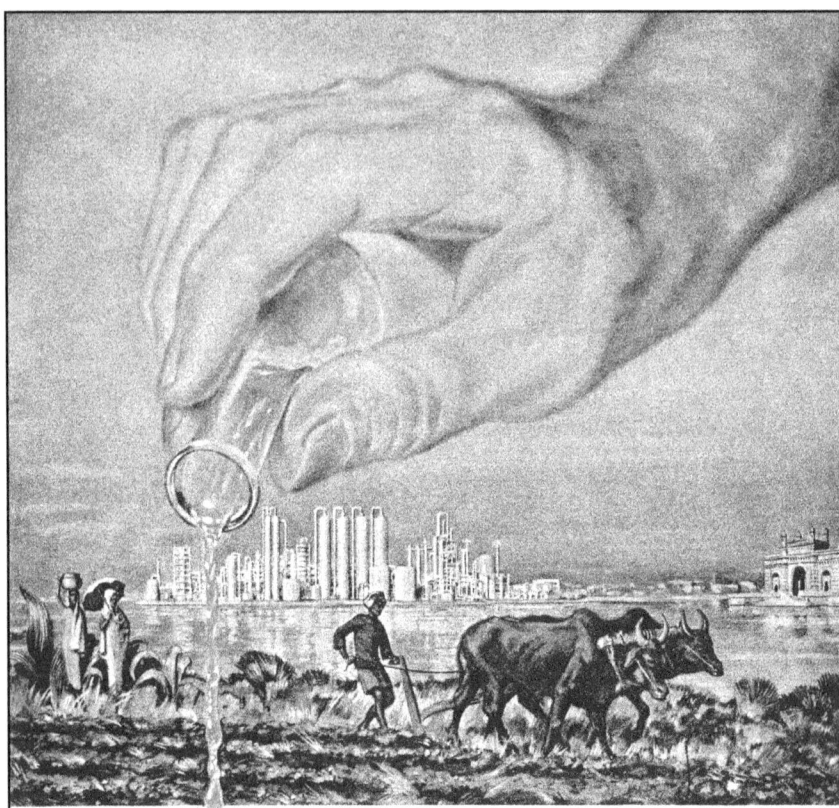

Fig. 3. Union Carbide Ad Campaign c. 1950s–1960s

agricultural enclosures. Following theorizations of the picturesque mode by critics like Richard Payne Knight in the eighteenth century, and more recent work on what Jonathan Barrell calls "the dark side of landscape," we can understand Animal's character to some extent as both picturesque object and requiem to late liberalism—his mutilated body not so much an homage to the civilizing narratives of developmentalism as much as a wretched spectacle for the liberal voyeur.

In Knight's 1806 *An Analytical Inquiry Into the Principles of Taste*, the critic posits a theory of the picturesque (as it obtains in both landscape gardens and portraiture) that understands so-called "rural virtue" in terms of a sort of "ruin"—whether of landscape or otherwise externalized objects like labor/laborers; that is, the object exists in a persistent state of decay that is strangely palatable to viewers, whether looking at images in a frame or wandering the countryside *a la* William and Dorothy Wordsworth. However much the rhetoric of a "wild" nature—uncultivated, in the parlance of Lockean conceptions of improvement, and existing somehow prior to the modern character of a highly industrialized English countryside (and labor force)—is a clear economic myth given the contemporaneity of the picturesque aesthetic tradition with the proliferation of the English factory system and the rise of fossil capitalism, the visual (and as I shall shortly demonstrate, poetic) rhetoric of the picturesque tradition effectively masked this sleight of hand. This was abetted by the imperial rhetoric of liberal capitalism and extant theories of the sublime properties of the putatively "inhuman."

Aligned with earlier ruminations on the sublime, like those championed by critic Uvedale Price and philosopher Edmund Burke, Knight was also interested in the physiological response of the implicitly European, liberal viewer/voyeur in the presence of such "inhuman" objects. Contra a Kantian metaphysics in which the sublime could catalyze a dialogic relationship between the knowing subject and observable object, here the picturesque object may be a source of pleasure and/or pain but resists sublimation as such. That is, Kant's notion of sublimation was grounded in a theory of cognitive synthesis—part of a Romantic lineage also evident in the work of Wordsworth and Samuel Taylor Coleridge, whose 1798 *Lyrical Ballads* would mark a departure from the dialectical thinking of Burke, and from a Newtonian understanding of the physical universe that would allow for a theory of matter as separable from the metaphysical forces acting upon it. The latter is a signature of the picturesque mode—a metaphysical explanation for the aforementioned gestures toward petrification. Knight, like Burke, favored a pre-Enlightenment conception of the human subject that allowed for the cultivation of class hierarchies by denying the physical possibility of synthesis—and thereby the impossibility of the intellectual cultivation of the working-class object. The laborer and the decaying landscape in which he toils, pace Burke, would remain a spectacle. As such, Animal, in resisting sublimation by the reader, conjures the Burkean spectacle that Knight imagines: his mutilated form instantiates the pleasure and pain of the picturesque mode—something that the reader is able to experience through such proxies as Sinha's predatory journalist.[3] The well-intentioned journalist concisely instantiates the liberal voyeur and is described in the novel as a "vulture" (*AP* 5).

In considering the genealogy of picturesque representation, it might be said that the Romantic figuration of the "rural subject"—the ideal poetic figure evoked by Wordsworth in his famous "Preface to the Lyrical Ballads"—serves a similar end to the picturesque object described above. In this sense, the laborers and soldiers rendered in *Lyrical Ballads* might be compared to the "laboring swain" of such picturesque poets as Oliver Goldsmith, whose 1770 *The Deserted Village* notably (and explicitly) erases the laborer through the trope of mourning. But however incomprehensible the musings of Wordsworth's "solitary reaper"—the highland lass, whose song is but a "vale" ("The Solitary Reaper," Line 7)—(or, for that matter, the disturbingly atomized soldier in the "Discharged Soldier" whose onomatopoeic murmurings are similarly incomprehensible), the picturesque tradition of petrifying labor works somewhat differently.[4] Wordsworth's reaper, for example, may at first glance appear static, but in the final stanza she is "singing [and] bending" while the speaker now appears "motionless." In contrast, Goldsmith's laborer is but a memory—erased with the "deserted village" that stands in for the rural virtue that the poet also mourns. In this sense, Goldsmith's is not an exploration of the "rural subject" but a lament for the loss of the rural *object*—the picturesque mode simultaneously foregrounding while effacing labor, a seeming paradox if the eighteenth-century laborer wasn't but a fungible object easily reducible to landscape. This aesthetic would dramatize ruin, or death, in a way not so dissimilar from the *memento mori* tradition in which the figuration of death, however central, worked to haunt not occupy the frame—the Arcadian myth disturbed, but left essentially intact.

All of this said, the *memento mori* also works differently than the picturesque mode; particularly so in Sinha's postcolonial rendition of the form. In *Animal's People*, the petrified object (i.e., Animal) is foregrounded in such a way as to force the viewer to grapple with his presence—the grotesque costs of development on display, and less an invitation for voyeurism than an indictment. The reader is not a proxy for the detached speaker, but instead for the aforementioned liberal predator. Significantly, this is later contrasted, as I shall discuss below, against a conventional illustration of the *memento mori* in the figure of an actual grave—clearly an omniscient wink at the reader belying Sinha's adaptation of the form.

In marshaling the trope of the *memento mori* toward a postcolonial critique of "Green Revolution" economic policy, Sinha's novel is also a far cry from what we might understand as a postcolonial picturesque—something that might be said of the novels of V. S. Naipaul or George Orwell, both of whom pedal primitivist portraits of colonial subjects. In *Animal's People* the petrified object of the otherized subject is forced into view and uncomfortably so; but it is the correlative critique of the market logic of neoliberalism that compels a radically different reception. Arguably, this is accomplished not merely through the mutilated protagonist—Animal's altered form conjuring earlier *pícaro* figures like the emaciated "Lazarillo" (of the 1554 *Lazarillo de Tormes*)—but likewise through the deployment of a picaresque temporality that arrests the reader in a relentless present.

Indeed, more than a critique of the magical erasures at stake in picturesque representations—in this context, of the fungible bodies of "cheap labor" regimes across the Global South, and the local communities who suffer the costs of globalization—through such tropes, Sinha adapts the historically antihumanist genre of the picaresque novel in the service of amplifying, not erasing, the material costs of development projects like those of Carbide. This is precisely why previous critics like Rob Nixon also understand the novel as picaresque indictment; here I expand this reading in order to consider how the figure of Animal operates beyond the conventional gambit of the *pícaro*—to see the picaresque *memento mori* as the perfect vehicle for communicating the necropolitical imaginary that subtends liberal ideology and the "enabling fictions" of classical and neoliberalism that have historically (and necessarily) eschewed consideration of the colonial *cum* corporate subject whose very body feeds the engine of global capital.[5] Such enabling fictions include the eighteenth-century autobiography, which we see parodied in the previous chapter, the nineteenth-century *Bildungsroman* or "coming of age" tale, and the "twentieth-century development dreams" that undergirded programs like India's "Green Revolution" (Tsing 2015, 4).

The Econopoetics of Developmentalism

While Animal's tale alternates with that of his city and his "people"—mostly fellow citizens who bear the brunt of MIC's long-term (if also teratogenic) effects, be they asthmatic children or lactating mothers producing poison—the novel is primarily a documentary of his survival and one that is both ruthless in its telling, and surely also in its form. Throughout, Sinha relies on the aforementioned picaresque convention of abjection in addition to the deployment of an unreliable narrator and an episodic structure to foreground what I am calling, after Pablo Mukherjee (2010), the "politics of global toxicity": the juridical gymnastics of company shareholders and their government proxies, and the corresponding narratives that sanction these institutions whether explicitly or implicitly. The novel parodies representational strategies that augment the project of global capitalism—specifically, the liberal narrative of development—through its episodic form, and with a narrator whose mutilated body illustrates the toxic underside of industrial progress, which is to say the lethal landscape of Sinha's fictional Khaufpur.

In order to illustrate the material conditions of Animal's world, the novel dramatizes the toxic ecologies born of what we shall discuss below as a form of "transcorporeality" wherein the porous bodies of figures like Animal are entangled within the blasted landscapes of an irradiated Khaufpur—where, per Elizabeth Povinelli, a global ecology can be properly understood not in terms of "sharp epidermal boundaries [but] fuzzy and open borders" (2016, 52). Here we see a shift "from simple local bodies to complex global patterns"—inclusive of sites of accumulation spanning the Global South and North (52). The latter is represented through the interlocking narratives of pesticide production in Bhopal/Khaufpur and the toxic steel mills of Coatesville, PA, where one of the liberal "Amrikans" in the novel is born and where her parents suffer the impacts of deregulation.

I shall turn directly to Animal's world momentarily, but it is worth noting that the example of Coatesville, PA, is a particularly fecund one for exploring the interstices of global regimes of capital and the vast tendrils of accumulation that enable new forms of entangled intimacy across a broader "topography of labor" (Pereira 2014). Coatesville presents a unique window through which to view such relationships: not only can the town boast of having produced the steel for the World Trade Center (something also mentioned in the novel as Animal watches horrified while the towers crumble); it likewise stands as a monument to a beleaguered American labor force whose treatment in many ways mirrored that of the Khaufpuri workers. The collapse of the union shop during the cold-war era as neoliberal economic reforms ravaged the working class is also alluded to in comments about mill workers entering a literal "hell":

> Forty feet below the main control floor, among furnaces that roared like volcanoes, was a tiny shack on whose door someone had chalked HELL HOLE. "Down there," said my dad's friend, "it's so hot it can burn the hairs right out of your nose. There's steel plates, glowing red as the

devil's eye, going by on a roller belt. Water's spraying on them but it bangs off, boom! Boom! Boom! Like a stick of bombs. Your dad's job is to step outside of the hell hole and check the plate.... He's got on fireproof gear and a face guard and he's holding four-foot-long calipers, even so he has only four seconds per sheet. Thirty seconds out there and protection or no, your skin is going to start blistering. One slip, you're history." It was a job for a skilled man with plenty of guys and a steady hand and my father was proud of it. "We built Amrika," he used to tell me. "We made the steel for the Walt Whitman Bridge and the World Trade Center.... The World is made of promises ... but noble ideas don't dull pain." (*AP* 201)

Despite the failures of such "noble ideas"—specifically the promise of uplift for workers in the now decimated steel belt—former US president Donald Trump's trade tariffs promise to auger a return of US industry, specifically in Coatesville if also in Pennsylvania and Appalachia more broadly. Surely, descriptions such as we see in *Animal's People* haven't sullied such promises. The destruction of the industry, although less spectacular than what Animal persistently refers to as "that night," which is to say the chemical leak at the pesticide factory, is itself a sort of *memento mori* to late capitalism; and both Khaufpur and Coatesville will continue to fuel the hyper-nationalist agendas of politicians whose adherence to a particular ideology of progress will necessarily depend on their sacrifice.

Of course, as a critique of the material costs of developmentalism the novel is certainly not unique: it aligns with a long tradition of commentaries on uneven development. As materialist critique, it joins a critical movement away from the so-called discursive turn in literary and critical studies and toward a more robust examination of not the ephemeral "hyper-object," but of the very matter of trade and ecological degradation. It likewise joins a myriad of working-class fictions of the sort that I take up in the next chapter—the proletarian poetics of a host of genres, from different regions and moments, which similarly critique the sacrificial zones of global capitalism. The picaresque form, as I have discussed throughout this study, is one in a long tradition of such "econopoetic" fictional indictments (Maiorino 2003); although its resurgence surely attests to its utility for incisive critique, perhaps over and against similarly critical narrative modes. As we discussed in the introduction, the genre has long satirized instances of economic and political injustice beginning with the sixteenth-century Spanish tradition and its illustration of poverty and displacement in rural Salamanca; but while the itinerant "Lazarillo" was similarly a product of dispossession, there was no pretense of mobility in early modern Spain. Thus, Sinha's unique contribution is his critique of the peculiar logic of capital ascent that ignores the material substrate of labor and suffering that makes capital accumulation possible. He achieves this through the abovementioned topography of labor as well as through the novel's episodic form. Structured as a series of recordings intended for distribution to Western readers, the novel asks: how does one talk of ascent or "progress" in a place like Bhopal—fictionalized as Khaufpur in the novel?

Clearly, the notion of uplift in the aftermath of such a catastrophe is absurd; and the novel drives this point home over and again. In insisting on stagnation over and against the putative mobility evinced by more triumphalist narratives of liberal capitalism, the novel in fact illustrates a sort of distorted logic. As Mukherjee argues, the explosion and its horrific aftermath "perfectly embodies the toxic logical outcome of the contemporary mantra of globalization and development"—a mantra that extols the gospel of free markets and whose exponents care little for its human costs (2010, 162). To wit, seven years after the accident, in December of 1991, then World Bank chief economist Larry Summers wrote the following in an internal memo: "I think the economic logic behind dumping a load of toxic waste in the lowest wage country is impeccable and we should face up to that" (Vallette 1999).

As we know from numerous critics of global capitalism and development—Neil Smith, David Harvey, and others—the uneven topographies of global capitalism have long demanded a tacit acceptance that third world toxicity is the necessary cost of global development and, consequently, first world prosperity. Western progress has hinged on such global asymmetries for centuries. When Animal proclaims that "they will build factories above our graves and use our ashes as cement," we are reminded of successive waves of dispossession that have historically been sanctioned by similar economic philosophies (*AP* 275). Accordingly, in her argument for the imbricated processes of colonial and slave labor and the rise of the first world bourgeoisie, Lisa Lowe cast this sort of logic in similar terms, albeit in a different historical context: "Colonized workers," she notes, "produced the material comforts and commodities that furnished the bourgeois home" (2015b, 30). She further remarks in reference to the ideological conditions that enabled (and continue to enable) such uneven geographies: "The modern distinction between definitions of the human and those to whom such distinctions do not extend is the condition of possibility for Western liberalism, and not its particular exception" (3). The "comparative [dis]advantage" with which such a model inheres was both the condition of possibility in the eighteenth-century context to which Lowe refers, and its latter-day correlate in the form of new modes of colonialism practiced by multinational corporations like Carbide as well as the myriad of multinationals still operating under the rhetoric of an agricultural "revolution" (Patnaik and Moyo 2011).

The proliferation of such developmentalist rhetoric—now deployed by Trump and also by Indian Prime Minister Narendra Modi—persists (and rather successfully) in the very same appeal to free markets that we critiqued in the context of colonial Bengal. So too, this rhetoric continues to marshal popular support despite its continued reliance on the "logic" that culminates in catastrophes like those in Bhopal, or the more recent instantiations of developmentalist fiction that understand Indian farmers as the necessary recipients of such improvement schemes as we see in the nation's cotton belt. As in the case of Ghosh's Bihari peasant farmers, contemporary farmers are similarly stripped of their land and forced into new forms of penury. If the case in Bhopal proves particularly resonant for the overwhelming arguments against corporate agriculture, the case of Monsanto's Bt cotton in the Indian state of Vidarbha should certainly resonate similarly, particularly given the fallout from such agricultural initiatives as we saw in Bhopal—the only "revolution" there one of cyclical return (*a la* Hannah Arendt's [1963] elucidation of the form's roots) in which historic modes of land dispossession are now being sanctioned under such paeans to industry as we see in Carbide's ad campaigns above.

Despite the global fervor around the Green Revolution, which many argue assuaged famine in postcolonial India, the human costs of agricultural reform were and are astounding. Beyond the thousands of Bhopali citizens who continue to develop life-threatening diseases, we are now confronted with the twofold reality of crop failure on the one hand (owing to a rather short-sighted commitment to monocropping), and the current epidemic of farmer suicides in rural states like Maharashtra where the mechanisms of free trade produce far more debt than food. Here, in the extractive zones of global capitalism, such rhetoric continues to shore up confidence even in the face of disaster. Adding to this, multinational corporations persist in skirting state legislation by appealing to free markets. Referring to the so-called "Maoist corridor" in Andhra Pradesh, activist and writer Arundhati Roy uses the term "Mouist corridor" to refer to the scores of memoranda of understanding (MOUs) that enable companies to prioritize market competition and profit over the welfare of local communities (2011, 25). Thus, the "horrendous logic" of corporate capitalism persists.

This logic, as I have argued thus far, is the ideological thrust behind *Animal's People* in which the author constructs a character, who blurs the distinction between liberal definitions of the human and colonialist typologies that produce its persistent other. Sinha's *pícaro* is an animal insofar as his persona evinces none of the trappings of the modern individual; or the ideal protagonist of such generic forms as the *Bildungsroman*, whose teleological sense of direction inheres with a sense of mobility foreclosed to people like him (Slaughter 2007). Animal thus begins his tale: "I used to be a human once. So I'm told" (*AP* 1). Sinha's ontologically amorphous *pícaro* is uniquely effective at exposing the sorts of global asymmetries that Mukherjee and Lowe describe, and which institutions like the World Bank persistently reinforce whether explicitly or "under cover of a free market ideology . . . where laws and loopholes are selectively applied in a marketplace a lot freer for some societies and classes than for others" (Nixon 2011, 46). This is because, as an animal, he cannot be the burden of what Joseph Slaughter has called "literary humanitarianism" (2007, 314). He is not human in the liberal sense of that word. He possesses neither the liberty, nor the political agency to exercise the requisite reason that such a category demands.

Animal may be a hero to his "people" to the degree that he is able to fight for them; but as we see at the novel's conclusion, the *pícaro* figure can only ever serve as an instrument of critique. Khaufpur will not be remediated; nor will Animal. Unlike the local plant managers, who avoided trial and thus prosecution, Animal belongs to Khaufpur's proliferating underclass and Sinha is careful to make this distinction. The beneficiaries of India's much-lauded development program—the "poison-wallahs" who figure as apologists in the novel—enjoy a very different fate. As such, Animal's character is a perfect model of postcolonial picarism. More than the wily outcast of the sixteenth-century *picaresco*—"Lazarillo" or "Don Pablos" in *Él Buscón*—Animal suffers the particular fate of the rogue in the postcolony. He is the grist of the economic system of global/late capitalism—as the erstwhile hands of empire; and he is likewise its excrement—that is, its *logical* product. *Memento mori* indeed, the novel persistently reminds the reader that death—whether the metaphorical death of liberal humanist ideals, or the literal death of the subaltern body—is always with them. As Animal remarks at the end of the novel: "Tomorrow there will be more of us" (*AP* 366).

Arguably, postcolonial literature may serve such a purpose *tout court*—the postcolonial other serving as a reminder to Western readers of the costs of "imperial liberalism"; but Sinha's novel bears little resemblance to the narrative realism of popular Anglophone works like Naipaul's *A Bend in the River* or Rohinton Mistry's *A Fine Balance* (Prashad 2007). *Animal's People* explicitly marshals the trope of the *memento mori* to drive home a particular point about dispossession. Sinha's readers are directly confronted with the material consequences of their bourgeois complacency; as with Poussin's tomb, Animal's deformed figure is a corporeal reminder, and one that insists on being seen.

"Like . . . most *picaros*," Animal is "sacrificed to the 'better' society . . . celebrated in 'great men' historical narratives"—the sorts of stories that obscure the fact of labor and suffering in their triumphalist tales of modern progress, or "development" broadly conceived (Maiorino 2003, 113). Adding to this, the arc of his character—framed as it is by "now-o-clock"—is a parody of the liberal pretense toward development, which is to be found in more aspirational genres: "Look, over there are the roofs of the Nutcracker. Know what time it's there? Now o'clock, always now o'clock. In the Kingdom of the Poor, time doesn't exist" (*AP* 185). This too is a stock convention of the picaresque novel—its episodic nature allowing for a temporal refutation of more teleological forms. Animal aspires to little other than carnal satisfaction: " 'My name is Animal,' I say. 'I'm not a fucking human being, I've no wish to be one' " (*AP* 23). He has no faith, and little sympathy. He, as did Lazarillo before him, survives on his wit and "pays his obeisance to bread, and not god" (Alter 1965, 5–6). Animal chastises his peer's religious faith remarking: "us animals, our religion's eating, drinking . . . the basic stuff you do to survive" (*AP* 88).

If the "grotesque fictions" of Western liberalism offer up "humanist similes [that point] toward divinity," *Animal's People* instead conjures "antihumanist analogies that [favor] elementary forms of survival" (Ghosh 2015b; Maiorino 2003, 22). In this way Animal is a perfect rogue—a *pícaro* par excellence; and he likewise serves as a stunning indictment to those who would continue to preach the gospel of development in places like Sinha's fictional Khaufpur. Despite former president George W. Bush's contention that "democracy, development, free markets and free trade . . . [will] lift whole societies out of poverty," the mechanisms of free trade as practiced by companies like Union Carbide, or Monsanto and Cargill for that matter, have certainly proven otherwise (Harvey 2005, 5).

This is again why I read Sinha's *pícaro* as a *memento mori* figure—a Faustian specter in an otherwise palatable narrative of Western progress. Less than a facile reminder to the reader of their own mortality, Animal embodies the economic logic that Summers extols, and that Lowe and Mukherjee critique. He likewise evinces the aesthetic logic that has produced this sort of character over and over again. The farmer magically extracted from Virgil's landscape, the nineteenth-century laborer removed from Jane Austen's countryside, or the displaced slum dweller lingering just beyond the utopian cities of the "new India," is bodied forth in the figure of Sinha's irreverent rogue. Animal is an abject reminder of the human cost of economic and ecological imperialism; and his tale forces the ideological and epistemological bases of liberalism into sharp focus. Liberal narratives of individual progress or social development are foreclosed, because Animal cannot be properly situated at the origin of such fictions.

Thus, the novel's *coup de grâce* is perhaps its parodic deployment of the picaresque convention of autobiographical narration—what Claudio Guillén

(1971) calls its "pseudo-autobiographical" nature. The novel mocks this "emancipatory trope" in rather clever ways to expose the sorts of developmentalist fictions that typically rely on human suffering and environmental devastation (Aravamudan 2011, 235). Animal's tale is in fact a superb "pseudo-autobiography": he narrates his story into a series of tapes for the Western "Eyes" that he imagines listening to them—the journalists and other "vultures" that prey on what Sinha characterizes as poverty porn. As Animal remarks: "Somewhere a bad thing happens, tears like rain in the wind, and look, here you come, drawn by the smell of blood" (*AP* 5). But rather than offer them blood, Animal proceeds to mock the very idea of such a narration with a series of perverse asides, outright lies, and even a vulgar nursery rhyme or two. He will not allow the Western imagination to produce another "poison victim," whose salvation hinges on their sympathy—an exchange, we should recall, governed by the same neoliberal logic espoused by Summers.

The "impeccable . . . logic" for which Summers notoriously argued directly undergirds the strangely parallel relationship between Animal and the "Eyes." So too, it bolsters the sorts of economic practices that have historically produced figures like Animal: Summers's "impeccable logic" in fact recalls the colonial logic of such liberal thinkers as John Stuart Mill, whose notion of liberty looked rather different in the context of Bengal during his tenure for the East India Company. As such, places like Khaufpur succinctly illustrate the shadow of both early and more recent modes of what Vijay Prashad aptly calls "imperial liberalism" (2007, 14). As with eighteenth-century Bengal where Mill (1990) would argue for the beneficence of the colonial occupation—the devastation of India's peasantry a reasonable cost for England's civilizing mission—twentieth-century Bhopal would also exist in a necessarily subordinate economic relationship to Delhi, if also Washington.

But while "colonized peoples [then and now] created the conditions for liberal humanism," European political philosophy has persistently disavowed the uneven topographies of global capitalism (Lowe 2015b, 39). Before Mill would apply a utilitarian calculus to justify Indian dispossession, John Locke would famously proffer a theory of "improvement"—whether of land or persons—that all but sanctioned colonial violence. Of course, and more germane to a discussion of Sinha's postcolonial picaresque, we might consider how the social contracts penned by Locke and also Jean-Jacques Rousseau laid the groundwork for a particular narrative form: emanating in a primordial "state of nature" from which the modern subject would necessarily emerge, Rousseau's 1862 *Social Contract* was a *Bildungsroman* par excellence. It also mirrored its generic contemporary, the autobiography—also an exponent of liberal capitalism when we consider the narrative *telos* of such canonical exemplars as that of Olaudah Equiano, whose capital enfranchisement was by necessity the presumed outcome of his eighteenth-century aspirations (Lowe 2015b).

The social contracts logically prefigured the narrative traditions of the autobiography and coming-of-age tales as well as such "enabling fictions" as those promoted by late-capitalist development initiatives—those of the IMF and the World Bank, for example, in the form of economic policy. Such narratives necessarily begin in poverty (or, in the parlance of the IMF, "under-development") and culminate in a narrowly construed mode of liberty, which is available only to a select few. Obviously, persons like Animal cannot count among those select few lest institutions like the World Bank wish to suffer economically and the planet burn more vociferously; hence Sinha's explicit repudiation of such a conventionally liberal *Bildung*.[6] At the end of the novel when faced with the option of corrective surgery—surely a metaphor for economic uplift—Animal refuses. The ending, I would argue, is a brilliant means of skewering farcical narratives about social mobility that have historically relied on the dispossession of figures like Animal—Sinha's *pícaro* a precise embodiment of a sort of social death (Patterson).

A Postcolonial *Memento Mori*

Animal's character is redolent with the political resonances of the pastoral, and surely also the picturesque, in which the aforementioned rustic subjects—what landscape artist Thomas Gainsborough would also refer to as "little dirty subjects"—or the images of low life foregrounded in the early picaresque novels played a similar role: their marginalization was a necessary condition for the emergent bourgeois subject (Bermingham 1986). Contemporary picaresque novels serve a similar end: the rogue in the postcolony is a reminder of the conditions from which the modern subject emerges and out of which his progress is made possible. This too is what is at stake in the *memento mori* tradition: as in Poussin's haunted landscape, the "neoliberal utopia" envisaged by imagined projections of the "new India" is similarly shrouded by the specter of death as embodied by figures like Animal (Ahmed 2011). Aligned with an ongoing history of aesthetic expression—from pastoral violence to new forms of aesthetic enclosure such as the *postcolonial* picturesque—*memento mori* is an apt description for conveying the material stakes of late liberalism. As well, for the long history of environmental tyranny on the subcontinent, and the imbricated chronologies of development and disposal upon which the rhetoric of developmentalism thrives. But more directly, the "home" that Animal cultivates out of the detritus of the Union Carbide factory is itself a sort of tomb—situated at the center of the novel and shrouding Sinha's storyworld with a reminder of the protagonists' mortality. The abandoned Kampani functions almost as a mausoleum. We might even argue that Sinha deploys the trope of the *memento mori* to invite closer scrutiny of the imperial geographies of empire for which Animal's world functions as a form of synecdoche. That the "Nutcracker" slum where Animal's people live is crafted out of the remains of the factory is of course symbolic; but, more than this, Animal lives within its crumbling walls—using its discarded records as a blanket no less. He describes the "silent spring" within the abandoned factory thus: "No bird song. No hoppers in the grass. No bee hum. Insects can't survive here. Wonderful poisons the Kampani made, so good its impossible to get rid of them, after all these years they're still doing their work" (*AP* 29). Surely the allusion to "no bird song" is no accident. Here we are reminded of the work of Rachel Carson (1962), whose investigation into what she termed a "biocidal" agent—the pesticide DDT—would be reviled by the very same forces of multinational agribusiness that would decimate rural India; indeed, Monsanto, interested to dispel fears about their products, would follow Carson's lead by employing the tropes of speculative fiction to terrify consumers with the very same rhetoric of revolution and development. Carson begins her tale with a prescient "fable for tomorrow" in which we see the ecocidal consequences of industrial agriculture; Monsanto, in retort, offers a horror story in which humanity was overrun by toxic insects (Carson 1962; Streeby 2018, 16–17).

Carson's documentary of ecological seepage into the nation's water supply, not to mention instances of environmental injustice such as were experienced by agricultural workers in California who would ingest the same toxic substances intended for the orange groves, ought to resonate here as well. I shall turn to a discussion of environmental justice and transcorporeal ecology below. Sufficed to say here that the "wonderful poisons" in which Animal's people must swim, and that they drink and breathe, will logically (and bio-logically) destroy them. This is how matter works. This is how ecosystems work. And indeed, this is why Animal is in fact a concise instantiation of the *memento mori*. The death of such inhuman bodies is a material inevitability—and a logical one it seems.

It is also worth mentioning that Sinha draws his own fallen Arcadia explicitly—perhaps an omniscient wink at the reader, or simply an inevitability in the denuded landscapes of Khaufpur. In an image that succinctly recalls Poussin's, he tells us:

> A little way off, across the tracks and near the factory wall, is a falling down tower of stone with grass growing out of its walls. Some bigwig

built it hundreds of years ago, in those days the factory lands were orchards. It was maybe a tomb, no one knows its purpose, when the poison factory came and threw its wall around the orchards, this ruin was left outside. (*AP* 43)

There is no shortage of images of what we might call the "structure of feeling" of enclosure and displacement, which is succinctly captured in the *memento mori* tradition (Williams 1977). Translated literally as "remember that you must die," such images remind the viewer that their imaginative pleasure hinges on the continuance of such violent modes of erasure as those which enabled the production of pastoral verse, picturesque landscapes, and more recent efforts toward "beautification" as were practiced in Indira's India, or Manmohan Singh's in which he promised a city that was "Delhi-ciously Yours." The tradition of emptying landscapes of labor (and of poverty) for our imaginative pleasure absolutely persists in our global imagination; as does the correlative anxiety, which is wrought from a similarly exploitative economic model—the surfeit of recent picaresque novels attesting to similar anxieties.[7]

Against the sorts of violent erasures cited above in the context of the pastoral and picturesque traditions—those explored in Raymond Williams's classic account of nostalgia, Arcadianism and the pastoral tradition, *The Country and the City*—picaresque novels like *Animal's People* foreground otherwise invisible labor regimes of the sort that I discussed above. The novel forces consideration of the fact that the pastoral frame or the multinational development initiative cannot exist without the correlative disposal of persons like John Clare, or the late farmer-poet Krishna Kalamb who took his own life due to the debts incurred from corporate agricultural initiatives in the nation's cotton belt: the poet's "death . . . like untimely rain."[8] Kalamb succinctly represents the precarious position of the Indian farmer who will suffer a new form of indenture in the form of peonage.

Arguably, Sinha's novel, like Kalamb's poetry, exposes the lie of such aesthetic enclosures. Far from masking the imperial imaginary of global capitalism, the narrative terrain of *Animal's People* conjures what we might call a sort of late-capitalist heterotopia. As aforementioned, the novel presents multiple sites—Khaufpur, Amrika, and Coatesville—whose remote geographies are sutured by both global capital flows and the toxic byproducts of the global commodity exchange. As the story of a "half-outsider," Animal's narrative keeps the disparate sites of this particular exchange—of pesticides, of steel, of poison, and of human lives—in tension (Guillén 1971). In this way, the novel also (and rather effectively) casts light on the material inequities that sustain what Edward Soja (2011, 159) has called the "postmodern geographies" of late capitalism—that is, the "contemporary restructuring of capitalist spatiality" wherein the hyper-subject, or Boyer's (2019, 3) term for what he elsewhere describes as the protagonist of "androleukoheteropetromodernity," thrives on the disposability of "cheap labor."

The movement of goods, and the consequent production and proliferation of global toxicity, that we see between Khaufpur and Amrika, instantiate networks of trade that thrive on the "turbid taxonomies" of neoliberalism that we discussed in the introduction—that is, the relegation of most persons to the category of waste, despite the role of the global majority as an unacknowledged labor source and thus the constitutive outside of global capitalism. This global model of transversality whereby the rogue in the postcolony is "half-outsider" within the larger matrix of global capital flows is concisely instantiated by Animal's character in many ways because of his mutilated form. In this way, Animal offers a praxis for thinking about the sorts of environmental toxicity taken up by thinkers like Alaimo (2010) who posits the aforementioned theory of transcorporeality in the context of environmental (in)justice—her argument in part adapted from earlier discussions of such socio-biological concepts as the "proletarian lung," which emerged following similar instances of worker dispossession and corporate violence (28). Referring to the concept of a "proletarian lung," Alaimo asks: "What does it mean for the body to 'know' something as seemingly abstract as one's place within a class system?" (27).

Of Bodily Natures

One of the centerpieces of Alaimo's (2010) critique is a reading of Muriel Rukeyser's (1938) *The Book of the Dead*, which focuses on another of Union Carbide's industrial disasters—that of the Hawks Nest Tunnel collapse in West Virginia. In the poem "Alloy," a section of the longer *Book*, Rukeyser reviles the slow violence of corporate managers, describing one as a "gangster" looming in the "murdering" snow of the silicon mine: "Crystalline hill: a blinded field of white / murdering snow, seamed by convergent tracks; / the travelling cranes reach for the silica" (lines 7–9). The analogy between the foreman of a mine where largely African American laborers were sacrificed in the extraction of rare earth, and a "gangster" with "gun smoking" is not so outlandish when we think of the casualties of such corporate mining projects (lines 1–2). Even more than the infamous collapse of the Hawks Nest tunnel were the labor conditions that caused scores of workers to contract silicosis: "Forced through this crucible, a million men. / Above this pasture, the highway passes those / who curse the air, breathing their fear again. / The roaring flowers of the chimney-stacks less poison, at their lips in fire, than this / dust that is blown from off the field of glass" (lines 19–24). This image is precisely why Alaimo begins her critique by citing Richard Lewontin and Richard Levins's *Biology under the Influence* in which they write: "Evidently your body knows your class position no matter how well you have been taught to deny it" (qtd. in Alaimo 2010, 27). Lewontin and Levins also coin the term "proletarian lung."

This example serves as the basis for Alaimo's theory of transcorporeality whereby human and more-than-human landscapes—bodies embedded in vibrant ecologies, no longer separated along Cartesian lines—move in and through one another. Transcorporeality is marked by porosity. The transcorporeal emerges at the breakdown of the facile understandings of the "human" and of "nature" (as bounded organisms) that served the interest of a "cosmology of the moderns"—conceived through a Cartesian ontology of material expression abetted by Judeo-Christian notions of human mastery, and cultivated through generations of political economy that thrived on the severing of the human from the nonhuman (or laborer from his land)—and which persist in bankrupt formulations of *Anthropos* (Debaise 2017). Per Didier Debaise's argument, following Alfred North Whitehead, such a "cosmology" expressly serves the interests of the agents of capital in so far as it provides the onto-epistemological criteria for modern development. Put more simply, without such a cosmology there is no "cheap nature" and surely no "cheap labor" (Patel and Moore 2017).

We have, per Bruno Latour and an army of new materialist thinkers, "never been modern in an ontological sense" despite the fact that "some humans have been behaving as though they were modern for centuries now—creating a potent instrumentarium for terraforming/anthroforming the planet for their convenience along the way" (Boyer 2019, 4). We are biosocial bodies forever bound in the material conditions of our environments, always subject to the vast destructions wrought by corporate industry and the *longue durée* of industrial development that I have critiqued thus far. As such, we must read Animal not as anomaly but indeed *memento mori*—an inevitability, a necessity. This is the "impeccable economic logic" of development for sure; but this is also the first law of thermodynamics. If matter cannot be created or destroyed, then we must be able to trace the material impact not of the "hyper-object," per se, but surely of the workings of the hyper-subject. A proper energopolitical reading of *Animal's People* (or Rukeyser's *The Book of the Dead*) necessarily leads us to a consideration of the porosity of bodies (human and non) and their positions in the shifting ecologies of late capitalism—energopolitical a term coined by anthropologist Dominic Boyer and just one in a series of potent neologisms, including Achille Mbembe's "necropower" and Povinelli's "geontopower," that call attention to the limited formulations of Foucauldian biopower. The latter, as argued by many critics including Kathryn Yusoff (2018), takes for granted that *bios* stems from a stable ontological niche—one cultivated through imperial-era notions of evolution and phylogenesis reliant on both Linnaean racism and what Yusoff calls the "white geology," a scientific category that posits as normative the same sort of species-level myopia attendant to the rhetoric of the Anthropocene. That is, within the logic of the Anthropocene the hyper-subject remains an omnipotent subject acting outside of/upon the material forces of his respective ecological niche—a unitary and discrete geological agent existing outside of the constituent Earth systems that constitute his being. Such a conception of *bios* is at the heart of conventional systems of governmentality that prioritize *human* populations and which marshal a particular—read Enlightened—definition of the human subject. Against an Anthropocene narrative that privileges the awesome power of the hyper-subject, and which relies on a teleological series of "golden spikes," Yusoff instead offers a "billion Black Anthropocenes" (2018) that make clear the material costs of each spike. We might understand Animal in terms of such costs.

Energopolitics names the entanglement of forces—energy, capital, and correlative forms of governmentality—that enables the conditions of power in our contemporary petrosphere and whose internal logic contests the anthropocentric impulse of a Foucaldian Cartesianism such as we see in the rhetoric of industrial development. In many ways, Animal's body serves as a conceptual limit for the Cartesian thinking that undergirds liberal notions of the human or of *bios*. As we see elsewhere in this project, the rogue serves as an explicit rejoinder to imperial subject formation: less an amorphous instantiation of vibrant matter than a commentary on the onto-epistemology of "colonial man" or *Anthropos*, Animal's figure—as, in Sylvia Wynter's (2003) formulation, a means of thinking through the human as praxis for the formation of the bourgeois subject—evidences the political history of *Anthropos*, or what Boyer (2019) and others refer to as a form of anthropolitics. Furthermore, the novel directly challenges conceptions of the human, while also posing new questions concerning biopolitics, if also Povinelli's notion of geontopower—a term that captures the heart of the carbon imaginary and which Povinelli defines as that which "does not operate through the governance of life and the tactics of death but is rather a set of discourses, affects, and tactics used in late liberalism to maintain or shape the coming relationship of the distinction between Life and Nonlife" (2016, 4).

"Nonlife" may here be understood as the "inhuman" subject of late liberalism—the toxified bodies sacrificed to the aforementioned economic "logic." Such bodies include the discarded human communities in cities like Bhopal along with the nonhuman environments in which they must vie for life—the "blasted landscapes" left in the wake of development schemes like those of Union Carbide (Tsing 2015). As we have just seen, the company's earlier projects—the aforementioned silicon mines, and the consequent death toll of the largely African American migrant labor regime in Hawks Nest, West Virginia—similarly conjure the impacts of a late-liberal geontopower. Perhaps this is why Sinha chooses to set his fictional Khaufpur against a more capacious world ecology that connects its crumbling factory to the denuded frontier of Coatesville. In both contexts, laborers are rendered fungible objects useful only for their role in the extraction of profit. Thus I understand what Yusoff calls the "biocentric subject of late liberalism" as a legatee of "colonial man"—the aforementioned hyper-subject—whose imperium is sustained through the maintenance of such extractive zones as those of Khaufpur and also Coatesville (2018, 11).

An Environmental Picaresque?

In order to render the sorts of ontological porosity at stake in Alaimo's formulation of transcorporeality or implicit to Povinelli's (2016) radical questioning of nonhuman life—"can rocks die"?—Sinha paints a landscape teeming with life, broadly conceived. Instead of counterpoising the "poison-house" *against* a living landscape, Sinha collapses the two sites: "Look throughout this place a silent war is being waged. Mother Nature's trying to take back the land. Wild sandalwood trees have arrived, who knows how, must be their seeds were shat by overflying birds.... Under the poison-house trees are growing up through the pipework" (*AP* 31). In this portrait of a defiant local ecology, the author endows the nonhuman landscape with a peculiar because unfamiliar sort of agency. Here the agentially rich landscape undermines the material (and conceptual) limits of a putatively static "nature"—inert and passive. Such scenes (of which there are several in the novel) are clear critiques of aesthetic renderings of "nature"—pastoral, picturesque, etc.—that continually deny the human and nonhuman presences that interrupt our imaginative pleasure.

It is this particular critique that helps Sinha to establish what Nixon would call an "environmental picaresque." That is, the novel isn't merely an instantiation of the picaresque form, but is according to Nixon somewhat *sui generis*. Sinha, argues Nixon, "singlehandedly" invented the genre of the environmental picaresque by deploying classic picaresque tropes in the service of exposing the sorts of environmental violence that we see in places like Bhopal (2011 46). Most notable is certainly Sinha's manipulation of linear time which,

Nixon argues, effectively duplicates the material and affective resonances of environmental violence—a violence whose temporal schema resists normative representation. "Time in paradise," Animal tells us, inheres with "the deep time when there was no difference between anything" (*AP* 352). Of course "paradise" here refers to the slum "covered in shit and plastic" where "Animal's people" lived (*AP* 106). Thus, picaresque indictment is transformed into tragic parody: more than a comic retelling of the exploits of the *pícaro*, here we see that the "Nutcracker" is a filthy place where Animal and his "people" must survive despite a dearth of clean water and other life-sustaining resources.

The strange timelessness of the picaresque form—in *Lazarillo*, in *Animal's People*, and elsewhere—has historically evoked the relentless present of the rogue, not the dreamy landscapes of more optimistic fictions. The picaresque novel thus serves a more material end—what Giancarlo Maiorino (2003) would also call its "econopoetics" to describe literary models that instantiate economic critiques, such as we see in the picaresque form. Maiorino looks to *Lazarillo de Tormes* as his central example; *Animal's People* operates similarly. As Animal remarks: "There is no night and day, only a vast hunger through which suns wheel, and moons wane and wax and have no meaning" (*AP* 186). By suturing the narrative with such corporeal desires—hunger over and against the loftier goals of the traditional hero and his "starry skies"—Animal tells a very different tale (Lukács 1974, 29). As in the picaresque tradition more broadly, "the acquisition of food weighs on matters of artistic representation" (Maiorino 23).

But the issue of time in Sinha's novel has already been sufficiently taken up by Nixon (2012), whose stunning critique links the novel's protagonist to the 1554 "Lazarillo" through such conventions as its nonlinear structure, which he argues is a perfect means of illustrating "slow violence." Nixon comments on the usefulness of nonlinearity for arresting the reader in the grotesque present of Bhopal—abjection here an aesthetic means of conjuring the particular condition of the *pícaro* in the Global South, and a tactic that was likewise employed in *Lazarillo*. In what follows, I read Animal accordingly; but I eschew an exhaustive discussion of time owing to Nixon's thorough treatment of this aspect of the novel. I will simply add that Sinha's manipulation of time—the recurrent motif of "now-o-clock," which recalls Salman Rushdie's "tick-tock," but in an even more sardonic homage to the violence of imperial teleologies—is a significant subversion of the aspirational tale of liberal ascent. Here, Sinha literally petrifies and protracts a single significant moment so as to render imaginatively the quarter-century long legacy of Union Carbide's presence in central India. Despite his constant disavowal of the primacy of "that night" as a marker of identity, it is nonetheless the temporal anchor of the novel. And the format—the episodically narrated series of tapes—allows for the reader to stay stuck in time. In this way, it is a superb "environmental picaresque" in so far as the reader is not able to bracket such forms of environmental violence. The explosion, the court case, the sickness . . . is never ending. We are stuck with Animal in its persistent present. As Animal also tells us: "Hope dies in places like this, because hope lives in the future and there's no future here" (*AP* 185).

I am interested here, though, in arguing for the rogue figure as a sort of antithesis to the liberal hero—a figure, who represents the "people of the Apokalis," and the "kingdom of the poor" (*AP* 63, 172). A Faustian specter indeed, one of Animal's "people" asks the Kampani lawyer quite presciently: "Mr. Lawyer, we lived in the shadow of your factory, you told us you were making medicine for the fields. You were making poisons to kill insects, but you killed us instead. I would like to ask, was there ever much difference, to you?" (*AP* 306). She likewise asks: "Is Khaufpur the only poisoned city?" (*AP* 296). The latter question gestures toward the larger matrix of global capitalism in which the uneven topographies of economic development have created many Khaufpurs. The closing line—"We are the people of the Apokalis. Tomorrow there will be more of us"—is more than a revenge fantasy (*AP* 366). It is a clear indication that, despite the promises of Western liberalism in the form of development, or progress, tomorrow there will surely be more casualties like Animal. Perhaps then, an even more chilling comment would be "Tomorrow, tomorrow, I want to cancel tomorrow" (*AP* 277).

As *memento mori*, the novel forces a consideration of such shadows of imperial liberalism as the aborted fetuses that likewise figure in the novel—a grotesque manipulation of the oft-cited trope of "midnight's children." The "Kha in the jar," who Animal befriends, tells him: "I am the egg of nature, which ignorant and arrogant men have spoiled" (*AP* 139). The Kha is literally an aborted fetus housed in a jar in a government clinic—an "egg" of a despoiled nature that such arrogant men as the "poison minister" and the Kampani managers have produced. Mukherjee also comments that "Animal and Kha mirror each other in that they have both been placed beyond the pale of normative humanity by the Kampani's poison gas"—the Kha, though, an even more terrifying illustration of the company's "impeccable" logic (2010, 153).

The Kha evinces, to a great extent, the structure of feeling of what we might call a sort of neoliberal Arcadianism—a perverted longing for a mode of life that explicitly requires the erasure of such local subjects as the "Kha in the jar," not to mention Animal himself. The Kha in the jar, and perhaps even more than Animal, is a succinct physical manifestation of the distorted logic to which I alluded at the outset of this essay. The local minister tells the American doctor "Elli," who had come to Khaufpur under humanitarian pretenses: " 'Please don't think worse of me if I tell you the truth. Those poor people never had a chance. If it had not been the factory it would have been cholera, TB, exhaustion, hunger. They would have died anyway'" (*AP* 153). As is made evident by such comments, the company's failures "were more than callous oversights; they were practices that illuminate the structural logic of the corporation's existence in India" (Mukherjee 2010, 140). This structural logic is succinctly captured in the figure of the Kha, and the community of aborted fetuses that populate Elli's clinic. This macabre display is also uniquely effective as antihumanist critique: reducible to the raw matter of life, the Kha evinces a fundamental instantiation of *bios* denied categorization as *Human*. Like Animal, the Kha cannot be *improved* in the Lockean sense. Both figures are effective reminders of the costs of imperial liberalism as well as tangible indicators of the political sentiment of contemporary Bhopal.

Animal's People and the Politics of Global Toxicity

Animal's People illuminates why real protests (in Bhopal and elsewhere) feature local residents comparing former Union Carbide CEO Warren Anderson to Osama bin Laden; but the novel's treatment of the fictional community's protest is more complicated. It attests to the tricky politics of resistance in which, as his character Zafar recurrently notes, residents must find strength in having nothing.[9] Zafar, who is an activist in the community but with no personal ties there, implores people to marshal their desperation into political action. This, he does, through such modes of resistance as hunger strikes and a proposed boycott of a new clinic, whose origins are unknown—some opining that it might be a response by the company to charges of criminal behavior, and thus a way of saving face. Zafar, who befriends Animal and employs him in the service of the movement, is one of many complicated figures in the novel—the progressive intellectual, whose elite education separates him from subjects like Animal, but whose (more) local origins distinguish him from such well-intentioned liberals as the foreign "Amrikan doctress" Elli.

Animal is also counterpoised against figures like Somraj, a former singer whose lungs were so charred "that night" that he can no longer sing, and who, like Animal, also lost his family—aside from Nisha, his daughter and Animal's muse. Consequently, he looks for music in the many mundane elements around him—frogs, the creaking of rickshaws, and so forth. Music, for Somraj, is a salve. It offers a "promise," an alternative logic that defies the logic of the company and the logic of those who protest the company's violence with different versions of their own (*AP* 201). Somraj's character—along with Animal's, Zafar's, and also Elli's—constitutes an element of the increasingly tangled mosaic of resistance and revolution that has been deployed over time against the company, and whose tactics repeatedly come into question as each ultimately fails. Animal, who sees no folly in violence—in contradistinction to Zafar's resilience, and Somraj's and Farouq's faith—stands apart. And his tactics—the accidental burning of the factory toward the end of the novel for example—also seem an omniscient wink at the reader that sometimes violence necessarily begets violence. Of course, Animal's form also reminds the reader that justice isn't merely an acknowledgment of past wrongs: "Justice should involve the Kampani facing trial" (Rickel 2012, 103).

In this way, the novel is certainly more complicated than what I have argued is its Spanish progenitor. Sure, like Lazarillo, Animal knows that only as a huckster would he survive. And both have no illusions about god, or innate human goodness. Both also symbolize the antihumanist discourse of the picaresque tradition, whose burden is the poverty and suffering of those for whom survival takes primacy over such false promises as social justice. But, and quite significantly, there are clear differences between *Animal's People* and *Lazarillo de Tormes*. The latter was a closed fiction in which the *pícaro's* narration was much more tightly circumscribed by his subjective experiences. *Animal's People* is a far more expansive story, with a host of different storylines—that of the Kampani of course, but also of the complicated local politics of Khaufpur. We learn much of characters like Nisha, Zafar, and also Farouq—their varied religious and philosophical beliefs, etc. Sinha offers frequent comments on their Hindu and Muslim affiliations, noting that such distinctions aren't relevant to the fight for justice—perhaps a nod to the false notions of national solidarity, which are continually marshaled against India's poorer castes.[10] And finally, Animal's narrative arc also departs in some ways from the classic picaresque form. He meditates on his own humanity—"if they kill me, what will die?"—as he experiences shame and love and pain (*AP* 313). Lazarillo embodies no such emotions. Thus, there is a progressive *Bildung* in regards to Animal's affective states, which contradicts common descriptions of the *pícaro* figure, who is generally reducible to a mere instrument for political critique.

Mukherjee also raises the issue of genre arguing that the novel is actually "an echo of [the] stylistics of north Indian classical musical performance" (2010, 162). He reads "Animal's traumatized imaginings about the night of the accident as the notes arranged . . . to create a *raga* of, as Animal calls it, *bhayanak rasa*—the mood of terror" (162). Mukherjee thus aligns the Sinha novel with a sixteenth-century Indian tradition, and not any Spanish one. Commenting on the leitmotif of music in the novel and the significance of Somraj's character, he further remarks: "As Animal sees it, a major task of his story is to convey this mood of sheer terror to his audience. In this—and it is clear by the term that he uses—he is very much like an Indian classical singer whose task is to pitch his melody and rhythm to express or evoke certain moods or *rasas*" (157).

I wonder, though, if we can't accept that Animal's "raga" is both a metaphor for an alternative mode of order—an alternative to both the violent logic of the Kampani's murderous business practices, and to the liberal ideology that understands the term "human" in rather limited ways—while also an instantiation of the picaresque form. That is, I argue that we can read the novel as a postcolonial picaresque, which illustrates the emergent realities of neoliberal capitalism as well as the residual cultural practices of both the classical Indian raga, and the Spanish picaresque novel. This, it seems, is what Maureen Moynagh meant by her comment, in the context of the Nigerian picaresque, regarding "the re-emergence of a picaresque sensibility . . . to explore and to protest the socio-political conditions that produce a new kind of rogue" (2011, 51).

We might also consider that the picaresque form is an incredibly generative means of socioeconomic critique. This is certainly the case in *Animal's People* even if we are to read it as a descendant of local aesthetic forms. The novel is absolutely a critique of both the neoliberal logic that would produce such figures as Animal, and of the larger matrix of global capitalism in which the structure of liberal humanitarianism effectively veils the transnational economic relationships that have in fact produced many Bhopals. To return again to Williams, if the dominant cultural ethos promotes a narrowly imagined sense of development or "uplift," I read the emergent aesthetic tradition of the postcolonial picaresque as its logical counter. Like Lazarillo before him Animal is evocative of the itinerant subject produced not by any "transcendental homelessness," but by a particular way of being in the world (Lukács 1974, 41). In the era of late capitalism, the "faceless average" evoked by Lazarillo emerges as so many "Animals"—a phenomenon that arises as new cycles of primitive accumulation produce ever more Bhopals (Maiorino 2003, 74).

Nonetheless, we must take seriously arguments like Mukherjee's; there is certainly a risk in such generic pronouncements. As Peter Hitchcock would also argue: "Too often genre is an alibi of cultural integration, a mode in which the African novel, for instance, is celebrated precisely because its 'local color' is rendered in a recognizable form" (2003, 323). But it is not my intention to gloss the novel in this way. I argue, rather, that Animal (as "faceless average") is uniquely effective in conjuring a new sort of proletariat owing precisely to Sinha's nuanced adaptation of the *pícaro's* tale.[11] In this sense, the novel may be situated in a burgeoning canon—that of similarly picaresque novels, which have lately captured the experiences of persons displaced across the Global South.

Tomorrow, There Will be More of Us!

Any distinctions notwithstanding, Animal's tale ends like Lazarillo's: both find love amidst the squalor of their lives. But while Lazarillo's tale ends in resignation, Animal's ends in triumph—that is, *Animal's People* culminates in a strange sort of revenge. Toward the end of the novel, after Zafar and Farouq have endured days of their hunger fast, and while the Kampani lawyers persist in their arrogance, Animal unknowingly causes a fire in the factory that reproduces (to a far lesser extent of course) the conditions of "that night." After ingesting the very pills that he had earlier used to poison Zafar in a futile attempt at suicide, Animal spins out into a hallucinatory frenzy during which he first starts the fire and then finds himself in the forest in fits of hysteria. Here, Sinha relies on a bit of magic to convey Animal's coming into consciousness. It is worth mentioning that this passage is reminiscent of the strangely miasmic aura of the Sundarbans in Rushdie's 1981 *Midnight's Children*—also a picaresque indictment, although of a different (but equally dubious) coming of age, this time at the moment of the nation's putative birth. But India's "tryst with destiny" in 1984 Bhopal was quite different from that of 1947 (Nehru 2007). And the revenge fantasy that Sinha creates at the end of the novel belies a very different political sensibility than we see in Rushdie's frequently maligned critique of India's post-independence history—particularly as regards Rushdie's almost caricatural representations of the nation's urban poor.

After the fast is ended, the Kampani lawyers resume their discussions, and the citizens of Khaufpur know the outcome. Justice will not be served, and so a bit of "poetic justice" is instead delivered:

> [The Kampani men] had begun their arguing and haggling when without warning their eyes began to sting. An evil burning sensation began in their noses and throats, a little like the smoke of burning chillies, it caught nastily in the throat, it seared the lungs, they were coughing, but coughing made it ten times worse. Something was in the room, something uninvited, an invisible fire, by the time they had realized this it was already too late. These big shot politicians and lawyers, they got up in a panic, they reeled around, retching, everything they did just made the pain worse. Tears streamed from their eyes, hardly could they see. One of the lawyers was trying to vomit, the rest of them ran in panic. They rushed from the room, jostling in the doorway each man for himself, the buffalo it seems being too bulky to rush, was left behind while the others scrambled to save their skins. These Kampani heroes, these politicians, they were shitting themselves, they thought they were dying,

> they thought they'd been attacked with the same gas that leaked on that night, and every man there knew exactly how horrible the depths of those who breathed the Kampani's poisons. (*AP* 360–61)

Poetic justice would have to suffice, because, as we learn in the novel, "gone" indeed are the days "when the starry skies are the map of all possible paths" (Lukács 1974, 29). Here instead, "the heartless stars glitter like knives above the city" (*AP* 327). And so, the ending is to be expected:

> Eyes, what else can I tell you? Life goes on. It will take time, so we're told, to appoint a new judge in the case, the hearing's again been postponed, the Kampani's still trying to find ways to avoid appearing. . . . There is still sickness all over Khaufpur . . . the factory is still there, blackened by fire it's, but the grass is growing again, and the charred jungle is pushing out green shoots. Moons play hide and seek in the pipework of the poison-khana still the foreign jarnaliss come. (*AP* 365)

But true to form, Animal punctuates this tragic fact—told with the signature wit and resignation of his character—with a nod to Lazarillo: he takes his wife and accepts his fate. And he promises the eyes to whom he has narrated his tale: "We are the people of the Apokalis. Tomorrow there will be more of us" (*AP* 366). As if to confirm the deadly truth of the novel, and the role of the form—a picaresque *memento mori* that reminds us that there are in fact many Bhopals—Animal beseeches the eyes thus: "Remember me. All things pass, but the poor remain" (*AP* 366).

The novel ultimately instantiates the econopoetics of the picaresque form in its representation of the necessarily failed *Bildung* of its protagonist. So too, the necessary failure of the movement against the company—necessary because of the extractive logic of global capital, which renders Animal as waste. In this sense, it is evocative of novels like Aravind Adiga's *The White Tiger*, which moves us from the econopoetics of the postcolonial picaresque to what I shall call, following Boyer's (2019) argument for energopolitics, the energopoetics of the carbon picaresque. In the following chapter, I investigate the nation's burgeoning coal industry—also an index of modernity, not unlike the agribusiness model that enjoyed favor under the "Green Revolution" and which decimated the nation's interior. Similarly a symbol of the waste of global networks of trade, Balram (like Animal) is a *pícaro* par excellence.

Chapter 3

Slum Ecologies: Figuring (Energy) Waste in Aravind Adiga's *The White Tiger*

Energopolitical analysis offers a different set of analytical attentions than those of biopower and capital and, as such, may enable us to tell different stories and imagine different futures.

—Dominic Boyer, *Energopolitics: Wind and Power in the Anthropocene*

Dubbed the "coal capital of India"—the third largest consumer (and producer) of coal-based energy after China and the United States—the mineral-rich city of Dhanbad, located in the state of Jharkhand, is home to 112 active mines producing 27.5 million tons of coal annually (Sardi 2018). Until 2020, the city was part of the state of Bihar—the region home to the English East India Company's original settlement. From the perspective of imperial Britain, it might appear that the EIC was responsible for midwifing the nation's coal industry: in the 1820s, its role in the production of steam-powered transport, vital to the Company's other holdings—namely opium and cotton—would secure its centrality in the nation's fledgling mineral economy. King Coal would auger " 'great steam highways for bringing cotton and other products of the interior to the coast, and for transmitting English manufactures in return,' at one stroke supplying Britain with an abundance of raw materials—apart from cotton, also silk, indigo, hemp, timber, rice, opium, tea—and a teeming market on which the surplus of manufactured goods could be dumped" (Malm 224). Mining the coal, however, was another question: while the Raniganj mine—now the longest-operating mine in India—would open and thus make "coal . . . the most highly prized resource of the Indian soil" given its potential to "ferry treasure" to the coasts, British officials saw local laborers from a Linnaean perspective that read Indians as somehow not fit for hard labor (Malm 224). Thus, potential miners would have to be subject to coercion and indenture—similar to the peasant laborers who I examined in the context of Amitav Ghosh's *Ibis Trilogy*: "A reasonably stable mining workforce could only be gradually molded through the constant application of extra-economic coercion over more than a century of British efforts to conjure the industry out of the ground" (Malm 228).

If Ghosh would temporalize Victorian India as the "age of flowers," in the present chapter I shall read this moment as the "age of coal"—a problematic distinction in so far as energy histories don't operate along such neat breaks, but a crucial one for understanding the role of coal in the formation of the subcontinent's infrastructural imaginary (Yaeger 2011). Coal would power the abovementioned "steam highway"; and it would fuel the nascent network of transcontinental locomotives that would enable connections between new sites of accumulation—also serving the imaginative end of independence-era notions of a bucolic countryside counterpoised against the nation's thriving metropolises. Of course, coal would also power the techno-socialist visions of the independent nation's first prime minister Jawaharlal Nehru (1947–64), whose five-year development plans hinged on the construction of giant (steel) dam projects—dependent as they were upon the metallurgical coal now central to the nation's fossil economy; hence the caveat regarding any discrete "age" in reference to energy histories.[1] As we shall see below in the context of Aravind Adiga's 2008 picaresque novel *The White Tiger*, while petrol also fuels much of India's industry, coal has retained its imperium well into the twenty-first century. Accordingly, scholars within the Energy Humanities have sought to problematize fallacious energy histories that eschew consideration of the overlapping trajectories of multiple energy regimes—including, for example, wind in the Victorian period—while forging new critical methodologies for examining the constellation of narratives that constitute modernity, a period that critics Imre Szeman and Dominic Boyer describe as "saturated" in fossil fuels (2017, 4). Indeed, and because "human civilization . . . did not begin on condition that, one day in his history, man would have to shift from wood to coal and from coal to petroleum and gas," in my consideration of coal's sustained hegemony I shall embrace a Thermocene model of environmental history (Chakrabarty 2009, 216). That is, and in lieu of a historically deficient Anthropocene timescale that ignores the uneven material histories of fossil capital, I shall embrace "a political history of CO_2," and one fueled by convergent regimes of extractive capitalism (Bonneuil and Fressoz 2016). And I shall read *The White Tiger* accordingly: as a carbon picaresque in its attention to the central role of fossil capitalism in Indian state-building; as a critique of such problematic timescales as obtain in Anthropocene discourse, employing instead a picaresque temporality; and also as a stunning portrait of worker dispossession and the human costs of the coal mining industry. It accomplishes the latter by foregrounding such precarious labor regimes as we see in the slums of Dhanbad and New Delhi—their precarity sustained through the sorts of taxonomic racism that renders working-class subjects as somehow inhuman.

But I shall in fact recognize an "age of coal" to the extent that I acknowledge the intimate link between King Coal's hegemony on the subcontinent and its role in shaping the nation's social and cultural landscape—whether in the age of Victoria or Narendra Modi, the nation's current prime minister. While Carl Trocki would argue (and rightfully) that "there [would have been] no [British] empire without opium" (1999, 59) here we must also consider that there would have been no opium economy without coal-powered steam ships.[2] As well, there would be no steel industry without coal—no dams, no factories; and perhaps too, there would be no democracy. And so, in the present chapter, we hail the age of coal—a period in which we continue to find ourselves despite popular narratives that would deny the immiscible chronologies of extractivist regimes on the subcontinent. As we shall see in the following discussion of India's carbon-fueled democracy, the umbra of coal-powered systems of governmentality stretches across normative historic, political, and regional periodizations. Not to mention, we must again question any timescale that reads the Anthropocene "as an event befalling a stable nature" and instead understand that the ontological fantasy of a "stable nature [is] a product of the European imagination"—an imagination responsible for the aesthetic greenwashing that has historically erased labor from the pastoral, picturesque, and postcolonial imaginations (Colebrook 16). The sort of greenwashing that I examined in the context of Indra Sinha's *Animal's People*—that which allowed for the developmentalist rhetoric of Union Carbide's ad campaigns to obscure the material violence inflicted upon Animal's community—is precisely what is operating in the late-capitalist landscape of New Delhi where Modi continues to boast of coal's civilizing potential (in the form of mass electrification for the poor) while ignoring the horrific conditions in which coal workers and local citizens must live. It is to the confluence, then, of such political drivers as Modi's electoral interests and the aesthetic traditions that have historically abetted the suppression of our collective energy unconscious, that I now turn in my discussion of carbon culture and the origins and proliferation of India's coal economy.

The "Age of Coal"

While coal's infrastructural imaginary would be largely drawn during the occupation of the Company and subsequently the British Raj, its centrality to India's GDP would be secured upon the nationalization of the industry in 1973. Meanwhile, efforts toward nationalization would begin in earnest in the 1940s when the onset of WWII would require that the industry be regulated and marshaled toward the war effort. Following the war, decades of political wrangling would then occur before its official nationalization by then Prime Minister Indira Gandhi—Gandhi's coal policies aligning with the agricultural programs outlined in the previous chapter, which also privileged the accumulation of capital over the livelihoods of the nation's vast *Adivasi* communities.

Often seen as a leftward shift in the nation's politics, it has been argued that nationalization was more likely indicative of what some scholars read as evidence of political ineptitude and the failures of the industry to self-regulate and thus remain sustainable (Kumar 1981a). Following the revocation of the East India Company's charter in 1857, and under the Raj, the Indian Mining Association (IMA) and the Indian Mining Federation (IMF)—the latter formed in 1925—would be established. A concise portrait of the sorts of public-private partnerships that monopolized the agrochemical industry under the auspices of the nation's "Green Revolution," private proxies of the IMA and IMF constituted 90 percent of industry holdings with the remaining mines governed by local speculators notable for endemic corruption and the cooptation of inequitable land distribution practices such as were practiced during the company's occupation.[3] The latter is also associated with local *zamindars*, not unlike the fictional "Stork"—one of a number of corrupt figures in *The White Tiger*, who "fed on the village" where Adiga's protagonist lived with his family, not to mention "everything that grew in it, until there was nothing left" (*WT* 21). The Stork also speculated in coal in addition to owning the local river that otherwise sustained regional fisherfolk.

Aligned with the conventional wisdom of EIC practices before them, in the 1920s and 1930s such smaller landholders began to lay claim to much of the nation's coal seams—the "land-intensive logic of extractive industries" like the mining of coal essentially "sediment[ing]" historical struggles over who is permitted to monopolize finite reserves of land and nature" (Shutzer 2021, 403). Associated with the IMA and IMF, these provincial landlords, argues economist Rajiv Kumar, were responsible for mining techniques that eschewed any consideration of the ecological sanctity of local landscapes and their respective communities. Such mine owners ostensibly sacrificed the lower depths of regional coal seams (many near the aforementioned colliery at Raniganj)—prospecting only the more perceptible surface strata—in a short-sighted effort to secure profit: "This caused the reserves, locked in the lower layers, to be lost forever, as water logging, subsidence and, worse still, underground fires, made it impossible to extract the coal" (Kumar 1981a, 758). More than an economic loss, this also served to establish practices that would continue to leave local landscapes in ruin. The material legacy of such practices persist in the enduring fires at Dhanbad, for example, and now serve as grounds for a host of geoengineering schemes geared toward environmental remediation:

> The history of subsidence, fires, flooding and other kinds of environmental hazards related to shallow coal workings in India goes back to colonial times some 300 years ago. As coal production accelerated in modern times, so did the environmental and socio-economic drawbacks related to exploitation. In the mid-1980s, a hydro-pneumatic sand-stowing method was developed to fill in abandoned galleries but their exact location had to be known. Unfortunately, most of these old workings are uncharted.(Maillol et al. 2003, 103)

Mine managers also disregarded labor regulations, which would have provided protection for seasonal miners—largely unskilled and directed only toward the shallow strata of the pits—who risked life and limb often without wages at all.

This is precisely the sort of ineptitude cited above that served as impetus for nationalization—a process which occurred really in two stages. The nation's power sector would be nationalized upon independence and thus the nationalization of coal—the primary source of Indian electrical power—would logically follow. So too, and owing to the need for coking coal which at the time constituted only 15–20 percent of total reserves (and is largely located in the fields of Raniganj and Jharia—adjacent to Dhanbad), nationalization is/was vital both to the steel industry and to the thermal power upon which most of the nation's industry depends (Kumar 1981a, 759). Nationalization, and consequent regulation, likewise proved a means of streamlining industry practice so as to avoid further exhaustion of resources. Kumar observes accordingly: "Given the particular market and production conditions in India, it was too risky to let the free market regulate the production and use of this crucially important exhaustible natural resource" (762). Despite the 1952 Coal Mines (Conservation and Safety) Act, for example, "by 1971, approximately 100 million tonnes of coking coal had been wasted in non- metallurgical uses" (762).

In short, prior to nationalization, the coal industry was marked by egregious labor conditions, short-sighted extraction processes that produced quick profit and destroyed reserves, and a commitment to profiteering and the requisite exploitation of the poor. Unfortunately, the latter is still a marker of the industry: approximately 90 percent of Indian coal is mined in southcentral Indian states like Odisha where Coal India Limited (CIL) was accused in 2016 of violating *Adivasi* rights—literally seizing and bulldozing Native land for mining operations.[4] Such acts continue to be sanctioned under the Coal Bearing Areas (Acquisition and Development) Act of 1957—areas including Jharkhand.[5] Significantly, legislation of this sort would also codify coal *as* property—a means of asserting rights to subterranean landscapes, which would present yet another frontier of accumulation and thus catalyze the further destruction of peasant landscapes and communal rights to land use.[6] Thus, Kumar concludes that nationalization was "at best an act of crisis management" and one that clearly fell short of systemic change (1981b, 829). To be sure, contemporary industry practice (as is evidenced by CIL) continues to come under fire—the extractivist logic employed during the Victorian period now reproduced in the era of late capitalism. Thus, Modi's promise of a fully electrified rural India in the coming year—electricity functioning as an index of modernity, and thus fulfilling the promise of India's first independent administration in 1947—has unsurprisingly been met with suspicion and vociferous protest. But with "coal provid[ing] about half of India's commercial primary energy supply," and with CIL (which is based in Bengal with subsidiaries across the nation) being "the world's largest coal mining company . . . [and producing] 84 percent of India's thermal coal" (thus providing electricity to some one billion Indians), Modi will likely succeed (Tangia and Gross 2019).[7]

Without rehearsing the excesses of colonial and corporate rule, the coal industry would likewise be marked by new mechanisms of dispossession, namely the abovementioned commodification of subterranean coal seams, the material legacy of which may be felt in the broader metropolitan region of Dhanbad where Adiga's protagonist and his family live. The fictional Halwais figure as a conventional representation of rural poverty; and Balram Halwai—Adiga's *pícaro*—emerges as an unlikely hero whose bawdy rhetoric and irreverent disposition will surely remind readers of Indra Sinha's "Animal," if also Lazarillo. The roguish Balram, who works for a coal speculator, will survive on his wit despite the material dearth with which he is constantly faced in the Dhanbad and, eventually, Delhi slums—sites that I shall read herein, in the parlance of Lockean notions of cultivation and improvement, as repositories for the human and nonhuman waste produced by India's spectacularly successful coal industry.

In this chapter, I read *The White Tiger* as a parody in which images of such waste—whether industrial sewage or persons—displace the conventionally optimistic visual rhetoric of the "new India," a moniker coined to mark the nation's period of economic liberalization which began in 1991 under then Prime Minister Manmohan Singh.[8] In this way, I perform a materialist intervention that foregrounds the slum ecologies of (in this case) the cities of Dhanbad, New Delhi, and Bangalore, and in so doing consider "slow violence" in the context of urban ruin—"slow violence" here understood as "a violence that occurs gradually and out of sight, a violence of delayed destruction that is dispersed across time and space, an attritional violence that is typically not viewed as violence at all" in part because of the invisibility of communities like Balram's, if also the distorted economic logic of extractivist industries like that of coal (Nixon 2011, 2).

Owing to the imbrications of extractive capitalism, electoral politics, and the proliferation of new modes of removal and forced apartheid—the latter emboldened by extant theories of the putatively Human, inhuman, and nonhuman—in what follows, I pursue three discrete questions in order to identify the intersections between global fossil capital, forms of waste (both wastelands and disposable populations), and the skeins of imperial ideology that produce figures like Balram: 1) the origins of such notions of *bios* as obtain in the category of the "Human" and its inverse—the inhuman subject laboring in India's coal mines and rendered as the refuse of fossil capital; 2) figurations of nonhuman waste in the form of coal ash and the toxic slum ecologies that flank cities like Dhanbad and New Delhi; and 3) the virtue of a speculative-critical reading praxis that centralizes energy (and energy regimes) for attending to cultural productions like *The White Tiger*. As Balram wryly remarks in reference to the coal barons who would determine his fate: "They talked about politics, coal, and about your country—China. Somehow these things—politics, coal, China—were linked to the family fortunes of the Stork and dimly I understood that my own fate, since I was part of this family now, was linked to these three things as well" (*WT* 60). Notably, Balram was a servant to "this family"—as much a "part of [it]" as Lazarillo was to his many masters.

Adiga's narrator is also a concise instantiation of the *pícaro* figure, if also earlier literary critiques of local waste economies such as were illustrated in works like Mulk Raj Anand's 1935 *Untouchable*. Here in the slums of empire, a new precariat, and one fueled by a global system of fossil capital, must vie for survival; and it is with this particular labor regime that I shall be centrally concerned. But before addressing the novel and its affordances for thinking through the enduring legacy of imperial ideology on the subcontinent—as it pertains to labor and extractivism—I first return to an exploration of the sprawling tendrils of the coal economy and its complicated history as well as to its impacts on cultural production.

Carbon Culture

Given the sustained hegemony of coal on the subcontinent—dating, as I've noted, to the nation's colonial period—it is in fact problematic to designate as age of coal. But I do so here in order to recognize the centrality of fossil-fueled systems of political economy such that I understand all cultural productions as inseparable from the material conditions in which they are conceived—that coal, for example, may serve as a more appropriate heuristic than such literary designations as a Romantic or Victorian age. To take but two examples, the Wordsworthian sublime or Dickensian satire are reproduced *ad nauseum* in so-called postcolonial texts, the latter also a rather problematic classification in its adherence to false political temporalities—per Balram, "the British left in 1947, but only a moron would think that we became free then" (*WT* 18). Accordingly, in the present discussion I understand independence-era films like the 1957 *Mother India* as an homage to Gandhian notions of an Arcadian return to the countryside, but one made possible by material networks of extraction and trade; and I likewise read postcolonial novels like *The White Tiger* not as a facile indictment of the putative "New India"—surely the most popular reading of the novel—but as a carbon fiction in its attention to the myriad of ways in which the nation's coal economy *fuels* such visions of modern India through its relationship with the nation's electoral politics. Indeed, we might say that the only way in which the oft-employed appellation "the world's largest democracy" (which Adiga's narrator refers to as a "fucking joke") is accurate is through the lens of Timothy Mitchell's argument regarding "carbon democracies."[9] Balram excoriates the nation's electoral politics at every turn—from the fraudulent voter cards that bear the imprints of neighbors coerced by local government officials, the "inky fingerprints which the illiterate person makes on the ballot paper to indicate his vote" (*WT* 81); to the Stork's appointment as a representative of the local Socialist party—the indication that the party is linked to his illegal dealings with the government-owned mines; to Balram's frequent jabs at the "Communist guerillas" with whom this nascent entrepreneur would never be associated (*WT* 69).

In Mitchell's argument it is the shift to petrol-dominant economies that correlates with a disintegration of forms of labor solidarity long associated with coal-powered factory culture—that is, a shift toward more itinerant (and putatively invisible) labor regimes such as we see evidenced by the migrant laborers moving from India's southern states to the Persian Gulf; but King Coal's continued dominance in India is also marked by the sort of precarity that we have come to associate with petroleum-based energy. If petroleum's slippery technics are easily out of sight to the elite consumer, because petroleum workers are sited in disparate choke points along transnational pipelines, the subterranean landscape of coal extraction produces a similar phenomenon of invisibility. The current migration of itinerant oil workers to the gulf follows an imperial trajectory of Indian and Chinese miners traceable to the nation's colonial period: the coalfields subtending the islands of the Malay archipelago, for example, which were worked by contingent labor regimes from the mainland, have been reproduced across the nation's coal belt and are worked by a similarly invisible population. Largely unseen, and surely less remarked than petroleum extraction, or the spectacular instances of displacement wrought by megadam projects like the Sardar Sarovar dam (which was opened after fifty years of protest), coal is the central economy upon which the subcontinent depends.[10]

Perhaps coal is less remarked than the emergent networks of petroleum extraction pulling laborers from the southern states not only because of the hegemony of petroculture, but also because of an ideological commitment to linear notions of industrial development such that India's modern history can only be understood in terms of successive increments—discrete state shifts, that is, between coal and petrol, or and as I shall demonstrate in the conclusion to this study, petrol and solar power. Such a logic—what has been termed "energologic" by Boyer—dismisses the historical simultaneity of energy sources in favor of the aforementioned hagiographic schema. In this sense then, and as we shall see evinced in remarks by the sarcastic Balram, coal instantiates the irrational inverse of a modern logic (what Ghosh terms the "bourgeois regularity" of modernity) that would understand energy forms as easily situated geographically, historically, ecologically, economically, and culturally: it is everywhere and nowhere; it is before and after petroleum; its continued prominence is a vestige of the East India's Company's occupation; and it is a hallmark of the independent nation's industrial virtuosity. To be sure, to "fuel [Indian] culture, coal must [continue to] burn" (Hatmaker 2017, 87). But according to Balram, nobody "pays attention to coal" (*WT* 182).

So too, the disposable labor regimes that constitute the material possibility of Indian autonomy must remain out of sight if only to reinforce the myth of a rising middle class, if also to comfort the elite consumer. Readers of *The White Tiger* would surely prefer the rags to riches story of films like *Slumdog Millionaire* (Boyle 2008)—dramatizing as it does the benevolence of liberal capitalism—to the images of irradiated slums and toxic bodies on display in the novel. It ought to be noted that the blockbuster film is riddled with images of slum life, but the conditions in which the fictional "Jamal" must vie for survival, rendered in flashbacks to the protagonist's childhood, serve only to further the developmentalist fantasy that is this particular mode of "ethnic *Bildungsroman*"—what Lisa Lowe describes in terms of the "subject's journey . . . to integrated citizenship . . . respond[ing] to the reconciliatory and universalizing functions of canonization" (1996, 45). Joseph Slaughter's (2006) indictment of this narrative form—the arc of which he describes in terms of incorporation into the system of capital—would aptly characterize the film as well. The slum of Jamal's childhood can be read in terms of the "state of nature" from which the capital subject will presumably emerge—that is, we can read Jamal as the raw nature of capital.

Contra the productive labor that Marx designated as "reserve" or "surplus"—land and labor understood as the fundamental bases of primitive accumulation, and a logical point of origin for colonialist notions of *Bildung*—such laborers as are represented in *The White Tiger* resist subsumption into such a logic. Instead, they seem to constitute the waste that is both a product of the inherent logic of global (fossil) capital and the evident material substrate of a global petroculture. Conventional wisdom reads the laboring body as indeed productive—of capital, that is, or of reifying raw nature into the commodity form; but here I want to return to our discussion of cheap nature and cheap labor (in the context of the *Ibis Trilogy*) to understand working bodies as not merely fungible but expendable. Perhaps we should think in terms of exhaustibility: once the working body is no longer productive, it may be rendered as waste. This, we know, was the fate of the plantation slave in the Americas and the indentured workers who I discussed in the context of the *Ibis Trilogy*. Of course, this might also be understood in terms of the "horrendous logic" of corporate profit that we critiqued in the context of *Animal's People*—a logic persistently marshaled against the global poor.

Accordingly, and similarly aligned with liberal apologists for empire—John Stuart Mill, and later Larry Summers, in India and elsewhere—contemporary regimes of liberal (fossil) capitalism are bolstered by the developmentalist rhetoric of leaders like Modi or former US president Donald Trump, both extolling a narrative of manifest destiny that continues to boast of civilizational progress and its necessary costs, whether human or non. In such narratives the exhausted laborer (and the fruit of their labors) is simply a byproduct of capital accumulation—the cost of progress as it were. Hence the need to offsite waste so as to maintain the developmentalist fiction of civilizational uplift. This is achieved through various forms of "wastelanding," including the construction and maintenance of what Macarena Gómez-Barris (2017) reads as "extractive zones," hitherto discussed in terms of zones of exception (Voyles 2015). These are regions where persons "historically and contemporarily . . . treated as fuel [are] a source of energy to be extracted, expended, and exhausted for the sake of someone else's good life" (Barney and Szeman 2019, 1). Such a model "relies upon the erasure, or at best subsistence, of large parts of the planet to ensure safe, quiet (almost pastoral) lives within cities in the disambiguated west" (Wilson 2018, 392). Extractive zones depend on both material violence as well as the onto-epistemological violence that renders figures like Balram as somehow less than human—subject to historically sanctioned categories of race which necessarily abetted the uneven development of the global petrosphere. The construct of race—read here in terms of a "white [biology]," and one bolstered by fallacious physiognomic theories such as we see parodied in *The White Tiger*—is what allows for the global stratification of class that produces the abovementioned extractive zones (Yusoff 2018).

It is for this reason too that I shall read Adiga's novel through the lens of the historically *inhuman* in order to examine the ways in which such "excremental populations" as Adiga's peasant laborers correlate—economically and ontologically—to the waste born of coal extraction within the global petrosphere more broadly, and in India specifically (Dawson 2011). Read as such, the novel sheds light on the intersecting histories of settler colonialism, extractivism, and environmental violence—the latter also felt in the wastelanding of both coal ash and the disposable populations who populate the Delhi slums. In the storyworld of the novel (and in the popular imaginary), the sooty stuff is indistinguishable from the "glistening bodies" charged with its extraction—both abstracted as so much cheap nature, and thus expendable fodder for the industry (*WT* 134). The latter, in part, accounts for why both coal and coal workers remain out of sight to liberal consumers in the Global North—rendered invisible through the logic of global extractivism. The invisibility of such laborers, it should be noted, accounts for arguments by scholars in the Energy Humanities for a renewed awareness of the "constitutive," really structural, absence of the global precariat, as well as a more robust interpretative framework for approaching such cultural productions as *The White Tiger*. This, of course, is a driving question in the field more broadly: how to *read* energy forms that are so embedded in contemporary culture as to be virtually invisible.

Adiga's carbon picaresque offers a model for thinking through such forms of invisibility. More broadly, the category of carbon fiction allows for a more expansive understanding of the carbon imaginary, engendering new questions about reading and form otherwise constrained by practices attendant to petrofiction—a genre focused primarily on the oil encounter.[11] Thus, in the remainder of this chapter I begin by examining the ways in which forms of extractive capitalism are narrated in our contemporary petrosphere so as to bolster economic programs that thrive on the maintenance of such "turbid taxonomies" as were conceived in the colonial period and propagated across the subcontinent through successive waves of accumulation by dispossession (Stoler 2006). I then attend to the ways in which energy and waste—both nonhuman in the form of coal, and inhuman in the case of the laborer—are dialectically bound such that the transversal relationship that I have discussed thus far (and which is immanent to the picaresque mode) emerges in the production of fossil capital and the fossil subject. In this way, I offer an energo-political analysis of the novel that interweaves questions of power, ontology, and energy: I trouble such onto-epistemological categories as "Human" and its inverse "inhuman"; and I examine forms of governmentality that hinge of the reduction of the latter to the waste of empire. Ultimately, I turn to the novel as a praxis for a more speculative-critical methodology—one increasingly favored by Energy Humanists interested in the evident material substrate of cultural production.

Narrating Extraction

A brief description of the novel's narrative terrain and the competing aesthetic histories of the modern Indian novel—moving between the abovementioned homages to Gandhian pastoral and biting social realism—will help to orient our discussion. The novel is a picaresque tale of a migrant worker turned criminal and huckster (and ultimately murderer), which critiques the nation's farcical democracy, linking coal speculation to electoral politics and making clear the intimacies between extractive capitalism and the dispossession of the poor. Adiga's *pícaro* Balram is a chauffeur for an America financier, "Ashok," who speculates in coal—more specifically who "tak[es] coal for free from the government mines" (*WT* 81). Mobilizing such picaresque tropes as itinerancy and precarity in addition to the nonlinear (and nonteleological) temporality of the *pícaro's* tale—this one told as a series of emails—Adiga adapts the genre in order to critique India's carbon democracy. To the extent that it recognizes the intimacies between fossil capitalism and voter (dis)enfranchisement, it aligns with similar critiques of extractivism. Where it departs is in its figuring of energy not as a thematic element, but as the very fabric of Indian modernity: coal—its ash, the noxious tailings that seep into the nation's rivers—is not separable from the social and political relations that it engenders. That is, and per Andreas Malm (2018, 17), "fossil fuels should, by their very definition, be understood as a social relation [because] no piece of coal or drop of oil has yet turned itself into fuel"; this then is the task of the inhuman, or the disposable figure who instantiates the inverse of what Denise Ferreira da Silva terms "*Homo Modernus*" to refer to the "post-Enlightenment version of the Subject as the sole self-determined thing" and the point of origin for a "global/historical consciousness" (xxii–xxiii).[12]

The transversal relationship that we see evidenced in *The White Tiger* wherein Ashok stands in for a sort of *Homo Modernus* is similarly dramatized in earlier renditions of the modern Indian picaresque novel. While independence-era films and novels issued a call for a sort of rural return, the gritty realism of novelists like Anand's *Untouchable* (1936) (or the beleaguered protagonist of his 1937 *Coolie*) dramatized something quite different—something aligned, that is, with the Nationalist politics of Rabindranath Tagore and B. R. Ambedkar, both of whom agitated for Nehruvian techno-socialism over and against the caste-based society that was essential to Gandhi's (and now Modi's) vision of a modern (largely rural) India. The former's 1918 *Nationalism* would indict Gandhi's bankrupt commitment to the pastoral—funded as it was by extractive industries, many steel barons (who, according to Balram, made the "coal men look like saints" [*WT* 105]); and the latter, the "great father's" commitment to caste as a means of upholding rural virtue in the form of dangerous labor for the poor (see Ambedkar 2014). Of course, this privileging of Arcadian myth was also central to Nehru's vision: "The word 'urban development' appears for the first time as a chapter heading [in one of Nehru's five-year development plans] only in 1974" (Doron and Jeffrey 2018, 50). This is so despite the material impacts of urbanization on the rural poor and the potentially disastrous impacts of such dam projects as are critiqued in Roy's stunning chronicle of Indigenous dispossession in *The Cost of Living* (1999).

This false dichotomy, which is to say that of the putative country (or rural idyll) and city, is perpetually reproduced in the era of late capitalism wherein Adiga's oft-remarked "darkness" and "light"—per Balram, the two poles of India's carbon democracy—are counterpoised in such paeans to the "new" India as Modi's *Swacch Bharat*, a beautification program that ostensibly promises to remove the poor; or those "working bodies" that are discarded alongside the tarry remains of fossilized plant matter, or the ashen particulates in the atmosphere of greater Jharkhand in Dhanbad (Chari 110). And it is a dichotomy that has historically been reinforced by the abovementioned aesthetic traditions—the quasi-picturesque rural virtue undergirding Gandhian philosophy, for example—that not only perpetuate a violent Cartesianism, but which allow for the masking of sites of extraction within India, if also on a global scale. The invisibility of extractivist violence, it should be noted, is not only a boon to industry but a key feature of the carbon imaginary. Hence the mandate by Energy Humanists to attempt to *read* energy and thus mitigate such forms of virtual invisibility.

Reading Coal

In our consideration of the coal imaginary—its narration as it were—it is significant, remarkable even, more in its absence from popular critiques than in its role in Indian state-building. The coal industry is, to be sure, an indispensable aspect of Indian modernity—its profits making possible Nehru's age of steel; the illicit relationship between multinational corporations like Tata Steel and the politics of Mohandas Gandhi; and Modi's dreams of a fully electrified countryside. But despite its economic and geographic centrality, the "coal capital" of Dhanbad is a succinct portrait of the constitutive absence of fossil capital's global hegemony—so ordinary, so mundane as to be everywhere and yet nowhere. As Adiga's *pícaro* Balram remarks: "People think it's only technology that's booming. But coal—the media pays no attention to coal, does it? . . . [Meanwhile,] millionaires are being made, left, right, and center" (*WT* 182). Referring to the "glowing pits" that account for India's millionaires, he further remarks:

> There was money in the air in Dhanbad. I saw buildings with sides made entirely of glass, and men with gold in their teeth. And all this glass and gold—all of it came from the coal pits. Outside the town, there was coal, more coal than you would find anywhere else in the Darkness, maybe more coal than anywhere else in the world. Miners came to eat at my tea shop—I always gave them the best service, because they had the best tales to tell. They said that the coal mines went on and on for miles and miles outside the town. In some places there were fires burning under the earth and sending smoke into the air—fires that had been burning continuously for a hundred years! (*WT* 44)

The "darkness" to which Balram persistently refers is the vast interior of the nation—endless fields of coal, and home to the majority of India's population. Nonetheless, Balram is quite right: "The media pays no attention to [coal]." This may also account for why the novel has never been read as a carbon fiction—why not a single critique has foregrounded coal.

It ought to be noted too that while the focus remains on coal in the present chapter, it must be said that petrol also figures rather centrally; and so too are there no critiques of the novel that substantively attend to the viscerally felt moments wherein the narrator revels in what he describes as the sublime properties of the diesel-saturated city air. Significantly, such passages might also be read as satirical allusions to the racialized narrative around the putatively miasmic air of India's capital city: the colonialist rhetoric made infamous by Romantic-era writers like Thomas De Quincey and propagated *ad nauseum* by a myriad of critics, including such progressive writers as Aldous Huxley.[13] Such writings, per historian Dipesh Chakrabarty, could "be read not simply as realist prose but also evidence of a particular way of seeing" (1992b,

541). Chakrabarty also reminds us that such modes of "seeing" are essential to sustaining both particular historical narratives and their attendant reading practices. In a similar vein, and responding to Nixon's provocation regarding a dearth of "arresting stories" attending to the atrocities of industrial development, Thom Davies remarks: "I do not think it is, as Nixon (2011) intimates, a lack of 'arresting stories, images and symbols' (3) that allows instances of slow violence to persist unchecked. . . . Rather, slow violence persists because those 'arresting stories' do not count" (2019,13).

Unsurprisingly, stories like those of the fictional Halwais, or the scores of mining industry laborers that populate the actual Dhanbad slums are no exception. Literary critics have, by and large, embraced the novel's surface narrative—that of the novel as a mere critique of "India Shining," or the "new" India per Singh (2012)—and thus an "ethnic *Bildungsroman*" par excellence despite the protagonist's criminal behaviors. To be sure, the novel excoriates Singh's notion of a "New India" in so far as the rags to riches scenarios implied by such fictions are so rare as to only be available to "white tigers"—Balram's adoptive title owing to the rarity of such beings. Yes, the novel is a critique of this neoliberal fantasy; but to sever the carbon economy from such visions of Indian political autonomy is to deny the material possibility of the nation's economic prosperity, and thus to participate in the very same rhetorical shellgame of figures like Singh (or Modi). Not to mention, to do so is to concede to the global forces of fossil capital that privilege developmentalist rhetoric over and against material cost, human and otherwise, fueling a collective ignorance that ultimately serves the interests of the nation's coal and petrol lobbies. Indian autonomy, it must be noted, was a hard-fought battle with its principal actors—namely Nehru, Tagore, Ambedkar, Gandhi, and Muhammad Jinnah—agitating for independence (and enjoying significant gains) well before Churchill would supposedly *grant* the nation its independence in 1947. But it is the nonhuman actor—coal, including coking or metallurgical coal— that would in fact bring the ages of steam and steel. Why is it then that we speak of cotton and bauxite and (rather recently) opium, but not of coal?

Critics of the industry do in fact attend to the waste born of such new "frontiers of capital accumulation" as are evidenced by the coal industry (Chari 2017, 110). However, the irradiated landscapes documented by, e.g., photojournalist Sebastian Sardi (2018), who describes the "glowing pits of fire" that have burned for over a century as the "gates to the underworld," have received less popular attention[14] than might be expected from an industry that has been overwhelmingly responsible for the nation's soaring GDP for over two centuries—traceable to the aforementioned Raniganj mine, which began operations in 1774. The mine is situated within a nexus of coal seams that sprawl across the Narmada Valley in Madhya Pradesh; Dhanbad, the so-called coal capital and partial setting for Adiga's storyworld is located some 1200 miles to its east. Dhanbad is also located just 600 miles to the northeast of the bauxite mines that Roy (2011) documents in her oft-remarked critique of Vedanta Limited's bauxite operations and the dispossession of the Adivasi-majority population of Andhra Pradesh. And it is a similar distance from the cotton belt, which has also endured successive waves of accumulation by extraction and dispossession—lately made infamous by the epidemic of farmer suicides that account for Vandana Shiva's coinage of the term "suicide economy." But it would seem that, whether in C19 Delhi or C21 Dhanbad, a "society that [depends] entirely on coal [can] barely, precisely because of that dependence, become conscious of [it] at all" (Hensley and Steer 2019, 67). This, we know, is the case with carbon culture, if especially petroculture, more broadly. To return to Szeman and Boyer: "It has been so difficult to grasp and grapple with so important an element [because] in many respects . . . fossil fuels are saturated into every aspect of our social substance" (2017, 6). This is precisely what we mean, within the Energy Humanities, by the term "energy unconscious"—a term employed by Patricia Yaeger (2011, 306) to characterize the underlying structure of feeling that subtends a host of modern novels ranging from Jack Kerouac's *On the Road* to Ralph Ellison's *Invisible Man* to Miguel Cervantes's *Don Quixote*. Arguably, this is a more appropriate means of characterizing modernity than Frederic Jameson's notion of a "political unconscious," because if we recognize that modern capitalism is fueled by fossilized carbon, then we cannot speak of one without the other. And yet, outside of the coterie of Energy Humanists who continue to reinforce this indisputable historical claim, many literary critics continue to do just this.

Perhaps, as Ashley Dawson also observes, "our failure to consider the origins of the coal-based power we consume is [simply] a particularly extreme version of [this] broader ignorance"—an imaginative failure that may be glimpsed ever more brightly as we now rely almost entirely on digital media (2021, 83). Despite coal's role in providing power for the digital utopia that many environmentalists see as a panacea in the face of imminent planetary disaster, coal manufacture is persistently conceived as somehow outmoded—a relic of the nineteenth century, now replaced by petrol. Such ignorance owes indeed to a "particular way of seeing" whereby we engage with fictions that illustrate "King Coal" as if its impact, and its detritus, is naught but a thematic element. If we are to recognize its presence, if also its seeming ubiquity, we must instead follow critiques like Dawson's (2021), whose reading of H. G. Wells's *The Time Machine*, for example, marshals a more speculative praxis, and one that employs coal as the interpretative lens through which to view Wells's novel. This is precisely how I read *The White Tiger*, which is partially set in the shadows of Dhanbad—the putative "darkness" that I shall seek to make legible by reading the text through the ephemeral technics of coal.

Coal enjoys a spectral presence throughout the novel—stretching indeed for "miles and miles," yet always shrouded in the "darkness." This characterization, perhaps intentionally, will surely evoke colonialist notions of sublime landscapes. I refer, of course, to Joseph Conrad's mythical Congo, or V. S. Naipaul's stunningly racist depiction of a nameless African country in the 1979 *A Bend in the River*. This darkness, however, not only sullies the pastoral vision of the nation's countryside—aligning in this sense with Conrad's sublime jungle; it infects the grand cities that would testify to India's emergence as a major economic power—the aforementioned miasmic landscapes of Delhi, for example, whereby the intentional/corporate enclaves of the well-healed figure as late-capitalist versions of the *cordon sanitaire*. I shall examine cities like Gurgaon below in the context of the slum ecologies that dot such strange late-capitalist off-worlds. Sufficed to say here that the perceived "light" of such places is buttressed by the imagined darkness of its artificial borders.

Reading *The White Tiger* as a carbon fiction, in my attention to the myriad of energy forms powering the plot, and not merely as a coal fiction—albeit one blanketed in coal ash—allows for a piercing of this darkness. Through such a reading, I engage the broader energopolitical imaginary that subtends Indian modernity; and I recognize the centrality of energy forms to our seeing and reading practices more broadly. As I discussed in the previous chapter, Boyer's notion of energopolitics—over and against the limited paradigm of biopolitics—refers to the political entanglements attendant to the carbon imaginary. Following theorizations of "necropolitics"—of Achille Mbembe's coinage, and a means of pushing back against the reductive discourse of biopolitics that denies the myriad forms of *bios* at stake in the carbon imaginary, if also the imperial origins of such anthropocentric positions—energopolitics recognizes that modern forms of governmentality are driven by the power to determine who may live and who must die in our contemporary petrosphere. Thus energopolitics names the overlapping of energy, power, and ontology in modern governance; and an energopolitical framework for understanding such carbon fictions as *The White Tiger* demands that we understand the formation of the fossil subject in terms of praxis. As in the formation of the Human subject—again, as a sort of *Homo Modernus*, or a product of the Enlightenment *Bildungsroman*—the fossil subject is similarly constituted through the interlocking forces of developmentalist rhetoric, imperial taxonomy, and global (extractive) capitalism.

Balram is a fossil subject—baptized both in the ashen waters of greater

Jharkhand and also in the greasy detritus of Delhi's petroleum-soaked slum ecologies: "Late every evening," he remarks, "I emerged from under a taxi like a hog from sewage, my face black with grease, my hands shiny with engine oil. I dipped into a Ganga of black—came out a driver" (*WT* 48). His account of the first time that he would behold the majestic diesel engine is similarly remarkable in its evocation of a sort of techno-sublime: "Remember, Mr. Premier, the first time, perhaps as a boy, when you opened the hood of a car and looked into its entrails? Remember the colored wires twisting from one part of the engine to the other, the black box full of yellow caps, enigmatic tubes hissing out steam and oil and grease everywhere—remember how mysterious and magical everything seemed?" (*WT* 95). The car with which he is charged to drive Ashok is also described as "moody . . . with a mind of its own" (*WT* 69).

Of course, against such excitations we are constantly reminded of the refuse of petroleum—those diesel particulates saturating the Yamuna River, the second largest tributary of the Ganga. As Assa Doron and Robin Jeffrey point out: "As India's car population rises, it will not be able to follow the twentieth-century strategy of the United States where, by 1970, it was estimated up to 30 million cars had been dumped in fields, lakes, and rivers. India's density of population leaves no room for such extravagance" (2018, 62). Coal also produces refuse: "As coal burns, it accumulates coal ash, a physical byproduct. As electricity flows constantly and invisibly, coal ash piles up across acres of land with every kilowatt-hour. This waste changes the look and feel, and the ecological interconnections, of the earth on which it sits" (Hatmaker 2017, 88). Although, while "coal ash landfills exist everywhere coal is burned," as with the broader veil of ignorance that shrouds coal capital, such landfills "attract relatively little attention" (88).

Notably too, the "problem of recalcitrant matter" is not a problem with which governments are prepared to reckon despite such blowbacks as we are now seeing in India and also China (LeMenager 2014, 229). Nor is the "recalcitrant matter" produced by the burning of petroleum or coal a problem that the aforementioned critical praxes, nor the onto-epistemological frameworks that subtend them, seem able to contain; that is, the ontological categories produced by the colonial-imperial episteme make no space for an examination of the historically non/inhuman, whether the raw nature of fossil capital, or those charged with its extraction. In this sense, the coterminous production of the productive subject and disposable object again emerge as constituent of the praxis to which I shall now turn—that is, to the onto-epistemological production of the "global" subject, and his inverse (and thus the transversal nature of capital); or in Balram's terms: "Inside that sealed car, master and driver had somehow become one body" (*WT* 169).[15]

On the "[In]human as Praxis"

Invoking a necropolitical planetary imaginary whereby such laborers as Balram are necessarily sacrificed, the novel enables consideration of such onto-epistemological frameworks.[16] So too, a consideration of correlative discussions around *bios* as subtend extractivist networks of accumulation reliant on the abstraction and commodification of the *inhuman*. I use the term "inhuman" to refer to such fungible objects as the slave or the miner, a term used as a means of describing those human subjects not accorded the characteristics of reason (and so forth) that mark the modern subject. A rejoinder to the "biocentric subject [which is to say the] dominant mode of subjectivity of late liberalism," such figurations of necropower—i.e., the reduction and manipulation of the fossil subject to raw life, and thus excluded from the material benefits of conventional forms of biopolitical governance—productively gesture toward the ways in which the discourses of life and nonlife make possible technologies of dispossession within contemporary regimes of waste colonialism (Yusoff 11). Significantly, the term "waste colonialism," which describes the off-siting of waste to the sacrificial zones of global capital, applies to both conventional images of "waste"—i.e., "garbage"—as well as to the excremental communities examined here.

Such sacrificial zones—the slums of Dhanbad for example—are in fact the condition of possibility for networks of extraction; so too, the ways in which such forced modes of invisibility are enabled: "Waste management makes things disappear by moving them elsewhere, and, like most infrastructures of liberal governance, waste management is considered most successful to the extent that its workings and flows remain invisible" (qtd. in Reno 2015, 561). Furthermore, waste management "is a process actively involved in reshaping our ideals and imaginations in turn"—cultivating, that is, "particularly ways of seeing" or not seeing the poor (558). This is abetted by what Amanda Boetzkes (2016) describes as the "paradoxical aesthetic of the current resource paradigm ... in which the ideals of a wasteless society are [not only] hinged to corporeal and environmental systems that are always already wasted" (5) but likewise to the "invisible ... forms of labor, energy expenditure, and ecological consequences on which the global resource system relies" (3). This again raises the question of invisibility—as obtains in discussions of both the inhuman and nonhuman; as well, the ways in which the global resource economy is aestheticized to serve the ends of global fossil capital.

Boetzkes's argument resonates in my earlier observations regarding the heterotopic landscape of an uneven petrosphere in which so many Bhopals or Dhanbads are rendered necessarily invisible to the end consumer—relegated to the outside, as it were, of autopoetic systems of production. To return to Chakrabarty: "The question of garbage . . . [raises] . . . the question of the 'outside.'. . . . It is the space that produces both malevolence and exchange between communities and hence needs to be tamed through the continual, and contextual, deployment of a certain dichotomy of the 'inside' and the 'outside.' This need to be tamed is what makes the 'outside' exciting, albeit in unpredictable and dangerous ways" (1992b, 544). In considering the lure of the outside we might consider how the slum has historically served to titillate the liberal voyeur. Not unlike the picturesque mode that we examined in the context of *Animal's People*, we can look to the slum tours of Charles Dickens's London, or in the same vein the popularity of contemporary works like Katherine Boo's *Beyond the Beautiful Forevers* (2012). Vik Muniz's 2010 documentary *Waste Land*—an exploration of Brazil's largest landfill and the *ad hoc* recycling culture that has emerged in the adjacent *favelas* of Rio—offers another example of such voyeurism and one perhaps more to the point: its central aim seems to be in the interest of garbage workers and their families; but the popularity of the film testifies to something else—something that Adiga is clearly critiquing. Such a critique is also at stake in Dutch artist Renzo Martens's chilling documentary *Enjoy Poverty* (2008)—a scathing indictment of this grotesque fascination with poverty through an examination of the roles of various NGOs in the Congo.

As mentioned at the outset of this chapter, the racialized bodies on display in such sites—which are surely evocative of a postcolonial picturesque—persistently figure as both imaginative and material waste, and thus instantiate the logical inverse of productive/laboring bodies within systems of (global) fossil capitalism. This is precisely the case with Balram and Ashok; so too with the scores of laboring bodies foregrounded in the novel who are consistently described in physiognomic terms—one colleague enjoying the moniker "vitiligo lips" to refer to the skin discoloration often caused by malnutrition. Such images serve as a clear commentary on the ways in which the working poor literally actualize what I am reading as the waste of imperial networks of production—the production, that is, of the citizen-subject by virtue of the ruination of disposable labor, or those persons who do not, indeed cannot, enjoy a colonialist *Bildung* because of the material finitude of natural resources. It is this finitude, significantly, that also accounts for the "horrendous logic" that Pablo Mukherjee indicts in his critique of *Animal's People*—a logic that demands that some communities be sacrificed for the welfare of others. In Ghosh's (2016) recent monograph *The Great Derangement: Climate Change and the Unthinkable*, he also remarks on this phenomenon while reminding his readers that if every family owned all of the trappings of modernity—a washing machine, two automobiles, etc.—"humanity would asphyxiate" owing to increased atmospheric carbon (92). Hence the perpetuation of the "turbid taxonomies" of imperial liberalism: it is critical that the elite consumer reads figures like Balram and his colleagues as somehow inhuman and thus beyond the pale of even the most impoverished of liberal humanitarian gestures.

Toward that end, and in line with Adiga's social critique, figurations of the inhuman are everywhere in this novel—not as grisly images for the liberal voyeur but as picaresque indictment of imperial liberalism: rickshaw pullers, who are banned from Dhanbad in favor of motorized/petrol-fueled transport, are described as "human beast[s] of burden" (*WT* 23). A local resident wanting to enter the gleaming mall where Ashok spends his money is denied and thus asks: "Am I not a human being too?" (*WT* 125) A café worker outside of Dhanbad is described as a "human spider" in his movement across the wet floor "crawl[ing] pushing a growing wavelet of stinking ink-black water ahead of him" (*WT* 227). And ultimately, in Balram's scathing indictment of the imposed resignation of the masses—the inability to protest born of extreme deprivation—as a rooster coop wherein "brothers" fight one another and "do not rebel" against their overlords. Specifically, he wryly remarks:

> The greatest thing to come out of this country in the ten thousand years of its history is the Rooster Coop. Go to Old Delhi, behind the Jama Masjid, and look at the way they keep chickens there in the market. Hundreds of pale hens and brightly colored roosters, stuffed tightly into wire-mesh cages, packed as tightly as worms in a belly, pecking each other and shitting on each other, jostling just for breathing space; the whole cage giving off a horrible stench—the stench of terrified, feathered flesh. On the wooden desk above this coop sits a grinning young butcher, showing off the flesh and organs of a recently chopped-up chicken, still oleaginous with a coating of dark blood. The roosters in the coop smell the blood from above. They see the organs of their brothers lying around them. They know they're next. Yet they do not rebel. They do not try to get out of the coop. The very same thing is done with human beings in this country. (*WT* 147)

Presumably, the roosters are like the men he described "making a line that no respectable human should cross"—the abovementioned construction workers openly defecating in a space adjacent to the earth-moving machinery that gouges the landscape of Delhi making possible further expansion and thus further forced removal and relocation (*WT* 222). Clearly riffing on the imaginary political lines that have been much-theorized by critics of the fledgling nation—perhaps most famously in Salman Rushdie's *Imaginary Homelands*

(1982)—this line of shit marks the literal border between the light of Delhi and the "underworld" from which the laborers emerge.

Descriptions of the denuded countryside, riven by the giant earth-moving machinery employed by the mining industry, are similarly corporeal in their depictions of workers. Referring to one such machine, Balram remarks:

> It was a monster, sitting at the top of the pit with huge metal jaws alternately gorging and disgorging immense quantities of mud. Like creatures that had to obey it, men with troughs of mud on their heads walked in circles around the machine; they did not look much bigger than mice. Even in the winter night the sweat had made their shirts stick to their glistening black bodies. (WT 134)

The "glistening black bodies" described herein resonate in Yusoff's discussion of such sacrificial persons, who are consistently reified as fungible objects in the production of fossil capital, or Raj Patel and Jason Moore's remarks regarding the material byproducts of such real abstractions as were coined by Linnaeus or John Locke: "[Carl] Linnaeus's typology did more than allow some human bodies to be considered property and instruments of debt. It went much further, providing a scientific basis for bodies and lives to be subject to government by a state run by humans who placed themselves at the top of this hierarchy" (2017, 188). This sort of taxonomic qua onto-epistemological violence is critical to an imperial imaginary—one sustained by Boetzkes's argument regarding the "paradoxical aesthetic" of (fossil) capital accumulation.

Figuring Waste

The inverse of *Homo Modernus* instantiates what I have discussed thus far in terms of unproductive labor, but so too, as Discard Studies scholars such as Josh Reno aver, "the moral-political waste that comes from systems of symbolic classification, such as rituals, religion, or racism" (2018, 2). Reno also contends that conventional categories of waste—"ecological [which] comes from living things or processes and is therefore *not exclusive* to human beings" or the "utilitarian waste that comes from the manufacture and use of utilities, and is therefore *mostly exclusive* to humans"—"are not unrelated and irreconcilable" from the symbolic forms of waste produced by moral-political signification, but roughly correspond to forms of "*vita active* [or] labor, work, and action" (2). If "labor" and "work" fall within a calculus determined by capitalism's ontological praxis within the ecological and utilitarian modes, "action" is here understood as the interaction between and within communities in the formation of hierarchies—"oppressor and oppressed" and so on (2).

It is within the category of "action" in which we might apply a Linnaean rubric—that is, a means of understanding the work of the inhuman and nonhuman laborer and the correlative production of itinerant labor regimes. Such a model, now updated with the hindsight of three centuries of imperial liberalism and its toxic aftermath, also allows for us to understand the so-called externalities associated with environmental pollution: it is both the recalcitrant matter that persists in the lethal atmospheres of cities like New Delhi as well as the occupants of the slums that successive federal administrations have attempted to raze. This is why we must also understand extractivist logic in necropolitical and not biopolitical terms. Departing from a Foucaldian biopolitics which articulates an anthropocentric approach to governance—*Anthropos* here also standing in for *Homo Modernus*—in considering Adiga's Balram we turn to Mbembe whose coinage of necropolitics charts a history of imperial liberalism marked by the "conflation of reason and terror" such as we see in development schemes that seek to demolish informal housing communities (2013, 19); or those produced by companies like Vedanta who are similarly responsible for forms of structural displacement. Such a conflation—of reason and terror, or that which allows for the *rational* subject to determine who or what may live—is also at the heart of geontopolitical forms of governance in which historically sanctioned understandings of the nonhuman allow for something like coal to be stripped of its vitality within the carbon imaginary.

Significantly, in my consideration of such nonhuman agents as coal, I explicitly acknowledge the agentic qualities of nonhuman matter while departing philosophically from posthumanist theories that might unwittingly collapse human and nonhuman communities. The latter has been indicted for stripping disenfranchised human communities of their historic due and rightfully so; as we discussed in the context of Ghosh's Plantationocene aesthetic, it is the production of the broader category of cheap nature that allows for this flattening in the Cartesian imagination, and it is a flattening with which we must continue to reckon. It is in this vein that I turn to nonhuman waste—specifically coal—recognizing its vitality, but also retaining a healthy suspicion of any theory that renders the miner indistinguishable from the commodity form.

Nonhuman Waste: Coal's Slum Ecologies

Aligned with Yusoff's (2018) argument for the "billion Black Anthropocenes" that subtend the material prosperity of Anglo-European modernity, those same "glistening black bodies" charged with the extraction of coal might be understood as human correlates to that other "glistening" stuff—the "total black, being spoken / From the earth's inside" (Lorde lines 2–3); or per Yusoff: "Coal was the inhuman corollary of those dehumanized black bodies" (15). In Audre Lorde's poem "Coal," the poet elucidates the phenomena immanent to Yusoff's theory through a discussion of such a collapsing of the inhuman and nonhuman: "I am black because I come from the earth's inside" (line 24). Lorde likewise employs "coal" as an agential speaker—"I / is the total black, being spoken / From the earth's inside" (lines 1–3). The "I" significantly refers to what materialist thinkers like Tsing would understand as a multispecies assemblage; for our purposes, we recognize that the agentially rich "I" stands in less as a form of more-than-human solidarity than a critique of fungibility. It is an "I" that encompasses the fossil subject and its inverse—the inhuman object; and pace Reno's discussion of waste, it is an "I" that resists the rhetorically qua politically flattening gestures of both posthumanist and Anthropocene discourse.[17]

Reading the figure of the inhuman "I" as both energy and waste, I understand the category of carbon fiction as a representation of coal tailings and petroleum dust for sure, but primarily of the social relations that enable its production—relations that also produce what I refer to as slum ecologies after Mike Davis's coinage to describe "poverty's niche in the ecology of the city" (2006, 121–22). Here the urban poor live in increasingly precarious conditions both because of unstable geologies as well as economic development in the form of mineral extraction (121–22). Geological hazards, inclusive of denuded soils contaminated by mining initiatives in the nation's interior as well as oversaturated soils—periodically inundated with floodwaters—also mark Adiga's landscape and clearly impact the itinerant communities living beyond the urban enclaves that otherwise stand as testaments to Indian progress. Such communities, it should be noted, are routinely bulldozed in the interest of urban development—also an illustration of the ways in which the slum figures as part of an urban ecology that is necessarily transformed in relation to the simultaneous production of the nation's bourgeoisie; this instantiation of infrastructural transversality is described by Balram in the context of the local market—that there is "always a smaller, grimier mirror image of the real market, tucked somewhere into a by-lane" (*WT* 173).

Here in the bowels of Delhi, we see the artificial frontiers "where civilization can appear and disappear within five minutes. On either side of us right now there was just wilderness and rubbish" (*WT* 241). Describing the workers who presumably live in the slums, Balram remarks:

The men were defecating in the open like a defensive wall in front of the slum: making a line that no respectable human should cross. The wind wafted the stench of fresh shit toward me. . . . These people were building homes for the rich, but they lived in tents covered in blue tarpaulin sheets and partitioned into lanes by lines of sewage. . . . The stench of feces was replaced by the stronger stench of industrial sewage. The slum ended in an open sewer—a small river of black water went sluggishly past me, bubbles sparkling in it and little bubbles spreading on its surface. Two children were splashing about in the black water. (*WT* 222)

From the perspective of the liberal voyeur, whether Ashok or Adiga's readership, it might be said that such images instantiate the very sensibility of Lorde's poem: here the slum dweller seems indistinguishable from the mined Earth that he presumably extracts in order to afford such meager conditions.

Images such as these are surely fodder for readings of the novel as a critique of the putative "new" India; but implicit to this scatological description is a direct critique of the infrastructural imaginary born of extractivism. As is showcased in the novel, and as has occurred in the actual city of Delhi, under each new development project, a cluster of slums appears to house the informal workers who are building them. These are figures like Balram himself: "Most slum dwellers are daily wage earners, laborers, guards, domestic workers, small shopkeepers and petty traders [who] constitute a key site of surplus extraction as 'informal' workers in Delhi's large and expanding urban agglomeration, a seemingly never-ending supply of flexible, contingent, and unprotected workers" (Kalyan 2014, 57). Balram and his colleagues—all chauffeurs for men of industry—live in similar conditions.

It ought to be noted that such informal slum communities also attest to a very different conceptualization of space—one that Partha Chatterjee, in *Politics of the Governed*, once described in terms of the "demographic categories of governmentality" (2006, 59). For Chatterjee, the nation must be understood through the lens of those who govern and those who are *governed*—a more nuanced approach to governmentality, he notes, that interprets "political society" in terms of the intersecting relationship between elite and subaltern groups.[18] This too might be understood in terms of praxis—the protean nature of class, and the construction of the bourgeoisie. Chatterjee's argument, Gramscian in nature, also reminds us that such governmental technologies as colonial-era land censuses, health and educational institutions, and a "host of other governmental functions" whose genealogy can be traced to British India, are constitutive of the postcolonial Indian state—materially speaking, manifested in the itinerant "frontiers" of communities like those of Balram and his colleagues. That is, the biopolitical rhetoric of development has produced the darkness and light—the blasted landscapes of the interior and the glittering streets of the new "global city."

In *The White Tiger* we are presented with two such conceptions of space—the modern city (whether Delhi or Gurgaon—the artificial playground adjacent to Delhi) and the slums that house its informal workers:

> Thousands of people live on the sides of the road in Delhi. They come from the Darkness too—you can tell by their thin bodies, filthy faces, by the animal-like way they live under the huge bridges and overpasses, making fires and washing and taking lice out of their hair while the cars roar past them. These homeless people are a particular problem for drivers. They never wait for a red light—simply dashing across the road on impulse. And each time I braked to avoid slamming the car into one of them, the shouting would start from the passenger seat. (*WT* 99)

Significantly, Balram does strike one such slum dweller, and he is quickly reminded that the safety of his Anglo passenger—Ashok's wife—takes priority over the sanctity of this homeless person's life.

Such descriptions of slum life also resonate with historically racist notions of India's sublime environment such as we discussed earlier: "India was uniquely mysterious and unhealthy . . . and it was India's climate and environment, not microbes, that made it so. India's diseases, this fantasy contended, were so exotic that they could survive only in India" (Doron and Jeffrey 2018, 21). The "filthy faces . . . taking lice out of their hair" are also a clear rhetorical legatee of the violent Orientalism of, for example, De Quincey. It comes as no surprise then that the slum dwellers are cast out of the artificial enclaves of the rich. This is what Chakrabarty also describes as "the language of modernity, of civic consciousness and public health, of even certain ideas of beauty related to the management of public space and interests, an order of aesthetics from which the ideals of public health and hygiene cannot be separated" (1992b, 541). Hence the strange off-worlds that appear in the novel—cities like Gurgaon:

> Gurgaon is fragile, but many NRIs [non-resident Indians] are happy to buy into it because they want to believe in the illusions it seems to support: the illusion of security, of the safety of gated communities, the illusion that one is not living in India because one is surrounded by Benetton, Nike, Pizza Hut, TGI Friday. But these are illusions that can

be sustained only because the drivers and domestics, the cleaners and sweepers, not to speak of the armed security guards, are all in place. I imagine that large numbers of executives fly into New Delhi's Indira Gandhi Airport in business class, and return to Paris or Düsseldorf three days later without having set foot in any part of India other than Gurgaon. (Subrahmanyam 2008)

But despite the proliferation of such intentional cities, the slum persists as the legacy of colonial-era development models, now in the shadows of these new "global cities": "The state's ongoing destruction of slum communities did not (and in fact could not) preclude the slum dwellers' ongoing presence in the city" (Kalyan 2014, 54). Indeed, and however much they try, the nation's leaders can't remove the poor like "laundry stains" (Roy 2011, x). Balram offers yet another description, this time markedly more sympathetic:

We were driving past a slum: one of those series of makeshift tents where the workers at some construction site were living. The Mongoose was saying something, but Mr. Ashok wasn't paying attention—he was looking out the window. My eyes obeyed his eyes. I saw the silhouette of the slum dwellers close to one another inside the tents; you could make out one family—a husband, a wife, a child—all huddled around a stove inside one tent, lit up by a golden lamp. The intimacy seemed so complete—so crushingly complete. (*WT* 161)

"So crushingly complete" indeed—perhaps particularly so in the wake of his having struck one such slumdweller.

This scene is then juxtaposed with a glimpse of the Mongoose—Ashok's brother, and one of the four landlords from Laxmangarh—devouring roadside sweets, the dribble off his grotesque paunch gleaming in the night. Descriptions such as these, it should be noted, are a critical departure from the signature wit and sarcasm of the roguish Balram. Similar (and conventional) critiques emerge in Balram's description of his class position: "The desire to be a servant had been bred into me: hammered into my skull, nail after nail, and poured into my blood, the way sewage and industrial poison are poured into Mother Ganga" (*WT* 165). Thus, when the reader is shuttled back to his parody of developmentalism, we are reminded of the stakes of the genre—a scathing critique of what Balram describes as the "narrative of the modern entrepreneur's growth and development," which is to say the aforementioned narrative of supposed enfranchisement (*WT* 194). Balram's story, punctuated with his slaying of Ashok with the butt of a whiskey bottle, makes a mockery of such narratives. His actual successes, while potentially illustrating a familiar boot-strap narrative and thus aligning with critics who see in the novel a sort of neoliberal Bildungsroman, seem beside the point of the broader critique of imperial liberalism.

In this sense, Balram is indeed a concise instantiation of the *pícaro* figure. He instantiates that "primordial urban contradiction" (Davis 2006, 137)—that is, "generations of human beings, out of whose lives the wealth of [the nation's elites are] produced [and who are] compelled to live in wealth's symbolic negative counterpart" (Marcus qtd. in Davis 137–38). There is perhaps no better example of "wealth's symbolic counterpart" than the criminal hucksters, like Balram, living on the streets and caricatured in the local comic *Murder Weekly*. These dime-store novels dramatize the perceived criminality of the poor—their spectacular crimes titillating local readers, including even Balram's colleagues. Balram's description of its role in simultaneously terrifying the rich while anesthetizing the poor is telling:

> It's sold on every newsstand in the city, alongside the cheap novels, and it is very popular reading among all the servants of the city—whether they be cooks, children's maids, or gardeners. Drivers are no different. . . . Now, don't panic at this information . . . it doesn't mean that they are all about to slit their masters' necks. Of course, they'd *like* to. Of course, a billion servants are secretly fantasizing about strangling their bosses—and that's why the government of India publishes this magazine and sells it on the streets for just four and a half rupees so that even the poor can buy it. You see, the murderer in the magazine is so mentally disturbed and sexually deranged that not one reader would want to be like him—and in the end he always gets caught by some honest, hardworking police officer (ha!), or goes mad and hangs himself by a bedsheet after writing a sentimental letter to his mother or primary school teacher, or is chased, beaten, buggered, and garroted by the brother of the woman he has done in. So if your driver is busy flicking through the pages of *Murder Weekly*, relax. No danger to you. Quite the contrary. It's when your driver starts to read about Gandhi and the Buddha that it's time to wet your pants, Mr. Jiabao. (*WT* 104–5)

Of course, Balram does eventually kill his boss; he "slit [his] throat" with a whiskey bottle—an ending that ought to infuriate liberal readers, who will come to sympathize with the Americanized Ashok, whose character stands in stark contrast to the Stork:

The most troubling aspect for progressive readers of all sorts is that it is the liberal Master who ultimately suffers, not the traditionalist, patriarchal, feudal Snake, Mongoose or Stork, all of whom seem so deserving of a whiskey bottle to the head. *The White Tiger* reveals liberalism for what it is. The vague sense of concern for the servant, the moralizing on family and rural values, and the lazy ignorance of and investment in inequity are shown to be what they are: a tragic emollient for rage. (Gajarawala 2009, 23)

Murder Weekly might be understood as a late-capitalist cony-catching tale—the genre that I discussed in the introduction, and a category of rogue literature credited with galvanizing popular support for England's notoriously violent Poor Laws; or the "false encounters" with peasant activists in the nation's so-called "MAOist corridor" that justify their eviction and occasional extermination (Roy 2011, 25). This explicit generic gesture also serves to remind the reader of the stakes of picaresque representation. But rather than belabor the point—that is, that *The White Tiger* is a postcolonial picaresque—let us instead return to our examination of the novel's carbon-soaked storyworld and read it not merely as a postcolonial picaresque but a carbon picaresque. More than an indictment of the distorted logic of economic liberalization in "shining" India, the novel affords its readers new avenues for critical inquiry wherein we might begin to read energy in more productive ways. Thus I turn finally to the emergent field of Energy Humanities and the stakes of a radical materialist critique of the novel.

Carbon Fictions: New Vistas for the Energy Humanities

Owing to its utility for thinking through the intersecting histories of coal extraction, urban development, and Indian democracy, the novel offers a perfect praxis for this broader category of carbon fiction, which I also see as a means of potentially imagining new vistas for the Energy Humanities. Using both energy and its detritus as interpretative lenses is a productive point of departure from normative literary exegeses that inevitably read both as leitmotif— settled ontologies over and against active participants in the creation of our material present and the perpetuation of conventional systems of energo-politics. In unsettling such presumably stable categories as energy, waste, and also that of the human, in addition to collapsing such facile periodizations as obtain in histories of energy that imagine clean breaks between coal and oil, or the plantation, the factory, and the oil field, carbon fictions like *The White Tiger* offer a generative praxis for a more speculative methodology, and one untethered from the prison-house of conventional literary criticism that privileges the stable theme and is thus constrained by its natural limits. In such a model, coal again is merely so much dead matter awaiting extraction—inert, brute, severed from the ongoing political imaginary that it continues to produce. That is, conventional critiques rely on "the resource logic of capitalism [which] presupposes that resources have no aesthetic whatsoever"—an "aesthetic [tradition] that effortlessly normalizes the brute inputs" of human and nonhuman labor (Bellamy, O'Driscoll and Simpson 2016, 2). A more speculative reading of coal, and thus a carbon fiction like *The White Tiger*, leads us instead to a radically different reading. Arguably, such a speculative praxis is critical to the cultivation of different ways of seeing—that is, of mitigating invisibility: "It does very little to point to the presence of fossil fuels in fiction, to go searching about for those few places where coal, gas or oil might resurface, receive mention or be extracted from the narrative. What we need instead is a new critical sensibility in our analyses of world literature" and one, I would add, that forces the reader to confront the stubbornly "recalcitrant matter" of the global carbon imaginary (Szeman 2017, 286). In this sense, we may also recognize the central role of energy in the production of all cultural forms—that energy forms might rightfully be considered the *mise-en-scène* of all aesthetic production in the putative "ages" of coal or petrol.

Such a speculative mode of reading also attends to the "imaginative challenges" presented by what Peter Hitchcock (2016) has described in terms of "constitutive limits," which is to say the aforementioned structural absence that forecloses our ability to read *The White Tiger* as a carbon fiction, or and quite significantly, coal as vibrant matter—the latter also troubling Malm's reading and again recalling Povinelli who recognizes that rocks do in fact live and "die."[19] Per Hitchcock, "to think energy is always to address constitutive limits"; and "the point in foregrounding such discussions within the humanities is not to forget about limits, but is rather to focus on the imaginative challenges they represent" (2016, 22, 24). Pace the voluminous work on "imagining anew" by Gómez-Barris, Shelley Streeby, Donna Haraway, and many others, it is to imagine ways of moving beyond impasse or limits. It is perhaps to follow Szeman's urgent call to cultivate new methodologies that employ energy as a heuristic over and against mere backdrop. Per Szeman: "What does it do to continue to critically attend to the literary using the rationales and orientations that we have garnered from a different perspective on history than the one we are left with after a confrontation with resources and energy?" (2021, 9). Instead privileging the speculative, we might posit the *limit* as a point of departure—seeing not the proverbial impasse but what critics like Szeman (2021) also read as a moment of "radical indeterminacy." This is perhaps also a means of reading what I shall provisionally call the spectral presence of energy.

In a sense, Adiga's novel marshals this speculative impulse in its almost spectral representations of coal and petrol—materially present, yet also, and most of the time, just out of the frame. The latter emerges in the gritty particulates choking the protagonist on the streets of Delhi; as sublime presence interpolating Balram's subconscious such that he describes himself as a diesel engine; and ultimately as an ephemeral haze blanketing the city. Of course, its material presence is felt here as well; the waste from coal production and petrol emissions permeates the landscape and its rivers such that the Ganga is described as a sea of black poison. Thus, to return to the question of limits as it obtains in the Energy Humanities, the oft-remarked trope of invisibility in our critical praxis—whether in reference to waste that is off-sited, or sacrificial populations whose labor greases the engine of the global petrosphere—may itself be a sort of impasse. Surely the violence of fossil-based energy extraction is invisible only to the naïve consumer. Thus, as scholar-activists we must ask: how do we make present such putative absences? Perhaps the answer lies in such critical practices.

To think in terms of limits and to employ the otherwise spectral presence of energy as a methodology, and as a lens through which to view culture, is to both recognize the generative potential of the speculative and to cultivate the aporic space between what Jennifer Wenzel (2016, 31) has described as the discrepant conditions of the "everyday tedium of filling the gas tank and the sublimely discrepant timescales at work in fossil fuels"—what Malm (2016a) also addresses when referring to climate change as being largely a temporal problem, or Rob Nixon (2011) when considering the problem of political timescales within petromodernity. Although, we might instead read energy as neither a purely spatial nor temporal phenomenon. Anthro- and terraforming practices historically reliant on extractivist logics follow a linear trajectory, but so too the central infrastructural mandate of global capitalism: the "spatial fix" (Harvey 2001). Furthermore, "[as] a spatial concept, slow violence"—the abovementioned form of structural violence that is generally associated with the protracted temporalities of environmental degradation—"invites us to include the gradual deaths, destructions, and layered deposits of uneven social brutalities" across vast geographic spaces (Davies 2019, 2). In short, we must consider at once the discrepancy between geologic time and the time of capital, while recognizing that new mechanisms of uneven development proliferate on a global scale owing to the underground vistas that constitute ever new frontiers for accumulation; not to mention new means of off-siting waste such that, and as we also see in *The White Tiger*, states like Jharkand (home to Dhanbad) come to evince a similarly uneven, heterotopic quality.

Conclusion

In all, and against more popular readings that focus on the novel's critique of India's period of economic liberalization—as if that could be untethered from coal—*The White Tiger* affords a unique perspective in that it moves between conventional critiques of toxicity endemic to such slum ecologies as are illustrated in the novel, and a more robust critique of the broader network of consumption and waste characteristic of our contemporary petrosphere. Additionally, it offers a masterful indictment of the biopolitical rhetoric of imperial liberalism and its *toxic* fruit. And finally, if read as a carbon picaresque, we not only complicate facile Anthropocene timescales that eschew consideration of the overlapping histories of energy, we are likewise forced to grapple with the "billion Black Anthropocenes" that are perpetually produced in the shadows of fossil capital (Yusoff 2018). That is, in foregrounding "the prefiguration of the human, in its inception within the technologies of the inhuman, a different model of extraction [emerges]" (Yusoff 18). Accordingly, I follow Mackenzie Wark in asking, "What happens when the Anthropocene [or Thermocene for that matter] meets Critical Race Studies?" Perhaps *The White Tiger* is a productive praxis for answering both. Furthermore, it might serve as a mirror for the centuries-old coal industry that is now facing additional scrutiny as rural Indians increasingly look to more sustainable (read renewable) energy sources like solar power. Although, if we are wont to see solar-powered energy as a panacea for India's beleaguered carbon democracy we must also confront the ways in which this putative alternative to conventional energopolitics seems only to perpetuate its violent logics. It is in this spirit that I conclude this study by turning to the follies of India's solar industry in my consideration of Indigenous futurisms and the radical movements that continue to agitate against projects that are predicated on the same extractivist *ethos* of the coal industry.

Conclusion

Beyond Extraction: Imagining Solarity in India's Mineral Belt

> If we only track the purview of power's destruction and death force, we are forever analytically imprisoned to reproducing a totalizing viewpoint that ignores life that is unbridled and finds forms of resisting and living alternatively.
>
> —Macarena Gómez-Barris, *The Extractive Zone: Social Ecologies and Decolonial Perspectives*

Indigenous communities have consistently agitated against forms of agricultural and industrial enclosure for centuries. Campaigns for equitable land use, for the preservation of communal water sources, and for political and economic enfranchisement, are daily being waged throughout the Global North and South. Pace Macarena Gómez-Barris's comments above, "forms of resisting and living alternatively" are to be found everywhere if only we, as scholars and activists, choose to expand our methodological scope beyond the "purview of power's destruction and death force" (2017, 3). We must instead seek out "useful[ly] utopian" examples of flourishing that defy the Lockean *ethos* of development critiqued throughout this study—those commoning economies who are thriving despite the hegemony of extractive capitalism (2021, 40). These are communities that instantiate the power of the collective—and the local—against the "death force" of global fossil capital; and it is through such models of creative resistance that we might begin to imagine a template for living beyond extraction.

The movements that I shall examine below offer a consistent rejoinder to the false belief that there is no narrative after extraction—that is, no alternative to the Anthropocenic eschatology whereby a beleaguered human mass uniformly marches toward the ever-looming "end of history." Significantly, each also attests to the falsity of the faux evolutionary psychology championed by apologists for capitalist greed and unfettered market expansion—i.e., that which bolsters the putative impasse that we face as advocates for energy justice, because it propagates the notion that the human species is hard-wired for selfishness, for the relentless individualism which only rose to prominence with the coterminous ascendancy of carbon capitalism. Unsurprisingly, this new "science" gained traction during the reigns of Ronald Reagan and Margaret Thatcher, giving additional sanction to violent regimes of economic liberalization fostered by the World Bank and the International Monetary Fund. But contra the absurd notion of an innate human selfishness, we need not look far to find myriad examples of collectivism—vibrant communities grounded in a spirit of conviviality.[1]

In the present discussion I consider alternatives to the neoliberal ideology championed by the likes of Reagan or Thatcher or Modi. Specifically, I examine the possibility of "life after extraction" as articulated in the work of communities like the Maldhari of Gujarat—native herdspeople who are contesting the enclosure of their land against the forces of solar capitalism. In so doing, I recognize that energy transition must be accompanied by a radical departure from the settler-colonial ideology that has historically shaped regimes of fossil capital—that a simple shift in fuel sources is insufficient to the task of achieving justice for the landless. So too, that "the logic of land as property" finds a viable alternative in the futurisms articulated by Indigenous groups across the globe who have consistently agitated for justice in the face of such corporate interests as Tata Solar Power—a subsidiary of Tata Steel (Boyer 2019, 69).

While I shall in fact focus on India's "sunshine state" in the present discussion, I shall first acknowledge those communities the world over who are indeed practicing forms of collective resistance, demanding political sovereignty and environmental justice: from the Standing Rock Sioux Community in South Dakota defending their water from corporate energy interests, including Energy Transfer Partners;[2] to the Karrabing of central Australia agitating against the mining of manganese for iron and steel;[3] to local communities in Detroit, Oakland, Newark, Flint, Philadelphia, and New York City (among others) fighting to preserve the sanctity of municipal water supplies and agitating for infrastructural justice—whether public transportation systems or the equitable distribution of bike lanes.[4] Many such communities have been successful in combating fossil-fueled terrorism on a local and global scale. As well, each effectively models what Shelley Streeby has described as a form of "world-making": "The transformative dimensions of the worlds and futures imagined by Indigenous people and people of color in confronting settler colonialism, environmental racism, and climate change" (2018, 149). In this sense, the Indigenous futurisms articulated by the Standing Rock Sioux or the Karrabing demonstrate the possibility of life after extraction—showcasing "useful[ly] utopian" alternatives that emphasize what Dipesh Chakrabarty has also described in his argument for planetarity. Here, Chakrabarty promotes a "perspective on humans and other forms of life without humans being at the center of the story" (2019, 14)—a perspective that would require "a new understanding of the changing place of humans in the web of life and in the connected but different histories of the globe and the planet" (29). Critically, this is not a plea to flatten *Anthropos* and thus to again ignore the unevenness of those "different histories"; it is instead an acknowledgment of the possibility, demonstrated by the Karrabing or Maldhari, of living in accordance with a more sustainable *ethos* of development.

Such a model is precisely what Indigenous communities are now demanding on every continent—fighting against resource imperialism in the Americas, across the African continent, throughout Asia and the Middle East, and on the subcontinent of India. In the Andean mountains of Peru, for example, residents of Pasco de Cerro—site of the centuries-old open-pit silver and zinc mines—are resisting the colonization of their land and water. Responding to soaring mercury counts in local streams, community members are taking on Cerro de Pasco Resources (based in Canada) and Volcan—two of many companies laying claim to the much-mythologized "veins of Latin America" (Galeano 1997). And in Bolivia, the indigenous confederation CONAMAQ (Consejo Nacional de Ayllus y Markas del Qullasuyu) is fighting to reclaim the commons from government-owned mining interests who stand to benefit from former president Evo Morales's mining reforms; specifically, and despite internal divisions, CONAMAQ was created to "restore [to] original nations . . . collective rights to land and natural resources [and the] re-definition of administrative units and self-determination exercised through indigenous autonomies and direct representation in state institutions."[5] And in Honduras, considered the most dangerous nation in the world for environmental activists, the legacy of slain environmental rights champion Berta Cáceres reverberates in the continued struggle of her comrades in COPINH (Civil Council of Popular and Indigenous Organizations of Honduras): the Agua Zarca dam project, which was proposed for the Gualcarque river—considered sacred by the Lenca people—has lost its principal investors and remains stalled owing to the justice work of COPINH.

Similar movements for land reclamation by Native communities in Nigeria are being waged across the Niger Delta where Dutch Royal Shell began drilling operations in 1958. It is here where activist and writer Ken Saro-Wiwa, who was murdered in 1996 by the federal government in consultation with Shell, founded the Movement for the Survival of the Ogoni People (MOSOP). MOSOP continues to fight against the material impacts of petro-violence, including environmental toxicity and internal displacement—their efforts now supported by the Movement for the Emancipation of the Niger Delta (MEND).[6] We can also look to the Asian continent where farmers from South Korea, Thailand, and elsewhere have aligned themselves with their comrades in the Americas under the banner of *"via campesina,"* or the peasant's way.[7] And I would be remiss, in a project centered on picaresque sensibilities, in not looking to the legacy of agrarian reform in rural Mexico: the seed of the current Zapatista movement, which Mariano Azuela beautifully depicted in his 1915 picaresque novel *Los de Abajo* (translated as *The Underdogs*)—a novel that Carlos Fuentes characterized as a "barefoot *Iliad* sung by men and women rising from the weight of history, like insects from beneath a heavy stone" (Weisman 2008, viii).

Also "rising from the weight of history" as it were, peasant resistance to corporate tyranny on the Indian subcontinent—from the 1857 Sepoy Mutiny that would expedite the removal of the English East India Company (and terrify the likes of Thomas De Quincey) to post-independence agitation against the enclosure of Native forests and grazing lands—has proven a consistent bulwark against generations of extractivist violence. Notable campaigns of peasant resistance during India's post-independence period include the Chipko Andolan, a form of *Satyagraha* (or nonviolent protest) in which local activists in Uttar Pradesh fought against corporate logging initiatives by hugging trees; following their lead, wasteworkers, in the wake of the economic liberalization campaigns of the 1990s, chose to hug dumpsters.[8] Both were successful in combating corporate initiatives designed to exterminate Native practice.

Also demonstrating the potential of Indigenous resistance to corporate enclosure, in India's mineral belt *Adivasi* (or Indigenous) communities like the Dongria Kondh in Odisha are fighting to reclaim the commons from the recently shuddered Vedanta Resources whose open-pit bauxite mines have rendered local water supplies lethal, and whose development program is a model for what Arundhati Roy describes as a "MOUist" corridor to refer to the scores of memoranda of understanding between such public and private interests. She remarks:

> The Fifth Schedule of the Constitution provides protection to *Adivasi* people and disallows the alienation of their land, but it doesn't seem to matter at all. It looks as though the clause is there only to make the constitution look good—a bit of window-dressing, a slash of make-up. Scores of corporations, from relatively unknown ones to the biggest mining companies and steel manufacturers in the world, are in the fray to appropriate *Adivasi* homelands—the Mittals, Jindals, Tata, Essar, Posco, Rio Tinto, BHP Billiton and, of course, Vedanta. There's an MoU on every mountain river and forest glade. We're talking about social and environmental engineering on an unimaginable scale. (Roy 2011, 25)

For the Dongria Kondh community, however, the mountain that houses the precious bauxite is sacred—a "protector of streams" and a source of life.[9] But because their forms of husbandry are not recognized by the federal government as viable modes of development they have been an easy target of mining companies like Vedanta. Galvanizing international support through their alignment with the Indigenous rights organization Survival, the Dongria Kondh continue to combat the destruction of their land and water.

Such movements instantiate what Ramachandra Guha and Juan Alier (1997) have famously dubbed "the environmentalism of the poor." This refers to grassroots initiatives that oppose post-materialist projects like the Sierra Club—an organization read by such critics as a champion of conservation imperialism, and one that has historically relied on ethically bankrupt notions of wilderness (as *terra nullius*), or those of "waste lands" such as have been marshaled against the Dongia Kondh. Organizations like the Sierra Club have historically done little more than propagate the myriad forms of Cartesian violence that I have discussed throughout this study: among their central guiding principles has long been that of wilderness conservation—championed early on by figures like John Muir on the occasion of the organization's founding in 1892. In 1994 their office of environmental justice was created, but it fell woefully short of addressing historic forms of environmental racism, including that of Muir himself—the great naturalist perceiving Yosemite more as a site for the well-heeled to enjoy majestic fauna than a source of water for working Californians living downstream. It ought to be noted as well that it was in fact the Sierra Club who published the 1971 book *The Population Bomb*—a tome that trucks in Malthusian fears of overpopulation, which are historically grounded in racist ideology and practice. While recently backpedaling on this outmoded position, the organization maintains its commitment to settler-colonial ideology, now in the guise of green capitalism. Former Sierra Club executive director Carl Pope published a book with former New York City governor Michael Bloomberg, which suggests to its readers: "Instead of arguing about making sacrifices, let's talk about how we can make money" (2017, 3). Such paeans to consumer capitalism are clearly incommensurable with environmental and social justice.

In North America, we can understand such *conservation* efforts historically in terms of the genocide of Native communities, and their means of subsistence, in the interest of such "civilizing" initiatives as the settling of the frontier and the founding of the nation's national park system.[10] The latter began in 1872 with the creation of Yellowstone—a moment that environmental historians conventionally associate with the removal of Indigenous communities, the enclosure of grazing land for bison, and the opening of so-called virgin (or "unused") lands to mining interests (see Spence 2000). Moving our lens back to India, we can read Native protests against such mining companies and, more recently, corporate solar projects, as the latest instantiation of an "environmentalism of the poor"—in both cases pushing back against forms of imperial liberalism historically aligned with the wilderness logic of the Sierra Club and the early modern theories of improvement upon which such perspectives rest; so too, against new development projects that remain tethered to the extractivist logics of colonial-imperial development models such as we have examined in the context of opium and coal. That is, the nation's move to solar power is naught but the most recent example of extractivist violence against the landless, with companies like Tata Steel, now Tata Solar, leading the charge.

In a sense, the solar parks being constructed in the nation's "sunshine state" may be almost as destructive as the coal mining operations discussed above: sanctioned by the federal government under the auspices of a green transition, and one aligned with the mandate of the 2015 Paris Agreement on Climate Change, the solar economy has effectively transformed tens of thousands of acres of commonly held pasture into fields of silicon. Commenting on India's putative transition to renewable energy in the form of solar-powered electricity, Charles Mann (2015) observes:

> From an airplane window, the coastal state of Gujarat seems like a monument to the ambitions of its native son, Narendra Modi. In a former badlands 100 miles from Ahmedabad, its biggest city, I could see sunlight reflecting from the Charanka solar park, Asia's biggest. Dozens of rectangular photovoltaic arrays, regular as Midwestern wheat fields, were scattered in a broad U over a mile on each side.

While the spectacular destruction of Native land, such as we see in the silver mines of Pasco de Cerro—following an imperial trajectory traceable to the genocides of the sixteenth and seventeenth centuries, and thus easy fodder for progressive critique—or the exploitation and destruction of Ogoniland for the purposes of oil extraction, surely resonate differently in the popular imagination than projects surrounding such "sustainable" resources as solar energy, as we shall see corporate solar projects are simply the latest actors in the centuries-long exploitation of the subcontinent through modes of resource imperialism that we have thus far traced from the East India Company to Tata. Nonetheless, when anthropologist Cymene Howe (in conversation with Indigenous Studies scholar and philosopher Kyle Powys Whyte) quips "what the fuck are we sustaining" in reference to such "sustainable" economies as Indian solar power, or various corporate efforts to assuage climate change, many readers might be taken aback: should we not celebrate Tata Steel's new solar ventures? Or those of British Petroleum or Texaco Chevron? Or, per Howe, should we recognize that a just energy transition for the global poor requires a hell of a lot more than shifting fuel sources? Otherwise, we are simply *sustaining* settler-colonial practices that depend upon resource imperialism and the continued enclosure of the planetary commons. Building upon Howe's prescient question then, along with the work of Guha and Aliers, in what follows I shall consider the implications of sustainability discourse as I explore the history of solar energy in India and its affordances for energopolitical critique.

While I have thus far attended to literary critiques of the nation's industrial modernization, correlative forms of economic liberalization, and an imperial ideology fueled literally by fossilized carbon and ideologically by an early Modern system of taxonomy (referred to herein as Linnaean imperialism), I now turn to Indigenous movements agitating for justice within the designated Special Economic Zones (SEZs) across India. Specifically, I shall look to those communities who are suffering the material impacts of India's *unjust* transition to solar-powered energy—an illustration of greenwashing that allows for corporate solar interests (Tata Solar Power among them) to reap the financial benefits of the SEZs, including duty-free commerce. Given the rare earth—i.e., silicon—and mineral resources required to produce the photovoltaic solar panels necessary for Modi's vision of energized rooftops (and endless fields of glass) across the nation by 2022, India's solar economy risks "[repeating] the expenditures, inequalities, and exclusions of the past," and thus demonstrates the folly of unjust transition for the nation's largely Indigenous poor (Howe 2019, 195). Such resource intensive initiatives force the further removal of communities like the Maldhari in Rajasthan.

The Charanka Solar Park: A Case Study in *Unjust* Transition

If successive instantiations of such Cartesian logics as obtain in the energopolitical forms of governance that we observed in the last chapter persist in the formation of new energy regimes—those supposedly geared toward sustaining planetary resources—then we must now consider the necessary shifts to political economy that ought to accompany any energy transition. We cannot simply and "convenient[ly] replace one form of energy for another and continue to live as we always have" (Wilson 2018, 380). Otherwise, we face the possibility that the sun will simply be "the latest frontier of an extractive enterprise whose names have [previously] been slavery, colonialism, industrial capitalism [and] imperialism" (Barney and Szeman 2019, 2).

This is surely the case in the SEZ in Gujarat—the westernmost Indian state, located immediately adjacent to the "sunshine state" of Rajasthan—where the construction of solar fields thrives on the very same colonial-imperial development model upon which opium and coal depended. Here, *Adivasi* communities—specifically the Maldhari, so named for their long time occupation as tribal herdspeople—have sustained a nomadic culture through usufruct land practices, both for agriculture and pasturage: "Charanaka village, next to which the solar park was developed, is a small, remote settlement . . . [it] has a population of about 1500, roughly 50% of which belong to one of the country's pastoral nomadic communities [who] travel for about eight months in a year, across two districts covering more than 200 km, in search of fertile land and food for their sheep and goats" (Yenneti and Day 2015, 666). The diverse Maldhari—including several communities belonging to the Rabari caste—have long used government-owned land for grazing. But in the construction of the Charanka Solar Park, the largest of its kind in the world—surpassing even the Golmud Park in China—corporate interests have marshaled the developmentalist rhetoric of improvement in order to classify such lands as "waste" and thus fodder (legally) for a new round of land grabs. Significantly, the municipal government protects private interests like the Gujarat Power Corporation over the welfare of the Maldhari community.

The Gujarat Power Corporation (Ltd.) describes grazing lands in Charanka as "unused land." This is so despite an official project map revealing that of the 5417 acres used by the park some 2000 acres are actually being cultivated through the Maldhari's commoning economy—the aforementioned deployment of usufruct right in the interest of grazing cattle. Harkening back to the original seizure of the commons in what Amitav Ghosh termed the "age of flowers" (when rent farming also emerged as common practice), the classification of peasant land as "waste" allows for private corporations to act with impunity. Adding insult to injury, such imperialist notions of cultivation have now been codified through the aforementioned clauses to the Indian Constitution. This is precisely the case in the Gujarat SEZ. Not to mention, and owing to the utopian narrative subtending "sustainable" resources like solar power in India and across the world, corporate energy regimes are now emboldened by a lack of federal oversight in the renewables economy. In the case of Gujarat, for example, "solar parks do not need environmental impact assessments before being commissioned . . . [and] the provision of [an] Environmental Impact Assessment Notification . . . is not applicable to solar PV [photovoltaic] power projects" (Hemalatha 2019). Of course, an environmental impact statement would not directly attend to the forced removal of the Maldhari, but it would surely reveal the impact of silicon extraction as well as the effects of the panels on local soils. So too, the reality that

> at an average of five acres of land needed for every megawatt of solar energy, some 140,000 acres or 570 sq km of land are already under solar panels across the country. If India is to meet its solar target of 100 gigawatts by 2022, which many analysts are skeptical about, nearly 3,000,000 acres or 1,214 sq km of land will have to be under panels across India. Of the 100 gigawatts target, 60 gigawatts would need to come from large solar parks and 40 gigawatts from rooftops. (Hemalatha)

Surely, to procure 3,000,000 acres of land, such communities must be removed; hence the imperative to designate peasant land as "unused." Unsurprisingly, "the villagers were livid at these labels": 'What do they mean that the land is unused and that it belongs to the government?' " asked one local livestock herder (Hemalatha). He continues: " 'We use it for grazing livestock, and our livelihood depends on this land. It doesn't belong to anyone, it belongs to everyone' " (Hemalatha).

But such a logic—that of the commons, or of a commoning economy that operates within a theory of habitability over and against "sustainability"—is anathema to modern development schemes such as we have critiqued thus far; "habitability," it ought to be noted, is the centerpiece of Chakrabarty's (2019) argument for embracing the planetary—that is, the narrative of sustainability must be immediately replaced with an emphasis on the habitability of the planetary commons. But to grant agency to the landless is to negate the very basis of modern governmentality—or biopolitical programs of enfranchisement tied to real property; and to acknowledge "occupational use [or] ecological importance" is to undermine the very foundation of capital—to thwart the reification of raw nature qua land into the commodity form (Kohli qtd. in Hemalatha 2019).

The logic of capital relies on the "logic of land as property" (Boyer 2019, 69); otherwise the folly of such developmentalist narratives as obtain in India's burgeoning solar industry would be exposed as obvious fictions serving the end of peasant dispossession and corporate profit . . . which they are: "The [solar park] project has . . . taken up nearly 2,000 acres of cultivated land around Charanka. While landowners got between Rs 80,000 and Rs 1.5 lakh per acre as compensation, the rest got nothing . . . [local laborers] are forced to travel to neighbouring villages because [they] can't find work as agricultural labourers in [Charanka] village" (Hemalatha). Another local resident remarked in reference to Modi's solar campaign: "He promised us free water, electricity and even a hospital. None of these promises has been fulfilled to this day" (Hemalatha). Notably, small landholders who held claim to adjacent lands were likewise removed through coercion—selling their land under duress in the hope that they might find employment in the solar park. But per one resident of Charanka, solar jobs are only viable during construction: "In operation, you don't require many" (Yenneti and Day 2016, 41). Commenting on the aforementioned infrastructural improvements, another resident coyly remarked: "The road is for the company and electricity for the government" (41).

As a result of such inequitable development projects, a new jobless precariat has been produced and one who will presumably be forced to move to the nation's urban slums—also sites of "waste" as we discussed in the context of Aravind Adiga's *The White Tiger*. Hence the imperative to cultivate systems of political economy framed by an understanding of land that values its "occupational usage" and "ecological" value—a development *ethos* steeped in collectivism, and one that marshals local knowledge systems in the creation of new lifeworlds. This may sound "utopian in the sense that [such a shift requires] mak[ing] a world that has not yet existed" (Howe 2019, 195). But, as we have seen above, such modes of world-making are indeed being practiced; and while solar projects like the Charanka Solar Park illustrate the perils of green capitalism, we might consider (as we shall below) the possibility of marshaling local knowledge toward the end of cultivating a system of shared governance within the solar sector—one reliant on a "logic of land" in which value is understood not in terms of the commodity form but communal use. Indeed, while there may be "no template" for a transition away from fossil fuels, there is surely a template for living otherwise (2021, 35).

Consequently, in the present discussion I consider resistance to corporate solar energy regimes. I look, for example, to the Indigenous futurisms articulated by local communities like the Maldhari. I likewise scrutinize historic approaches to solar energy, utopian in nature, that see the limitless power of the sun as a silver bullet against the threat of energy scarcity—a vast and expansive frontier in the face of the finitude of fossilized carbon—in order to debunk utopian narratives that are not at all "useful" in building a habitable world. That is, and pace anthropologist Jamie Cross's work on the promise and peril of renewable forms of electrification for India's rural poor, I examine the ways in which "solar energy has been morally encoded with a spirit of social and ecological entrepreneurialism" that has the potential to reinforce extant forms of extractivist violence (2019, 3). And I also recognize that forms of "solar communism" historically promoted by those privileged enough to live "off the grid" find a viable counter in the arguments of solar champions like Herman Scheer who instead seeks to transform the grid—to invite the sorts of local grid initiatives that are also being practiced in communities throughout the subcontinent.

Thus, I shall consider both the perils of unjust energy transition as well as the possibility of solar-powered cultures that depart materially and ideologically from such settler-colonial imaginaries as are implied by terms like "wasteland." I begin, however, with the former and the potential for any *unjust* transition to solar-powered electricity to risk reproducing what Prashad describes as the "assassination of the Third World" through new mechanisms of extraction and trade (2007, 3). I then look to the nascent solar industry in India, and the ways in which rural (solar-powered) electrification promises to improve lacking infrastructure, and whether such promises must be framed by the extractivist logic of the fossil fuel industries, or whether the possibility of just transition might be glimpsed in Indigenous development projects predicated on the possibility of "solarity" (Barney and Szeman 2019). The latter is a political condition in which the "limitless" power of the sun is governed by an "ecologic" wherein "land is understood in terms of communal right . . . and not private property, and where [solar power] is a lifeforce and not a commodity" (Balkan 2021b, 31). Ultimately, in examining modes of unjust transition and looking to "solarity" over and against mere solar, I make clear that energy transition must be accompanied by a radical shift in political economy, and that such transitions must in fact be initiated from "below." That is, "solarity" demands that "those who have experienced globalization from the bottom" are no longer reducible to fodder for extractivist regimes, even *sustainable* ones like the optimistically entitled "Solar India" initiative (Lopéz). As we shall see below, this is but another example of the public-private partnerships that dominate Indian industry, and which are, despite the role of public interests, framed by an *ethos* of corporate privatization.

The Sunshine State: Transitioning from Coal to Solar

"Solar India" was initiated by former PM Manmohan Singh, who may also be credited with *beautifying* the nation through the violent razing of urban slum communities. The project began in earnest in 2010 when the champion of economic liberalization would remark:

> National Solar Mission has the pride of place in India's National Action Plan on Climate Change. Its success has the potential of transforming India's energy prospects, and also contributing to national as well as global efforts to combat climate change. We will pool our scientific,

technical and managerial talents, with sufficient financial resources, to develop solar energy as a source of abundant energy to power our economy and to transform the lives of our people. (qtd in Joshi and Yenneti 2010, 1)

Singh, who served as finance minister under Prime Minister P. V. Narasinha Rao (Rao also presiding over the first stages of economic liberalization—including the 1995 GATT agreements, which would secure India's position in the Washington Consensus) would, during his administration, usher in a new age of privatization and a renewed commitment to global trade. So too, projects like Solar India, which would place India at the forefront of environmental mitigation projects despite the nation's continued prominence in the global coal arena.

But how and why did the nation shift from coal to solar? That is, and as we discussed in the context of *The White Tiger*, coal has ostensibly produced the modern nation and secured India's autonomy. And despite Modi's much-remarked solar initiatives, the PM remains wedded to King Coal, which is consistently cheaper and whose power (unlike solar) is not intermittent—a problem for the rural poor who continue to await the promise of electrification. If electricity is an index of modernity, surely the intermittent nature of solar-powered electricity (at least from the perspective of industry critics and local citizens)—waning as it does at sunset if there is no viable means of capture and storage—is a marker of the persistent unevenness of Indian development:

> Solar panels generate electricity only between sunrise and sunset—from about 6:45 am to 6:45 pm during my visit. To provide electricity at night, power generated in daylight must be stored for later use. Typically storage systems employ the sun to heat a liquid (water, say, or molten salt); at night the stored hot liquid drives a steam turbine, producing electricity. In 2010, India announced seven solar-energy storage projects, one of them in Gujarat. (Mann 2015)

Thus, the shift to solar power must indicate something other than economic sense, grid parity, or environmental justice:

> Despite its dramatic cost declines, solar energy was not cost competitive with electricity produced from domestic coal in the period 2014–17. Yet, the Indian government made a concerted effort to bring about a dramatic growth in solar energy. This suggests that while techno-economic

factors certainly facilitated the solar scale-up, they do not fully explain it. This also implies that political drivers were important (Shidore and Busby 2019, 1182).

Perhaps in the face of the Paris Agreement, and recognizing that India houses approximately 25 percent of the planet's population, this shift was of an existential nature: we simply wouldn't survive as a species with close to 1.5 billion people emitting carbon dioxide at a rate comparable to rich nations like the United States.

Thus, we might consider such political drivers as climate change mitigation in our examination of India's energy transition. Perhaps, however, there is a less palatable justification. We know that state shifts between energy regimes have historically aligned with political ideology—that is, and undermining the myth of scarcity, fossil fuels have historically been embraced because of popular sentiment, whether or not said sentiment is informed by verifiable science or even economic sense. Fressoz and Bonnueil remind us of just this in the context of Victorian-era wind power—that wind remained a prominent energy source in nineteenth-century Britain, but "the steam engine ... despite being more expensive, constituted a flexible, modular and individual source of energy that matched very well the ideology of English textile capitalism of the 1830s" (2016, 109). That is, the success of the steam engine—owing to its ability to succor new labor protocols that would align with the rise of the factory and thus the autopoetic fantasies of the post-industrial entrepreneur—would be enabled not by economic need or ecological sense, but the capitalist fictions attendant to the rise of the modern factory system and the oft-remarked revolution in industry during the mid-nineteenth century. The subcontinent's embrace of solar would similarly rely on the enabling myths of global capitalism and the promise of new frontiers of accumulation—the latter effectively masked by the narrative of sustainability attendant to solar capital.

While the cost of solar was higher than coal in 2015, it was in fact a shift in popular sentiment following Paris that nudged the industry. This is also clear in then minister Modi's embrace of solar in Gujarat: "Perhaps the strongest indicator that rapid emergence of grid parity did not drive Modi and his team in 2014 was Modi's approach to solar in Gujarat well before 2014, when solar was far more expensive and cost reductions were even less expected" (Shidore and Busby 1183). Contra any economic incentive, "Modi saw solar as a way to project an image of a future-oriented modern reformer" (1184):

> The BJP led the national election campaign of 2014 projecting Modi as a can-do modernizer. The "Gujarat development model was held up as a

standard that the country would achieve under his leadership. The model emphasized a build-up of modern infrastructure and industry through state-facilitated private investment." (Pathak 2014) This pitch was strongly linked to technology. For example, Modi's campaign speeches were projected as holograms to many Indian small towns and villages (Nelson, 2014) and had a major impact on rural, less educated voters. Solar energy was thus a part of the general message of modernization and development. (Shidore and Busby 1184)

To the extent that Modi's election signaled a shift in India's energy policies—and thus a watershed moment for industry—his alignment with corporate solar (ironically also with Tata) recalls Nehru's alignment with the steel industry: both figures occasion at least a visible state-shift in energy regimes; and both were intimately linked with corporate interests.

Furthermore, and more than political capital for Modi's domestic policy, solar projects would galvanize international recognition of India as a leader in climate change mitigation efforts. What's more: solar could help the nation to achieve energy independence. This, however, would also be achieved through maintaining, and in fact increasing, investment in the nation's coal industry; hence again, our need to scrutinize fallacious energy histories such as I critiqued in the previous chapter. To be sure, "on coming to power, the Modi government initiated a major expansion in *both* coal and solar. By ramping up domestic coal production from the state-owned monopoly coal mines, coal shortages in power plants turned into surpluses by the middle of 2015" (Shidore and Busby 1186). But despite Modi's continued commitment to coal, he has retained his position as an environmental leader whose fundamentalist policies he now explains in terms of religious faith: "Extolling Hinduism's ancient environmental beliefs, the BJP promised in its election manifesto to 'put sustainability at the center of our thoughts and actions' " (Mann 2015). Ironically, this is also so despite his later hedging: shying away from any radical departure from fossil capital, Modi would also invoke the metaphysical in an argument denying climate change. Apparently, " 'climate has not changed. We have changed . . . God has built the system in such a way that it can balance on its own' " (Mann). What this latent climate change denier also doesn't mention is that "87 percent of Indian household electricity is subsidized, but less than a fifth of the subsidies go to the rural poor for whom they were intended, and the [government-owned] utilities have little incentive to spend what it would take to connect them" (Mann 2015). Hence, the Charanka resident's remark regarding Modi's empty promises.

Relying on solar power to fulfill such promises is perhaps even more problematic given its putatively erratic ontology; but the Gujarati sun is a prime source of Modi's political capital, and despite his own quibbles with the science of global warming, solar does seem to be the new coal—an abundant resource, if one shrouded in myriad forms of violence against Native communities. While the subcontinent is notable for its ample waters—from the much-mythologized Ganga to the glacial runoff from the Himalayas—and thus a prime site for the deployment of hydropower (as is evidenced in the labyrinthine networks of megadams, and ones constructed out of steel and thus also the product of coal), it is likewise a noteworthy recipient of abundant sunshine:

> With over 300 days of sunshine, solar radiation of 5.6e6.0 kWh/m2 per day and the availability of large tracts of "waste" land, the State of Gujarat in India has a huge potential for generating solar energy (GEDA, 2009). Realising this potential and the benefits that solar energy can bring in addressing climate change and energy security issues, the Government of Gujarat released the Gujarat Solar Power Policy (GSPP) in 2009, making it the first of India's states to do so. This was a year before the release of the National Solar Mission (NSM) of India . . . Apart from supporting individual solar photovoltaic (PV) power projects, the GSPP 2009 was also an experiment by the State government to develop a series of public-private partnership based large-scale "solar parks" in the state. (Yenneti and Day 2016, 35)

The region more broadly is marked by an extremely arid climate. The state of Gujarat is flanked by Rajasthan, which is in large part desert.

Gujarat is also notable for its mineral stores: like most Indian states, its subterranean resources—including bauxite, lignite, and limestone—have attracted speculation from a myriad of mining firms, many of which are government owned. While solar power does not (on the surface) instantiate a conventional form of extraction, such public-private entities—the portfolios of which remain dominated by fossil capital and precious metals—are increasingly turning to solar capital. What we might traditionally think of as a mineral belt—such as we see, for example, in the eastern states of Odisha and Andhra Pradesh—is being somewhat transformed in the context of Gujarat where solar capital is dominant; although, the state also boasts the largest output of silica—the primary material used in the construction of photovoltaic solar panels. Hence, solar power is in fact an extractive economy, if one that enjoys far better PR than coal.

Solar Fetishisms

While the perception of solar energy is often rather utopian—an alternative to extractivist violence, and one whose environmental benefits also promise the ability to *sustain* the rather unsustainable habits of the developed nations—solar power is also encoded socially and culturally in a fairly conventional way: "Electricity is always mediated, and thus is from the very beginning a social and cultural thing . . . the anthropology of electricity can help us understand the relationship between sources of energy and social and political arrangements" (Gupta 2015, 562–63). Similarly, and in terms of the nation's energopolitics, "the solar lamp has come to serve as a benchmark of whether or not people have access to the most basic level of clean, efficient energy deemed necessary for human life" (Cross 2017, 5). But, asks Cross, "How is this so? How did ideas about what constitutes a basic level of access to electrical power become equated with the solar lamp?" (5). His answer: "As a little development device and a humanitarian good, the solar lamp meets a minimum basic need while opening pathways to new electric desires and aspirations" (23). Thus, solar capital emerges as both an index of development and "social reform" as well as an instantiation of an " 'energopolitics' married to market expansion" (5, 7). Consequently, Cross ultimately asks whether the "low-cost solar lamp [is] an appropriate solution to energy poverty, infrastructural failure, and climate change" given that solar marketeers have come to understand electricity refugees as "potential future markets for low-cost solar-powered devices" (12, 20). It isn't surprising, given the history of solar power, that such a dichotomy would emerge: solar as both humanitarian good and new extractivist frontier. That is, "solar power seems to have been uncoupled from the decentralized postscarcity society that [Murray] Bookchin imagined; it remains nested within dominant systems of energy production and distribution and must confront the formidable challenge of grid parity" (Boetzkes 2017, 316). In her entry on solar power for *Fueling Culture: 101 Words for Energy and Environment*, Amanda Boetzkes remarks on the paradox that this putatively utopian energy source provides: "The history of solar power invites us to consider the difference between a form of energy that shapes cultural exchange and a resource that merely fuels production" (2017, 314). That is, if energy has historically been understood as that which fuels development, we must also remember—pace the above discussion about coal—the ways in which energy forms also fuel culture: modern capitalism would not exist without fossil fuels; and the social infrastructures that support global fossil capitalism now directly enable the accumulation and distribution of solar capital. As well, the narrative of manifest destiny that undergirded historical approaches to extractivism was merely emboldened with the discovery of the solar cell. Cross also cites a 1954 *New York Times* op-ed that makes this abundantly clear: "The solar cell 'may mark the beginning of a new era, leading eventually to the reclamation of one of mankind's most cherished dreams—the harnessing of the almost limitless power of the sun' " (2019, 5).

This "limitless" power has also invited geoengineering schemes globally, and in India, that marshal the sun's energies toward climate change mitigation. Chief among them are solar geoengineering schemes that propose the "injection of aerosol precursors such as SO2 into the stratosphere to form sulfate aerosols and deflect about 1%–2% of the incoming solar radiation" (Bala and Gupta 24). Thus, solar power promises not only limitless energy, but likewise a viable means through which to assuage the impacts of fossil-fueled climate violence. Of course, "these schemes do not address ocean acidification, which could be detrimental to marine life, and they also commit us to maintain them for decades to centuries until atmospheric CO_2 levels fall to sufficiently lower values" (Bala and Gupta 24). Comparable schemes, which seek to harness the hydropower of the monsoons and the glacial waters of the Himalayas, are similarly short-sighted; and neither takes into consideration the human costs of such putatively "green" ventures—namely the displacement and/or drowning of Native communities, whether in the interest of solar fields or new dam projects.

As nations continue to look to the utopian promises of renewable energy systems, specifically solar power, it is imperative that each also considers its human and nonhuman costs. The case of Charanka is an obvious testament to the material impacts of extractive (solar) capitalism in terms of such costs—that is, the destruction of Native lands and thereby the means through which the local community can sustain itself. Looking to its ecological costs more broadly, we might also consider that "solar energy is one of the most land-intensive sources of power [whereby] large tracts of arid and semi-arid land are being covered by solar panels" (Hemalatha). To wit, India's current solar economy seems to be the farthest thing possible from a utopia; to the contrary, it illustrates a level of social and environmental injustice matched only by the petrochemical industry. Although the latter at least doesn't promise to assuage energy poverty through "social and moral reform." Big Oil makes no claims to justice, only the "energy-intensive freedoms" that we have come to associate with modernity (Chakrabarty 2009, 208). But Big Solar not only makes such promises, unlike the fossil fuel industries (and as aforementioned), corporate solar projects in India are not beholden to any federal oversight: "Concerns . . . are often overlooked [because of] the perception of solar energy as a clean, climate-friendly technology, deployed in unused, 'desert' areas . . . despite their massive scale, solar parks in India are exempt from any requirement for an environmental or social impact assessment" (Yenneti and Day 2015, 665). In short, projects like the Charanka Solar Park have come to symbolize the very worst of energy capitalism—a dystopia on par with that of coal-soaked Dhanbad. Although I wonder if we might look to Charanka differently—that is, if we might engage in the speculative in order to imagine what may have happened if the Gujarat Power Corporation had consulted the Maldhari community in their decision-making.[11]

Solar Dystopia or Glimpse of Solarity: The Charanka Solar Park

A concise portrait of environmental and procedural injustice, Charanka has not only suffered the indignity of having their grazing land deemed "waste" and thus fodder for development. Local citizens were not even notified of the construction of the park: "They became aware of the project only when several excavators entered their village to clear land" (Yenneti and Day 2015, 668). A local resident told researchers: "We were aware [of the construction] through a land acquisition public notice. As our village Charanka is under 'Group Panchayat', the public notice was sent to our main Panchayat office which is in Bhabra village' " (668). The Panchayat Raj system was incorporated following independence to ensure Indigenous sovereignty through collaborative electoral units; and it likewise stands in as a means of collective bargaining with government land holders who are required under the 1894 Government of India's Land Acquisition (LA) Act to publish official notice prior to all construction projects on government land—i.e., that which the Maldhari community use in common for their livestock.

Such notice would have served to invite local knowledge about the landscape and thus enhance the efficacy of the park while limiting its impact on local villagers—the laborers who are "endow[ed] with intimate knowledge about geographical and environmental conditions" and could thus potentially serve the interests of the company (Yenneti and Day 2015, 670):

> According to the "Detailed Project Report" of the solar park, the location of Charanka was selected due to factors such as high solar radiation, availability of a large chunk of government land (at a single location) and acquirable private farm land (with single cropping patterns), and the relatively small population of the village. However, according to the local perspective, this decision was neither sound nor necessary. The

acquisition of a large plot of in-use land (both government land and privately owned plots) from one single village was lamented by several interviewees. They said that using different pieces of land from different villages could have had less severe livelihood impacts on the pastoralists and farmers: "About 10,000 ha of waste land, located on the other side of the hill, is neither being used for agriculture nor for grazing. If the government used that, there would not have been any problem for farmers or Rabaris (Respondent #1, Male, Rabari)." (669)

Had the government and its corporate proxy sought local knowledge, the project may actually have been more successful—particularly given suspicions by many rural Indians regarding the unreliability of solar-powered electricity; but, as we have seen, local residents were largely ignored.

Consequent to such forms of procedural injustice, the Ministry of Justice and Empowerment of the Government of India established a "Nomadic Commission" along with the creation of an act to ensure The Right to Fair Compensation, Resettlement, Rehabilitation and Transparency in Land Acquisition in 2014 (Yenneti and Day 2015, 671). The latter promises new forms of participatory justice. But improved "participatory justice" doesn't necessarily address the problem of resource imperialism; nor assuage the long-term impacts of such settler-colonial development models, reliant as they are on the enclosure of the commons in the service of bolstering energy markets. Thus, Szeman and Boyer continue to argue: "It is difficult to see how we might engage in the energy transition we need without plans that bring together scientific knowledge about the causes and consequences of global warming with social and cultural insights into the shape and character of our [energy] subjectivities" (2017, 7). That is, "the question is not whether markets are good or bad but rather what it means for our energy ethics when it is almost impossible to imagine a future without them" (Cross 2019, 17). If according to George Bataille, in *The Accursed Share*, "economic science merely generalizes the isolated situation . . . [and] restricts its objects to operations carried out with a view to a limited end" then we must imagine alternatives to market-driven energy solutions that deny the validity of local cultures and forms of geographical and ecological knowledge (23).

But how do we shift from stock in fossil fuels to the potentially unlimited potential of the sun without reproducing such modes of social inequality and environmental injustice as have been practiced in Charanka? Does this not require a shift away from the extractive logics that fuel fossil capitalism? If "energy is dialectically bound to economic history—not a concept or variable dependent of it, but a structuring force without which capital could not operate"—then we must envisage new forms of political economy that are framed by a different logic altogether, and one that acknowledges the validity of common right (Bellamy and Diamanti 2018, x). This demands a departure from the autopoetic impulses of liberal capitalism—the Kantian cum Reaganesque narrative of self-reliance and uplift that has ensured the destruction of all forms of collectivity; and it would likewise require a re-imagining of energy grids—what some Energy Humanists see as Edison's greatest legacy, which is to say more so than the bulb: "Edison's major innovation was not the filament that would illuminate a glass bulb, but the grid that would distribute electricity from the point of its generation to the point of its consumption. He created the mechanism whereby energy could be brought to market" (Bellamy and Diamanti 2018, xxv).

Markets have allowed for the decentralization of energy such that local communities have come to rely on distant power grids; and those same markets are now governed by the sorts of public-private partnerships that we see in Charanka. Thus, solar champion Herman Scheer argues that an "effective use of renewable resources requires a radical rethinking of the supply and redistribution networks" (2002, 77). Such a model of Scheerian thinking, Boyer argues in his recent *Energopolitics*, "[seeks] to harness renewable energy sources to transform and improve the social and political conditions of humanity, to bring justice and empowerment to long-marginalized communities in the postcolonial world" (2019, 59). This is accomplished in large part, per Scheer, through the construction of a local grid—one that could capture and store solar energy within a finite region. Less interested in grid parity—or the emphasis on cost—than cultivating social justice through the implementation of a means through which local communities like the Maldhari can achieve energy sovereignty, Scheer promotes the idea of "electricity without supply chains" (75).

This would require a radical shift in energy policy and municipal relationships to/with markets. Thus I return to the central question animating energy justice advocates: in what ways might we decentralize energy markets and uncouple energy policy from the logic of extraction? And is this even possible? Sheena Wilson suggests that we must also ask: "What from the age of oil is not working? And, most critically, for whom is it not working?" (2018, 377). Obviously, Wilson, continues, "switching energy sources alone will not reconfigure our problematic relationships with one another, or our natural and built environments. To think otherwise is to fetishize oil"—or coal or solar in the case of India (401). And surely, to continue to rely on centralized energy grids is merely to reproduce said inequalities through the dispossession of local communities through forced dependence on extant markets.

We must, therefore, consider the logics animating our reliance on a conventional energopolitics. And we must, in this sense, and pace Donna Haraway, revisit "the thoughts [that we use] to think thoughts" (2016, 35). And we must finally, per Powys Whyte (2019), understand "nature" and "environment"—and thus "energy"—as a set of relationships predicated upon accountability and consent. That is, we must emphasize "accountability and consent" over and against profitability and the sorts of illicit practices that we see in the Charanka Solar Park where the government flouts "consent" so egregiously (Powys Whyte 2019). Of course, this would fly in the face of a development model that hinges on dispossession and the enclosure of the commons; but if there is no material shift away from such a model, we face (with certitude) environmental catastrophe if not complete Earth systems collapse. Indeed, "if it took Britain half the resources of the world to be what it is today, how many worlds would India need" (Gupta 2015, 566).

It is in this spirit that we recognize Maldhari culture as a model for "solarity"—that is, for the potential of groups like the Maldhari to marshal local knowledge and land use practices in the pursuit of environmental justice. While their pleas for inclusion were largely ignored in this particular instance of solar capitalism, the sentiments of local laborers make clear that their knowledge may have helped to galvanize support for development projects that emphasize shared governance—the federal and municipal government, the corporate proxy of the day, and the Panchayat. So too, in marshaling not only local knowledge but sanctioning the legitimacy of the Maldhari's commoning economy—through an acknowledgment of their political sovereignty—a different development model might indeed emerge, and one that follows the charge of Scheerian thinking and thus liberates local communities from centralized energy markets that thrive on the dispossession of their families and the destruction of their ecologies. Anthropologist Ankhil Gupta actually cites Gandhi on this score: "Gandhi's critiques of electrical power was the worry that it would bring centralized control over the lives of people in remote villages and prevent communities from becoming self-sufficient for their energy needs" (2015, 565). Noting, however, that such a position also effectively cut "remote villages" off in ways that would create more harm, Gupta advocates for a recognition of "different ideas about the future" and the urgent need to cultivate forms of development that do not repeat the aforementioned "expenditures of the past" (566).

One such effort to cultivate energy justice can be glimpsed in the mini-grid economy. Working toward grid parity, there are initiatives in the sunshine belt centered on the construction of mini-grids that are working with local communities to opt out of the central power grid. Such campaigns would surely align with Scheer's imperative to create "electricity without supply chains." But such projects—like the organization SELCO—have their drawbacks.[12] While SELCO is laudable for efforts toward shared governance, it likewise promotes opportunities for "entrepreneurship" that could potentially undermine local autonomy through conventional profit motives; SELCO is also aligned with multinational energy corporations who will surely benefit from the SEZs in the same ways as Gujarat Power. And thus we arrive again at the question, or the possibility, of just transition and life after extraction. By way of conclusion, I shall attempt to address this question, which is in fact a veritable impasse: just how do we transition away from the extractivist *ethos* governing the age of fossil capitalism in its many guises? In order to answer this question, I engage the speculative in an attempt to imagine otherwise.

After Extraction

Rogues in the Postcolony began as a project about narrative and form—how the picaresque novel, in its nonteleological mode, allows for an imaginative departure from the developmentalist temporality undergirding conventional political and economic narratives. I now return to questions of representation by asking "how to frame the 'unimaginable' " (Szeman 2016, 39). That is, what would a "useful[ly] utopian" narrative look like? (40). And what mode of political economy would "[enable] new forms of collaboration and action" while encouraging a sympoetic (or collectively produced) understanding of the nonhuman landscape (31). Rather than focus primarily on literary critiques of solar capitalism—even such wonderfully nonlinear (perhaps picaresque?) works as graphic novelist Ganzeer's dystopian *The Solar Grid*, or the more optimistic "Solarpunk" movement—here I look to local initiatives framed by a sense of Indigenous futurity, and a viable one at that.[13]

Of course, it is worthwhile mentioning that there is in fact a robust genealogy of literary works that attend to the solar economy—from the dystopian projections of an irradiated landscape singed by a relentlessly encroaching sun, to works that foreground the beneficence of the sun's warmth and radiance. As well, there is a long tradition of South Asian dystopian science fiction, including Ruchir Joshi's *The Last Jet-Engine Laugh* (2001) and Shovon Chowdhury's *The Competent Authority* (2013), that offers biting critiques of India's complicated and often-contradictory political landscape (see Khan 2016). It is surely a matter of time before there is a solar picaresque excoriating "Solar India"—perhaps one not unlike *The Solar Grid*. That said, the narrative terrain of Ganzeer's serialized novel stretches across a vast transnational (and intergalactic) geography while shuttling its protagonists back and forth in time—its formal elements thus mimicking the global imaginary of extractivist fictions like *The White Tiger*. In this sense, and pace Amitav Ghosh's oft-remarked argument regarding "petro-fiction"—that it is a necessarily transnational genre given the geographic scope of the oil industry—*The Solar Grid* may in fact be an appropriate commentary on something like "Solar India" (1992). If so-called "petro-fictions" require a transnational political terrain as their narrative backdrops, it might be said that fictionalized corporate solar economies (as we see in *The Solar Grid*)—in their reproduction of such economic models—ought to follow suit. Surely a picaresque critique of "Solar India" would present such a terrain—any inclusion of grid parity to be glimpsed in the sorts of Swiftian moments that we occasionally find in *Animal's People* or *The White Tiger*.

Exquisitely Swiftian in its aims, yet appropriately dystopian in its affinity to "cli-fi," Ganzeer's geographically sprawling graphic novel foregrounds the collapse of Earth systems, opening with the "wretched of the Earth" in the year 949 AF (After the Flood). At this point a dystopian geoengineering project entitled "The Solar Grid" has been constructed to restore the drowned landscape—a product, the reader learns, of drastically rising sea levels. The grid would transform life by providing limitless power: "a spectacular network of satellites that beam sunrays onto the planet in the dead of night! Such Power!" (Issue 2) But this malevolent scheme proves a far cry from the solar utopia imagined elsewhere—here in the "Wastecount[ies]" of the galaxy, the "Sisyphean" figures of Mehret and Kameen live as scavengers, careful to stay out of the sun's path for fear of burning their skin.

Images of peak Earth abound in this veritable necroscape; and the novel moves through the incremental changes to the global fossil economy—beginning in the immediate aftermath of the flood—which ultimately culminate in Ganzeer's spectacularly rendered dystopian present. Readers learn of the monomaniacal founder of "Skyquench," another geoengineering project, this one promising to assuage global thirst through a conventional privatization scheme that ultimately leaves most of the global poor without water; and a myriad of political grotesqueries follow—from the militarized surveillance of journalists to the sexual assault (by state police) of a local street artist. A mosaic of constructed artifacts—newspaper clippings, museum archives, and traditional paneling—this visual landscape offers a compelling indictment of extant geoengineering schemes that are naught but monuments to imperial hubris. There are even explicit allusions to current projects, including former president Donald Trump's "Space Force." This is an obvious critique of the settler-colonial *ethos* powering the state's desire to cultivate new avenues for territorial expansion. There are in fact several nods to the US's settler-colonial history, including a reference to the dispossession of Native communities like the Lakota Sioux. Caricaturing a white nationalist in a "Don't Tread on Me" tee, Ganzeer delights his readers with a magical realist gesture in which the prodigal snake ultimately ravages the raging supremacist. Less comical intimations of the novel's political aims include the presence of a sort of revolutionary archive: apparently there had been much resistance to the solar grid project at the outset.

In the final installment of the novel, at least the most recent one published (August 2020), the artist turns to a striking commentary on the power of the aesthetic—thus offering a metacommentary on the role of the novel itself. Shifting to a somewhat linear narrative, there is a long passage about the evolution of street art—evolving (or devolving) from politico-aesthetic intervention to highly prized commodity in the context of a rapidly gentrifying intergalactic capitalist dystopia; Mars is now a playground for the elite. This may be read as self-effacing: here the artist explicitly meditates on the cooptation of street art and thus the futility of his own project; or perhaps this metacommentary on form signals the artist's desire to move beyond the satirical mode.

The last chapter ultimately returns to a critique of the utopian fantasies of limitless solar power and the folly of such hubristic schemes as are evidenced by the "grid." While this serialized graphic novel remains unfinished, at least for now we are left wanting a more viable way to move forward. In short, *The Solar Grid* is a productive condemnation of neoliberal privatization schemes that will ultimately ensure the ruination of the planet and all who dwell within it, but one that also leaves its readers mired in tragedy. I shall thus conclude with a different means of speculating on possible futures by embracing the mandate of the Petrocultures Research Group (PRC).

In the collective's collaboratively authored "Principles of Intentional Transition"—a set of principles designed to ensure a more equitable energy transition—the PRC outlines six criteria for an intentional, or just, transition, and one whose constituent steps I shall apply to the commoning economy of the Maldhari community in an effort to imagine a material praxis for such an endeavor. The principles are as follows: 1) agency and mobilization: "conscious participation and mobilization of peoples and communities" (Szeman 2016, 25); 2) collective stewardship: "right of people and their communities to own, manage, and develop the energy resources . . . that support their ideals" (25); 3) Equality: all people must have access; 4) Ethics of use: ethical dimensions of energy; 5) Sustainability: pushing back against the culture of obsolescence that ignores the increasing obsolescence of the fossil fuel industry; and 6) Redefinition of growth: growth must be tied to a new ethics.

The practical application of each principle may in fact be glimpsed in the case study of Charanka if only we employ the subjunctive—a strategy that I model after Cymene Howe's imaginative work on corporate windpower in Mexico (see Khan 2016). "Conscious participation" in all energy decisions would mean that India's federal government comply with the 1894 and 2014 acts. "Collective stewardship" would require that the Panchayats are always consulted, but more so that communities like the Maldhari have the right to "own, manage, and develop" a solar economy on their own terms and with the hindsight of centuries of local knowledge. Equality and access would require that all members of the community have access to grazing land—that the notion of "use" be radically transformed in the interest of land equity. An ethics of use must include consideration of such relationships to the land as are practiced through usufruct right. A new conception of "sustainability" must be cultivated in the interest of not *sustaining* the settler-colonial practices of the fossil fuel industries, which rely on obsolescence. And growth shall be understood as the growth of community and life-sustaining forms of world-making tied to habitability.

Such a redefinition of India's solar economy requires the sort of philosophical anthropology for which Chakrabarty calls, if also the vision of social and environmental justice being demanded by the broader nexus of "Animal's people" who continue to agitate against global extractive capitalism in its myriad forms—communities who remind us that "the lands which have been engrossed by this deleterious culture should be returned to uses not incompatible with human life, virtue, and happiness" (*RS* 504). Perhaps we must now consider how the "deleterious culture" of liberal capitalism more broadly can never be "[compatible] with human life, virtue, and happiness," and instead embrace a vision of world-making of the sort that Streeby promotes—one that she likewise reminds her readers may be glimpsed both in speculative fiction as well as in the examples of Indigenous movements that we have examined here. For it is in the protests of the Chipko Andolan, the Dongria Kondh, and the Maldhari that new worlds are being forged and ones that are indeed compatible with life.

Notes

INTRODUCTION

1. In "The Global City: Introducing a Concept," Saskia Sassen explains the economic dynamics of the global city—contra the world city—as "a strategic site for a whole range of new types of operations—political, economic, 'cultural,' subjective." So too, "one of the nexi where the formation of new claims, by both the powerful and the disadvantaged, materializes and assumes concrete form" (2005, 40). Such an imagined terrain is concisely instantiated by Lagos—a city organized by transnational networks of global fossil capital, and stratified by the "powerful and the disadvantaged," whether international elites or migrant labor regimes from the nation's interior settling in sites like those illustrated by Abani.
2. I read the novel as such in Balkan (2015) "Rogues in the Postcolony: Chris Abani's *GraceLand* and The Petro- Picaresque," *The Global South* 9(2): 18–37.
3. I distinguish *Lazarillo* as a text that popularized, rather than created, the form because its genealogy can be traced much farther back historically and is generally contested. For example, Abdullah Al-Dabbagh (2009) argues that "the hero of Al-Harîrî's *Mqrâmât*, is the true model of the Spanish *pícaro*, and a precedent for the characters of Guzman de Alfarache and Estibanillo Gonzalez, the heroes of the two most renowned Spanish picaresque novels written in 1599 and 1646 respectively" (21).
4. See, for example, *Oil Fictions: World Literature and Our Contemporary Petrosphere*, edited by Stacey Balkan and Swaralipi Nandi, Penn State University Press, 2021.
5. See work on petrocultures and petromodernity, including Imre Szeman and Dominic Boyer's recent anthology *Energy Humanities* (2017). The third chapter of the present study, "Slum Ecologies: Figuring (Energy) Waste in Aravind Adiga's *The White Tiger*," builds upon extant discussions within the Energy Humanities expanding arguments regarding "reading energy" to include new praxes for literary critique—that is, coal or petrol as heuristics through which to understand plot and story.
6. I use the term "late capitalism," following Ernest Mandel, to refer to the postwar period. See *Late Capitalism* (1999).
7. Lasting from 1975 to 1977, the "Emergency" refers to the Prime Minister Indira Gandhi's federally sanctioned suspension of civil liberties in favor of security—a period notable for severe forms of violent oppression and the "beautification" of cities *via* the bulldozing of slum communities.
8. See also Jacques Derrida's discussion of rogue states and the economic function of the constitutive outside in *Rogues: Two Essays on Reason* (2005).
9. For a discussion of "enabling fictions" see also Joseph Slaughter's (2006) "Enabling Fictions and Novel Subjects: the *Bildungsroman* and International Rights Law."

10. As I discuss in the context of Ghosh's *Ibis Trilogy*, this particular convention manifests differently in *Sea of Poppies* wherein the polylingual terrain of Indian Ocean trading networks replaces the narrower storyworld of the typical *pícaro*. The neopicaresque novels of Adiga and Sinha do in fact employ this trope.
11. See also Sourayan Mookerjea's (2018) stunning elaboration of the subaltern's multitude contradiction in "Accumulated Violence, or, the Wars of Exploitation: Notes Toward a Post-Western Marxism," *Mediations* 32(1): 95–114.
12. See Micheal Rumore's (2021b) discussion of Shailja Patel's *Migritude* and the project's unsettling of normative ontological categories like "Asian" and "African"— both imperial fictions constructed in the interest of sustained resource colonization in, for example, Kenya and India—in "Black Water: Race and the Human Project in the Indian Ocean Imagination."
13. It is also worth recalling Ursula Le Guin's essay "The Carrier Bag Theory of Fiction" in which the famed speculative fiction writer examines the origins of such imperialist notions of *Bildung* as are demonstrated in conventional—read heteropatriarchal—cosmogenies of modernity.
14. In J. M. Neeson's *Commoners: Common Right, Enclosure, and Social Change in England, 1700–1820*, she states: "Enclosure meant the extinction of common right and the extinction of common right meant the decline of small farms" (1996, 15). She, like John Barrell in his *Dark Side of Landscape* (1983), argues that "the" industrial revolution—that is, the enactment of large-scale agriculture, and the consequent (and exponential) enclosure of land—was a protracted phenomenon that lasted some three centuries and which effectively destroyed an entire class. Neeson also notes: "Most commoning economies were extinguished by enclosure at some point between the fifteenth and the nineteenth centuries" (5). Statistically, some six million acres of common land were enclosed by 1840.
15. Locke also remarked: "God, who hath given the world to men in common, has also given them reason to make use of it to the best advantage of life and convenience" (2002, 12). See also Gyan Prakash's comments on "land as object" and the legacy of seventeenth-century economic doctrine in his *Bonded Histories: Genealogies of Labor Servitude in Colonial India* (1990).
16. In G. A. Cohen's discussion of value in *Self-Ownership, Freedom and Equality* (1995), he notably points to an elision (within Marxist arguments around Locke) of any consideration of an *a priori* value in the "ground which produces the materials" (Locke qtd. in Cohen, 1995). In my reading of Ghosh's *Ibis Trilogy*, I attend to this prominent elision—one that also instantiates the violent Cartesianism of Marx's rift paradigm.
17. The "cony-catching" pamphlets, popularized by such examples as Thomas Harmon's *A Caveat for Common Cursitors Vulgarly Called Vagabonds* (1566), are one species of rogue literature.
18. See Pablo Mukherjee's discussion of a "postcolonial picturesque" in the context of Anglophone Indian Realist novels in his *Postcolonial Environments: Nature, Culture and the Contemporary Indian Novel in English* (2010).
19. This theory also resonates in the eighteenth-century picturesque context—images of gypsies, beggars, and disabled veterans foregrounded as objects in traditionally pastoral settings.
20. See also E. P. Thompson's discussion of moral economies and the ways in which emergent theories of free trade—such as were presented by Thomas Ricardo, and which are satirized in the *Ibis Trilogy*—scandalizes and erodes the moral and

ultimately material/political fabric of commoning economies in eighteenth-century England. See, for example, "The Moral Economy of the English Crowd in the Eighteenth Century," *Past & Present*, no. 50 (1971): 76–136.
21. See Joya John's "From Political Climate to Climate Politics: Traces of Energy in the Hindi Literary Archive (1972–1990)," ACLA Annual Convention, March 10, 2019.
22. In C16 Spain, criminality *via* itinerancy was similarly produced by new property laws.
23. In Ashley Dawson's "Surplus City: Structural Adjustment, Self-Fashioning, and Urban Insurrection in Chris Abani's *GraceLand*," under the section header "Excremental Urbanism," he notes that such "persons are literally treated as excrement" (2011, 20).
24. Maiorino (2003, 7) defines the *converso* thus: "Arab peasants and Jewish craftsmen and merchants who became Christian to avoid persecution."
25. Gayatri Spivak has recently indicted the term "Global South" as problematically reductive and thus potentially a vehicle for "reverse racism." In her essay in the Spring 2018 *PMLA*, she makes this claim citing earlier interventions by the Subaltern Studies collective. The inaugural volume of the journal *The Global South* makes clear that Spivak's argument eschews the myriad of nuanced treatments of this vastly pluralized region. See Alfred Lopéz's (2007) "Introduction: The (Post) Global South" in *The Global South*.
26. See also Naomi Klein's discussion of "sacrificial zones" (in the context of global climate change) in *This Changes Everything: Capitalism vs. the Climate* (2015).
27. See also Dipesh Chakrabarty's (2009) "The Climate of History: Four Theses," in which he interrogates questions of subalternity and agency in the context of the Anthropocene. Chakrabarty remarks: "What scientists have said about climate change challenges not only the ideas about the human that usually sustain the discipline of history but also the analytic strategies that postcolonial and postimperial historians have deployed in the last two decades in response to the postwar scenario of decolonization and globalization" (198).
28. See also Pheng Cheah's discussion of heterotemporality and worlding in *What Is a World?: On Postcolonial Literature as World Literature* (2016).
29. In the *raiyati* system, rights were collectivized as in a commons system. Under the *zamindari* system, peasants were taxed directly. See also Gyan Prakash's (1990a) discussion of land tenure in *Bonded Histories: Genealogies of Labour Servitude in Colonial India*.
30. *Midnight's Children* has received a great deal of critique for a perceived endorsement of liberal capitalism. Amongst its virtues, however, is certainly its representation of a sort of "multiculture" from below, rendered in the bloody scenes that accompanied the language marches for example.
31. See Frauke Huber and Uwe Martin's documentary film *White Gold: Killing Seeds* (2009) for further discussion of what Vandana Shiva calls "suicide seeds."
32. I take the term "transcorporeality" from Stacy Alaimo's *Bodily Natures: Science, Environment, and the Material Self* (2010) wherein she describes the mutually constitutive role of human and nonhuman agents in their respective ecologies. The term "geontopower" is defined by Elizabeth Povinelli in *Geontologies: A Requiem for Late Liberalism* (2016) as a mode of power framed by the distinction between life and nonlife—a critique of notions of *bios* such as are employed in conventionally biopolitical readings of power.

33. I take the term "wastelanding" from Traci Brynne Voyles's *Wastelanding: Legacies of Uranium Mining in Navajo Country* (2015).
34. See again Ghosh's "Petrofiction: The Oil Encounter and the Novel" (1992). See also Szeman's (2017) "Conjectures on World Energy Literature: Or, What Is Petroculture?" for a discussion of oil fiction as well as Szeman and Boyer's introduction to the anthology *Energy Humanities* (2016).

CHAPTER ONE

1. See Carl Trocki's remarks in *Opium, Empire, and the Global Political Economy: A Study of the Asian Opium Trade* (1999).
2. See the final report of the 1894 Royal Commission on Opium. John Richards asserts: "Clearly, the attack on Indian opium use was a form of cultural imperialism. The reformers unanimously regarded opium consumption (other than for the most direct medical purpose) as disgusting and degrading. This was a foreign judgment that had its roots in European or western culture and society. It was a judgment that, among many others, condemned the practices and customs of India and the Orient. It was also a judgment intimately tied to that version of Protestant Christianity practiced in the British Isles in the late nineteenth century and disseminated by missionaries in India. As their testimony to the Royal Commission on Opium revealed, British and American Protestant missionaries were the most fervent anti-opium witnesses" (418). Timothy Mo's 1986 novel *An Insular Possession* dramatizes the impact of the Opium Wars on Hong Kong and Canton, also tracking the trade between China, India, and England; but the geographical locus is primarily on the Chinese side of the trade.
3. Lascar is "a fluid term used to describe sailors from the Indian Ocean region employed on European vessels. Although sometimes used only to denote south Asian seafarers, it might also include those of south-east Asian, Arab, or African origin" (Jaffer 2013, 153).
4. Matthew Edney refers to the English victory at the Battle of Plassey in 1757, and the subsequent granting of the *diwan* as a sort of accident—a happy coincidence, that the British happened upon one of the "richest provinces of the Mughal empire" almost by chance (1997, 8). Adding to this, it was military force that secured their dominance: their seizure of the trade from the Mughal (or Malwa) regions joins an existing British program in which land tenancy was being transformed under British rule.
5. See discussions around transversality and the production of the "Human" as an onto-epistemological outgrowth of eighteenth-century science in the introduction. See also Mill's *Considerations on Representative Government* (1861).
6. "This era of primitive accumulation gave rise not only to the 'accumulation of capital' and the 'accumulation of men' (Foucault 1977, 221), but also a new world-praxis: Cheap Nature. This praxis was one of accumulating and organizing not only human bodies, but of assigning their value through the Humanity/Nature binary. That so many humans could be reassigned to the domain of the not-human (or not-quite human) allowed capitals and empires to treat them cheaply—even as this cheapening was fiercely resisted" (Moore, 2017, 600).
7. 1838 marks the opening of the novel; the EIC charter is dissolved in 1857.
8. As aforementioned, in Malm's *The Progress of this Storm: Nature and Society in a Warming World* (2018), he indicts new materialist critiques that afford agency to

coal or other nonhuman actors within the industrial revolution in England. Contra Malm's contention regarding the brute stuff of coal, anthropologist Elizabeth Povinelli avers that rocks can in fact live and die, and do so through their interactions with other ecological actors.
9. See Carl A. Trocki's discussion of "port polities" and "isolated production zones" in *Opium, Empire and the Global Political Economy* (1999).
10. See my discussion of Bakhtin's "chronotope of the road" and its relevance to the picaresque tradition in the introduction.
11. See Gilroy's discussion of the chronotope of the ship in his *Black Atlantic: Modernity and Double Consciousness* (1993).
12. See Meena Alexander's remarks in "Indian Ocean Crossings," Lecture, February 27, 2015.
13. The Ghazipur and Patna opium factories were the primary sites of opium production in the Bengal region at the time.
14. In De Quincey's essay entitled "Ceylon" (1890a), he refers to British rule as so much "vernal rain." He remarks: "True it is that the best of our gifts—peace, freedom, security and a new standard of public morality—these blessings are like sleep, like health, like innocence, like the eternal revolutions of day and night, which sink inaudibly into human hearts, leaving behind (as sweet vernal rains) no flaunting records of ostentation and parade" (454).
15. Speaking in the context of anti-apartheid discourse in South Africa, Isabel Hofmeyr (2019) notes: "One feature of this nationalist antiapartheid discourse was a turning away from the ocean, the site of imperial incursion, toward the land, the locus of the desired nation. More recently, a group of postapartheid black feminist scholars (of which Putuma forms a part) has sought to shift this balance, by reclaiming the ocean from a decolonizing perspective, foregrounding the histories of slavery that it brought, but also examining how one might unseat and reimagine these genealogies."
16. Significantly, Hofmeyr's model of "cosmopolitanism then, nationalism now" is itself problematic. As I discuss in the second chapter, there is neither such a neat cleavage between these two moments; nor should we romanticize early modern trade networks. The latter move has been criticized by scholars interesting in exposing the tyranny of free markets, which were quite rapacious in earlier periods as well. Nonetheless, Hofmeyr is quite right in that the "older diasporic networks" further complicate the aforementioned "neat thesis about continuity" or discontinuity.
17. Lin Zexu was the Chinese Imperial Commissioner during the Opium Wars.
18. See also E. M. Forster's 1924 novel *Passage to India* for Orientalist/popular representations of the sublime.
19. See also Mike Davis's *Late Victorian Holocausts: El Niño Famines and the Making of the Third World* (2002) for a discussion of how imperial strategies transformed naturally incurring drought-induced dearth into famine as well as Janam Mukherjee's discussion of the 1946 famine and the persistence of artificially induced famines in *Hungry Bengal* (2015).
20. See work on tropicality, the sublime, and the production of the other: Aldous Huxley's "Wordsworth in the Tropics" is a notable example of such positions; Arnold and Guha's *The Problem of Nature: Environment, Culture and European Expansion* (1996) also offers a robust critique of such conceptions of "nature"; Richard Grove's *Green Imperialism: Colonial Expansion, Tropical Island Edens and the*

Origins of Environmentalism (1996), albeit more conservative, serves as a useful companion to Crosby.
21. Several such painters also feature in the novel as a means of illustrating yet another colonial reality: "Indian painters and draftsman were now employed on a massive scale in these colonial institutions to execute maps, landscapes, and some of the great herbals of the late eighteenth and early nineteenth centuries" (Schiebinger and Swan 2005, 269).
22. The term is translated literally as "searcher" and is the title of a famous picaresque novel by Francisco de Quevedo—*El Buscón* (1626).
23. See Gayatri Chakravorty Spivak's *Nationalism and the Imagination* (2015) for a discussion of sepoy losses in WWII.

CHAPTER TWO

An earlier version of this chapter appeared in the Winter 2018 volume of *ISLE: Interdisciplinary Studies in Literature and Environment*. In his critique of *Animal's People*, Pablo Mukherjee cites the "politics of environmental toxicity" (2010, 134). In substituting "global," I refer to a global apartheid system that thrives on the persistent dispossession of places like Bhopal.

1. See William S. Gaud's "The Green Revolution: Accomplishments and Apprehensions," Presented at the Society for International Development, Washington, D.C. (8 March 1968). See also Akhil Gupta's *Postcolonial Developments: Agriculture in the Making of Modern India* (1998) and Benjamin Robert Siegel's *Hungry Nation: Food, Famine, and the Making of Modern India* (2018). For a substantial gloss of the perils of the "Green Revolution," see also Benjamin Siegel's "Whither Agriculture?: The 'Green Revolution' @ 50," publicbooks.org, January 14, 2019.
2. I refer to Oliver Goldsmith's characterization of the "laboring swain" in the 1770 *Deserted Village*. The picturesque tradition, however, is marked by such rhetoric more broadly.
3. John Barrell's *The Dark Side of Landscape: The Rural Poor in English Painting, 1730–1840* explores the human and more-than-human costs of such aesthetic traditions. Notable also for his work on Thomas De Quincey—*The Infection of Thomas De Quincey: A Psychopathology of Imperialism* (1991)—Barrell is interested in the "dark side" of aesthetic expression more broadly and the ways in which nineteenth-century landscape aesthetics aligned with the imperial interests of the British Empire.
4. It is imperative to note here the complicated and contested terrain of Wordsworth studies in which scholars might read the "Solitary Reaper," or "The Discharged Soldier," as gestures toward animating an otherwise atomized subject. But in his preface to the 1798 *Lyrical Ballads*, which is often understood as a sort of Romanticist manifesto, the poet makes clear the ways in which such figures are but "rustic subjects" appropriate for poetic representation and aesthetic inquiry. Notably too, "The Solitary Reaper" is written as the poet and his sister would travel the recently cleared Highlands region of Scotland; and the solitary song of the poetic subject is indeed, in the poem, rendered but an aspect of the broader "vale" that constitutes the Romantic vista of the Wordsworths' imaginations. Thus, we can understand the poem as a departure from Goldsmith, but must also remain alert to such problematic political representations.

5. See again Joseph Slaughter and arguments regarding "enabling fictions" in the introduction.
6. In Ghosh's *The Great Derangement: Climate Change and the Unthinkable*, the novelist also comments that such a wholesale development program—that which would include the billions of Indian citizens now excluded from such capital schemes—would culminate in the asphyxiation of much of the global population.
7. See discussion in introduction regarding Chris Abani's 2004 *GraceLand* and Daniel Alarcón's 2003 novella *City of Clowns*.
8. Kalamb's poem is featured in the documentary *Nero's Guests* (2009, dir. Deepa Bhatia) which scrutinizes consumer complicity in the farmer suicide crisis in a manner similar to the critique marshaled in *Animal's People*.
9. See also Jesse Oak Taylor's (2013) discussion of the "power of zero" in the context of international aid organizations such as we see fictionalized through Sinha's American doctor Elli's clinic.
10. Amongst the many volumes that attend to this historical phenomenon, Arundhati Roy's *The Doctor and the Saint: Caste, Race, and Annihilation of Caste* (2017) is very useful in its documentary of India's independence-era and post-independence caste politics.
11. In Patrick Chamoiseau's 1992 picaresque novel *Texaco*, the author describes the displaced communities of Fort du France (Martinique) as a "new proletariat without factories and without work."

CHAPTER THREE

1. Malm (2016b) defines the "fossil economy . . . as one of self-sustaining growth predicated on the growing consumption of fossil fuels and therefore generating a sustained growth in CO_2 emissions" (222).
2. See Carl Trocki's remarks in *Opium, Empire, and the Global Political Economy: A Study of the Asian Opium Trade* (1999). See also our discussion in chapter one.
3. Following the lead of the opium economy, local speculators were emboldened by company agents who would coopt the extant *Zamindari* system. See also Amitav Ghosh's representation of *asami* contracts in *Sea of Poppies*.
4. See Vidhi Doshi's essay "Coal India accused of bulldozing human rights amid production boom" for a discussion of eviction, dispossession, and human rights violations at the hands of CIL: https://www.theguardian.com/global-development/2016/jul/13/coal-india-accused-of-bulldozing-human-rights-mining-operations-amid-production-boom-amnesty-international.
5. For further discussion of land dispossession in coal bearing states, see also Patrik Oskarsson and Siddarth Sarren, "Adivasiness as Caste Expression and Land Rights Claim-Making in Central-Eastern India," *Journal of Contemporary Asia* 50.5 (2020): 684–95.
6. For further discussion of subterranean land rights in relation to India's colonial-era coal economy, see also Matthew Shutzer's "Subterranean Properties: India's Political Ecology of Coal" (2021).
7. See the complete report on "Coal in India": https://www.brookings.edu/wp-content/uploads/2019/03/fp_20190731_coal_in_india.pdf.
8. India's period of economic liberalization is marked by its entry into the so-called Washington Consensus—a series of free market economic policies represented by institutions like the World Bank and the International Monetary Fund. The 1995

GATT (General Agreement on Tariffs and Trade) is often seen as a pivotal turn in the nation's economic landscape.

9. In Timothy Mitchell's *Carbon Democracy: Political Power in the Age of Oil* (2011), the author traces the coterminous genealogies of fossil capital and the rise of modern democracy through the advent of new forms of labor solidarity in the age of coal-power—specifically within the context of the modern factory system—to its disintegration in the face of petroleum-based economies whose itinerant labor regimes lack the centralizing infrastructures to form labor unions.

10. The Sardar Sarovar dam, which is the second largest concrete dam in the world, is located on the Narmada River in Gujarat—Modi's home state and now the site of the nation's premier solar parks. Promising to offer electricity, via hydroelectric power, to millions of Indian citizens, the park received funding through the World Bank. Its construction was delayed for decades owing to the strident protest from community members and activists concerned about internal displacement.

11. See Amitav Ghosh's (2005a) aforementioned "Petrofiction: The Oil Encounter and the Novel," wherein the author coins the term in reference to explicit oil narratives. Energy Humanists have sought to expand this category in order to interrogate the centrality of fossil-fueled energy to artistic production more broadly. For a discussion of "oil fictions" and the genealogy of the genre, see Stacey Balkan and Swaralipi Nandi's "Reading our Contemporary Petrosphere" in *Oil Fictions: World Literature and our Contemporary Petrosphere* (2021).

12. I cite Malm here—the statement is to be found both in *Fossil Capital* (2016) and *The Progress of This Storm* (2018)—with the caveat that Malm's Cartesian perspective on the human and nonhuman subject, and correlative dismissal of Anthropocene timescales/narratives that push back against the Anglocentrism that he endorses, will be contested later in this chapter through a close reading of Yusoff's work and that of Critical Black Studies scholars interested to interrogate the imperium of what Yusoff calls the "white geology" and its impacts on the racialized discourses of biology and geology beginning in the nineteenth century.

13. See Ramachandra Guha and Juan Alier's discussion of Huxley's essay in their introduction to *Varieties of Environmentalism: Essays North and South* (1997).

14. By popular, I refer to the reception of such narratives in the Anglosphere. As I shall demonstrate in the conclusion, local resistance to extractivism is beginning to pose a viable threat to the industry; or perhaps beginning to make clear its deleterious impacts on local communities and their respective landscapes.

15. I read Balram and Ashok as such with the following caveat: the inverse of da Silva's *Homo Modernus* is not an amorphous subaltern, but an explicitly racialized subaltern subject living and agitating in informal sectors from Delhi to Gaza to Oaxaca to Dhanbad.

16. I use the term "praxis" following Sylvia Wynter's (2003) theorization of the category of Human within Enlightenment discourse.

17. There is ontological utility in recognizing the vitality of nonhuman actors, particularly when recognizing the correlative production of putatively inhuman and nonhuman subjects in the accumulation of cheap nature qua capital; and such utility—particularly in the cultivation of anti-imperialist conceptions of land use and development—it ought to be noted, is generally the purview of new materialist critiques of the sort that Tsing launches rather than conventionally posthumanist arguments.

18. Foucault's theory of "governmentality" upon which Chatterjee relies may be understood as "the way governments try to produce the citizen best suited to fulfill those government's policies"; "the organized practices through which subjects are governed"; and "the techniques and strategies by which a society is rendered governable." See Foucault (1991) *Discipline and Punish* and his lectures at the Collége de France (2010). Prashad also comments on the complicated relationship between national peasantries and industrial elites who would forge anticolonial relationships.
19. While it may be argued that the speculative is always already framed by the same imperial impulse that drives extractivism in the first place, we might instead consider Macarena Gómez-Barris's argument for the speculative as a model for organizing and resistance beyond the limitations of given forms—in her argument, the nation-state, here conventional reading practices.

CONCLUSION

1. In her exquisite indictment of neoliberal mythology, *A Paradise Built in Hell* (2009), Rebecca Solnit also considers the "surge of citizenship" that continually arises in the wake of disasters. Similarly, Ashley Dawson offers a stunning critique of such false beliefs in *Extreme Cities: The Peril and Promise of Urban Life in the Age of Climate Change* (2017). Here Dawson chronicles the spirited movements for social justice that arose across the denuded landscapes of New York City following Hurricane Sandy in 2012.
2. In a recent court decision, Energy Transfer Partners has been ordered to empty the Dakota Access Pipeline of all contents. See Jacey Fortin and Lisa Friedman's "Dakota Access Pipeline to Shut Down Pending Review, Federal Judge Rules," *New York Times*, July 6, 2020.
3. See Elizabeth Povinelli's discussion of the Karrabing in *Geontologies: A Requiem for Late Liberalism* (2016).
4. On infrastructural justice, see John G. Stehlin's *Cyclescapes of The Unequal City: Bicycle Infrastructure and Uneven Development* (2018).
5. National Council of Ayllus and Markas of Qullasuyu. See http://www.conamaq.org.
6. A decision by the Dutch Appeals Court (December 18, 2015) to allow for litigation by Nigerian farmers was the result of such campaigns. See "Dutch appeals court says Shell may be held liable for oil spills in Nigeria," *The Guardian*, December 22, 2015.
7. See again Dawson (2017). La Via Campesina is an international peasant movement that works to combat economic policies that favor capital-intensive agricultural programs over local peasant populations.
8. See Assa Doron and Robin Jeffrey's discussion of waste-picker protests and the legacy of environmental activism in *Waste of a Nation: Garbage and Growth in India* (2018).
9. See the full etymology of the name Dongria Kondh on the Survival International site—an international organization with whom they have aligned to fight against Vedanta Resources: https://www.survivalinternational.org/dongria.
10. Frederick Jackson Turner's frontier thesis epitomizes the supposed mandate of manifest destiny—the core of the civilizing campaigns of the mid- to latter nineteenth century which ostensibly aligned democracy with genocide. For an

incisive critique of the thesis and correlative aesthetic movements, see William Cronon's "The Trouble with Wilderness, or, Getting Back to the Wrong Nature" (1995).
11. This rhetorical move is directly inspired by Cymene Howe's speculative imaginings in the recent *Ecologics: Wind and Power in the Anthropocene* (2019), in which the anthropologist deploys the subjunctive in her critique of corporate windpower projects in the Mexico's isthmus of Tehuantepec.
12. See http://www.selcofoundation.org/aboutus.
13. See A. C. Wise's collection *Sunvault: Stories of Solarpunk and Eco-Speculation* for examples of the genre. See also the *Cultures of Energy* podcast episode with Rhys Williams: www.cultures of energy.com

References

Abani, Chris. 2004. *Graceland*. New York: Farrar, Strauss & Giroux.
Adeney, Katherine, and Lawrence Sáez, eds. 2005. *Coalition Politics and Hindu Nationalism*. London: Routledge.
Adiga, Aravind. 2008. *The White Tiger*. New York: The Free Press.
Agamben, Georgio. 2005. *State of Exception*. Chicago: University of Chicago Press.
Agrawal, Arun, and K. Sivaramakrishnan, eds. 2000. *Agrarian Environments: Resources, Representation, and Rule in India*. Durham, NC: Duke University Press.
Ahmad, Aijaz. 2005. "The Making of India." *Social Scientist* 33(11/12): 3–13.
Ahmed, Siraj. 2011. *The Stillbirth of Capital: Enlightenment Writing and Colonial India*. Stanford, CA: Stanford University Press.
Ahmed, Siraj. 2013. "Notes from Babel: Towards a Colonial History of Comparative Literature." *Critical Inquiry* 39(2): 296–326.
Ahmed, Waquar. 2011. "Neoliberal Utopia and Urban Realities in Delhi." *ACME: An International Journal for Critical Geographies* 10(2): 163–88.
Ahuja, Ravi. 2006. "Mobility and Containment: The Voyages of South Asian Seamen, c. 1900–1960." *International Review of Social History* 51(S14): 111–41.
Ahuja, Ravi. 2012. "Capital at Sea, Shaitan Below Decks? A Note on Global Narratives, Narrow Spaces, and the Limits of Experience." *History of the Present* 2(1): 78–85.
Alaimo, Stacy. 2010. *Bodily Natures: Science, Environment, and the Material Self*. Bloomington: Indiana University Press.
Alaimo, Stacy. 2019. "Afterword: Crossing Time, Space, and Species." *Environmental Humanities* 11(1): 239–41.
Al-Dabbagh, Abdulla. 2009. *Literary Orientalism, Postcolonialism, and Universalism*. New York: Peter Lang Publishing.
Alexander, Meena. 2015. "Indian Ocean Crossings." Lecture, Graduate Center, City University of New York. New York, NY. February 27, 2015.
Almond, Ian. 2006. "Rogues of Modernity: Picaresque Variations in the Postcolonial Genre of the Enlightenment Missionary." *Orbis Litterarum* 61(2): 96–113.
Alpert, Michael, trans. 1969. *Lazarillo de Tormes and The Swindler: Two Spanish Picaresque Novels*. London: Penguin.
Alter, Robert. 1965. *The Rogue's Progress: Studies in the Picaresque Novel*. Cambridge, MA: Harvard University Press.
Ambedkar, B. R. 2014. *Annihilation of Caste: The Annotated Critical Edition*. New York: Verso.
Amrith, Sunil. 2011. *Migration and Diaspora in Modern Asia*. Cambridge: Cambridge University Press.
Amrith, Sunil. 2013. *Crossing the Bay of Bengal: The Furies of Nature and the Fortunes of Migrants*. Cambridge, MA: Harvard University Press.

Anand, Mulk Raj. 2000. *Coolie*. Gurgaon: Penguin India.
Anand, Mulk Raj. 1940. *Untouchable*. New York: Penguin.
Anderson, Clare. 2013. "The Age of Revolution in the Indian Ocean, Bay of Bengal, and South China Sea: A Maritime Perspective." *International Review of Social History* 58(S21): 229–51.
Andrade, Susan. 2011. *The Nation Writ Small: African Fictions and Feminisms, 1958–1988*. Durham, NC: Duke University Press.
Andrade, Susan. 2012. "Representing Slums and homes: Chis Abani's *Graceland*." In *The Legacies of Modernism: Historicising Postwar and Contemporary Fiction*, edited by David James, 225–42. New York: Cambridge University Press.
Arasaratnam, Sinnappah. 1986. *Merchants, Companies and Commerce on the Coromandel Coast, 1650–1740*. New Delhi: Oxford University Press.
Aravamudan, Srinivas. 1999. *Tropicopolitans: Colonialism and Agency, 1688–1804*. Durham, NC: Duke University Press.
Aravamudan, Srinivas. 2011. *Enlightenment Orientalism: Resisting the Rise of the Novel*. Chicago: University of Chicago Press.
Arendt, Hannah. 1963. "The Meaning of Revolution." In *On Revolution*, 11–48. New York: Penguin.
Arnold, David. 1996. *The Problem of Nature: Environment, Culture and European Expansion*. Cambridge, MA: Wiley-Blackwell.
Arnold, David, and Ramachandra Guha, eds. 1996. *Nature, Culture, Imperialism: Essays on the Environmental History of South Asia*. Delhi: Oxford University Press.
Arora, Anupama. 2015. "The Sea Is History: Opium, Colonialism, and Migration in Amitav Ghosh's *Sea of Poppies*." *ARIEL: A Review of International English Literature* 42(3–4): 21–42.
Azuela, Mariano. 2008. *The Underdogs: A Novel of the Mexican Revolution*. Translated by Sergio Weisman. New York: Penguin.
Baber, Zaheer. 1998. *The Science of Empire: Scientific Knowledge, Civilization, and Colonial Rule in India*. New Delhi: Oxford University Press.
Baden-Powell, Henry. 1907. *Land Systems of British India: Being a Manual of the Land Tenures and of the Systems of Land Revenue Prevalent in the Administration of Several Provinces*. London: Oxford.
Bakhtin, Mikhail. 1937. "Form of Time and Chronotope in the Novel." In *The Dialogic Imagination: Four Essays*, 84–258. Austin: University of Texas Press.
Bala, G., and Akhilesh Gupta. 2019. "Solar Geoengineering Research in India." *Bulletin of the American Meteorological Society* 100(1): 23–28.
Balkan, Stacey. 2015. "Rogues in the Postcolony: Chris Abani's *GraceLand* and the Petro-Picaresque." *The Global South* 9(2): 18–37.
Balkan, Stacey. 2016. *Rogues in the Postcolony: The New Picaresque and the Making of Modern India*. PhD diss., City University of New York.
Balkan, Stacey. 2021a. "Documenting 'Cheap Nature' in Amitav Ghosh's *The Glass Palace*: A Petro-Aesthetic Critique." In *Oil Fictions: World Literature and Our Contemporary Petrosphere*, edited by Stacey Balkan and Swaralipi Nandi. University Park: Penn State University Press.
Balkan, Stacey. 2021b. "Energo-poetics: Reading Energy in the Ages of Wood, Oil, and Wind." In "Fossil Subjects," edited by Pablo Mukherjee, special issue, *Revue Etudes Anglaises* 74(1): 12–33.
Balkan, Stacey, and Swaralipi Nandi. 2021. "Reading our Contemporary Petrosphere." In *Oil Fictions: World Literature and our Contemporary Petrosphere*, edited

by Stacey Balkan and Swaralipi Nandi. University Park: Penn State University Press.
Barney, Darin, and Imre Szeman. 2019. "Solarity: Energy and Society after Oil—An introduction to *Solarity*." *Solarity*. www.afteroil.ca.
Barrell, John. 1983. *The Dark Side of Landscape: The Rural Poor in English Painting, 1730–1840*. Cambridge: Cambridge University Press.
Barrell, John. 1991. *The Infection of Thomas De Quincey: A Psychopathology of Imperialism*. New Haven, CT: Yale University Press.
Bartosh, Roman. 2012. "The Postcolonial Picaro in Indra Sinha's *Animal's People*: Becoming Posthuman through Animal's Eyes." *Ecozone* 3(1): 1–10.
Bataille, George. 1991. *The Accursed Share*. New York: Zone Books.
Batra, Kanika. 2013. "City Botany: Reading Urban Ecologies in China through Amitav Ghosh's *River of Smoke*." *Narrative* 21(3): 322–32.
Bayly, Christopher Alan. 1990. *Indian Society and the Making of the British Empire*. Cambridge: Cambridge University Press.
Bayman, Anna. 2007. "Rogues, Conycatching and the Scribbling Crew." *History Workshop Journal*, no. 63(Spring): 1–17.
BBC. 2010. "Bhopal Trial: Eight Convicted over India Gas Disaster." June 7, 2010. http://news.bbc.co.uk.
Bellamy, Brent Ryan, and Jeff Diamanti, eds. 2018. "Materialism and the Critique of Energy." Special issue, *Meditations* 31(2).
Bellamy, Brent Ryan, Michael O'Driscoll, and Mark Simpson. 2016. "Introduction: Toward a Theory of Resource Aesthetics." *Postmodern Culture* 26(2). doi:10.1353/pmc.2016.0010.
Benanav, Michael. 2020. "Portraits of Everyday Life in the Indian State of Gujarat." *New York Times*, June 18, 2020.
Benito-Vessels, Carmen, and Michael Zappala. 1994. *The Picaresque: A Symposium on the Rogue's Tale*. Newark: University of Delaware.
Bennett, Jane. 2010. *Vibrant Matter: A Political Ecology of Things*. Durham, NC: Duke University Press.
Berlant, Lauren. 2011. *Cruel Optimism*. Durham, NC: Duke University Press.
Bermingham, Ann. 1989. *Landscape and Ideology: The English Rustic Tradition*. Berkeley: University of California Press.
Bhattacharya, Soumya. 2008. "*The White Tiger* by Aravind Adiga: Tales from the Shadowy Side of Booming India." *Independent*, April 11, 2008.
Bhatia, Deepa, dir. 2009. *Nero's Guests*. Mistral Movies.
Blackburn, Alexander. 1979. *The Myth of the Picaro: Continuity and Transformation in the Picaresque Novel, 1554–1954*. Chapel Hill: University of North Carolina Press.
Bloomberg, Michael, and Carl Pope. 2017. *Climate of Hope: How Cities, Businesses, and Citizens Can Save the Planet*. New York: St. Martin's Press.
Blum, Hester. 2010. "The Prospect of Oceanic Studies." *PMLA* 125(3): 670–77.
Boetzkes, Amanda. 2016. "Resource Systems, the Paradigm of Zero-Waste, and the Desire for Sustenance." *Postmodern Culture: Journal of Interdisciplinary Thought on Contemporary Cultures* 26(2). doi:10.1353/pmc.2016.0008.
Boetzkes, Amanda. 2017. "Solar." In *Fueling Culture: 101 Words for Energy and Environment*, edited by Imre Szeman, Jennifer Wenzel, and Patricia Yaeger, 314–17. New York: Fordham University Press.
Bonneuil, Christopher, and Jean-Baptiste Fressoz. 2016. *The Shock of the Anthropocene: The Earth, History and Us*. Translated by David Fernbach. New York: Verso.

Bose, Sugata. 1993. *Peasant Labour and Colonial Capital: Rural Bengal since 1770*, Cambridge: Cambridge University Press.
Bose, Sugata. 2009. *A Hundred Horizons: The Indian Ocean in the Age of Global Empire*. Cambridge, MA: Harvard University Press.
Boyer, Dominic. 2019. *Energopolitics: Wind and Power in the Anthropocene*. Durham, NC: Duke University Press.
Boyle, Danny, dir. 2008. *Slumdog Millionaire*. Celador Films and Film4 Productions.
Broughton, Edward. 2005. "The Bhopal Disaster and Its Aftermath: A Review." *Environmental Health* 4. doi:10.1186/1476-069X-4-6.
Burke, Edmund. 1887. "Ninth Report of the Select Committee of the House of Commons on the Affairs of India. June 25. 1783." In *The Works of the Right Honourable Edmund Burke in XII Volumes*. London: John C. Nimmo. Project Gutenberg.
Burton, Antoinette. 2012. "Amitav Ghosh's World Histories from Below." *History of the Present* 2(1): 71–77.
Carter, Marina. 1992. "Strategies of Labour Mobilisation in Colonial India: The Recruitment of Indentured Workers for Mauritius." *Journal of Peasant Studies* 19(3/4): 229–45.
Carter, Marina, and Khal Torabully. 2002. *Coolitude: An Anthology of the Indian Labour Diaspora*. London: Anthem Press.
Chakrabarty, Dipesh. 1992a. "Decoloniality and the Artifice of History: Who Speaks for 'Indian' Pasts?" In "Imperial Fantasies and Postcolonial Histories," special issue, *Representations*, no. 37, 1–26.
Chakrabarty, Dipesh. 1992b. "Of Garbage, Modernity and the Citizen's Gaze." *Economic and Political Weekly* 27(10): 541–47.
Chakrabarty, Dipesh. 2000a. *Provincializing Europe: Postcolonial Thought and Historical Difference*. Princeton: Princeton University Press.
Chakrabarty, Dipesh. 2000b. "Universalism and Belonging in the Logic of Late Capital." *Public Culture* 12(3): 653–78.
Chakrabarty, Dipesh. 2007. " 'In the Name of Politics': Democracy and the Power of the Multitude in India." *Public Culture* 19(1): 35–57.
Chakrabarty, Dipesh. 2008. "The Public Life of History: An Argument out of India." *Public Culture* 20(1): 143–68.
Chakrabarty, Dipesh. 2009. "The Climate of History: Four Theses." *Critical Inquiry* 35(2): 197–222.
Chakrabarty, Dipesh. 2019. "The Planet: An Emergent Humanist Category." *Critical Inquiry* 46(1): 1–31.
Chakravarti, A. K. 1973. "Green Revolution in India." *Annals of the Association of American Geographers* 63(3) 319–30.
Chambers, Claire. 2005. " 'The Absolute Essentialness of Conversations': A Discussion with Amitav Ghosh." *Journal of Postcolonial Writing* 41(1): 26–39.
Chambers, Iain. 2010. "Maritime Criticism and Theoretical Shipwrecks." *PMLA* 125(3): 678–84.
Chamoiseau, Patrick. 1997. *Texaco*. New York: Vintage.
Chandler, Frank Wadleigh. 1907. *The Literature of Roguery*. New York: Houghton Mifflin.
Chari, Sharad. 2017. "Detritus." *Fueling Culture: 101 Words for Energy and Environment*, edited by Imre Szeman, Jennifer Wenzel, and Patricia Yaeger. New York: Fordham University Press.

Chatterjee, Partha. 1993. *The Nation and its Fragments*. Princeton: Princeton University Press.
Chatterjee, Partha. 1998. *The Present History of West Bengal*. New Delhi: Oxford University Press.
Chatterjee, Partha. 2006. *The Politics of the Governed: Reflections on Popular Politics in Most of the World*. New York: Columbia University Press.
Chatterjee, Upamanyu. 1997. "Rambling at Fifty." *India Today*, August 18, 1997.
Cheah, Pheng. 2016. *What Is a World?: On Postcolonial Literature as World Literature*. Durham, NC: Duke University Press.
Chew, Shirley. 2013. "Roots and Routes: On Amitav Ghosh's *Sea of Poppies*." In *Writing India Anew: Indian English Fiction 2000–2010*, edited by Krishna Sen and Rituparna Roy, 47–58. Amsterdam: Amsterdam University Press.
Choudhury, Chandrahas. 2011. "Fashioning Narrative Pleasures from Narcotic Ones." Review. *New York Times*, October 7, 2011.
Cohen, G. A. 1995. *Self-Ownership, Freedom and Equality*. Cambridge: Cambridge University Press.
Cohen, Margaret. 2006. "The Chronotopes of the Sea." In *The Novel: Volume II, Forms and Themes*, edited by Franco Moretti, 647–66. Princeton: Princeton University Press.
Cohen, Margaret. 2010a. "Literary Studies on the Terraqueous Globe." *PMLA* 125(3): 657–62.
Cohen, Margaret. 2010b. *The Novel and the Sea*. Princeton: Princeton University Press.
Cohn, Bernard S. 1980. "History and Anthropology: The State of Play." *Comparative Studies in Society and History* 22(2): 198–221.
Cohn, Bernard S. 1996. *Colonialism and Its Forms of Knowledge: The British in India, Princeton Studies in Culture/Power/History*. Princeton: Princeton University Press.
Colebrook, Claire. 2017. "We Have Always Been Post-Anthropocene: The Anthropocene Counter-Factual." In *Anthropocene Feminism*, edited by Richard Grusin. Minneapolis: Minnesota University Press.
Connelly, William. 2017. *Facing the Planetary: Entangled Humanism and the Politics of Swarming*. Durham, NC: Duke University Press.
Cronon, William. 1995. "The Trouble with Wilderness, or Getting Back to the Wrong Nature." In *Uncommon Ground: Rethinking the Human Place in Nature*, edited by William Cronon, 69–90. New York: W. W. Norton.
Crosby, Alfred. 2004. *Ecological Imperialism: The Biological Expansion of Europe, 900–1900*. New York: Cambridge University Press.
Cross, Jamie. 2017. "Solar Basics." In "Little Development Devices / Humanitarian Goods," *Limn* 9 (November). http://limn.it.
Cross, Jamie. 2019. "The Solar Good: Energy Ethics in Poor Markets." *Journal of the Royal Anthropological Institute* 25(S1): 47–66.
Cutt, Elmer H. 1953. "The Background of Macaulay's Minute." *The American Historical Review* 58(4): 824–53.
Dalrymple, William. 2007. "Plain Tales from British India." Review. *New York Review of Books*. April 26, 2007.
Dalrymple, William. 2015. "The East India Company: The Original Corporate Raiders." *Guardian*, March 4, 2015.
Dasgupta, Rana. 2009. "Capital Gains." *Granta*, no. 107 (Summer): 77–107.
Dasgupta, Rana. 2014. *Capital: The Eruption of Delhi*. New York: Penguin.

Dasgupta, Sugata. 1968. *A Great Society of Small Communities: The Story of India's Land Gift Movement*. New Delhi: Indraprastha Press.

Datta, Ayona. 2012. " 'Mongrel City': Cosmopolitan Neighbourliness in a Delhi Squatter Settlement." *Antipode* 44(3): 745–63.

Davies, Thom. 2019. "Slow Violence and Toxic Geographies: 'Out of Sight' to Whom?" *Environment and Planning C: Politics and Space*, 1–19. doi:10.1177/2399654419841063.

Davis, Mike. 2002. *Late Victorian Holocausts: El Niño Famines and the Making of the Third World*. New York: Verso.

Davis, Mike. 2006. *Planet of Slums*. New York: Verso.

Dawson, Ashley. 2009. "Another Country: The Postcolonial State, Environmentality, and Landless People's Movements." In *Democracy, States, and the Struggle for Global Justice*, edited by Omar Dahbour, Ashley Dawson, Heather Gautney, and Neil Smith. New York: Routledge.

Dawson, Ashley. 2010. "Introduction: New Enclosures." *New Formations*, no. 69: 8–22.

Dawson, Ashley. 2011. "Surplus City: Structural Adjustment, Self-Fashioning, and Urban Insurrection in Chris Abani's *Graceland*." *Interventions* 11(1): 16–34.

Dawson, Ashley. 2015. "Introduction: Radical Materialism." *Social Text*, no. 122. http://socialtextjournal.org.

Dawson, Ashley. 2017. *Extreme Cities: The Peril and Promise of Urban Life in the Age of Climate Change*. New York: Verso.

Dawson, Ashley. 2021. "Energy & Autonomy: Worker Struggles and the Evolution of Energy Systems." In *Oil Fictions: World Literature and our Contemporary Petrosphere*, edited by Stacey Balkan and Swaralipi Nandi. University Park: Penn State University Press.

De Quincey, Thomas. 1890a. "Ceylon." In *De Quincey's Collected Writings, Volume VII*, edited by David Masson, 427–56. Edinburgh: Adam and Charles Black.

De Quincey, Thomas. 1890b. "The Chinese Question in 1857." In *De Quincey's Collected Writings, Volume XIV*, edited by David Masson, 345–67. Edinburgh: Adam and Charles Black.

De Quincey, Thomas. 1890c. "The Opium Question with China in 1840." In *De Quincey's Collected Writings, Volume XIV*, edited by David Masson, 162–205. Edinburgh: Adam and Charles Black.

De Quincey, Thomas. 1890d. "The English in India." In *The Uncollected Writings of Thomas De Quincey*, edited by James Hogg, 298–353. London: Swan Sonnenschein.

De Quincey, Thomas. 1966. "West India Property." In *New Essays by De Quincey: His Contributions to the Edinburgh Saturday Post and the Edinburgh Evening Post 1827–1828*, edited by Stuart M. Tave, 358–87. Princeton: Princeton University Press.

De Quincey, Thomas. 1985. *Confessions of an English Opium Eater*. In *Confessions of an English Opium Eater and Other Writings*, edited by Grevel Lindop, 1–80. New York: Oxford University Press.

Deb, Debal. 2009. *Beyond Developmentality: Constructing Inclusive Freedom and Sustainability*. New York: Routledge.

Debaise, Didier. 2017. *Nature as Event*. Durham, NC: Duke University Press.

Deckard, Sharae. 2019. "Land, Water, Waste: Environment and Ecology in South Asian Fiction." *The Oxford History of the Novel in English, Volume 10: The Novel in South and South-East Asia Since 1945*. London: Oxford University Press.

Deckard, Sharae, Nicholas Lawrence, Neil Lazarus, Graeme Macdonald, Pablo Mukherjee, Benita Parry, and Stephen Shapiro. 2015. *Combined and Uneven*

Development: Towards a New Theory of World-Literature. Liverpool: Liverpool University Press.

Delaney, Martin. 1971. *Blake, or the Huts of America*. Boston: Beacon Press.

Derrida, Jacques. 2005. *Rogues: Two Essays on Reason*. Stanford, CA: Stanford University Press.

Derrida, Jacques, and Avital Ronell. 1980. "The Law of Genre." *Critical Inquiry* 7(1): 55–81.

Desai, Darshan. 2013. "The Sunshine State." *The Hindu*, May 5, 2013.

Desai, Gaurav. 2004. "Old World Orders: Amitav Ghosh and the Writing of Nostalgia." *Representations* 85(1): 125–48.

Desai, Gaurav. 2007. "The Scholar and the State." *The Global South* 1(1): 98–108.

Desai, Gaurav. 2010. "Oceans Connect: The Indian Ocean and African Identities." *PMLA* 125(3): 713–20.

Desai, Gaurav. 2013. *Commerce with the Universe: Africa, India, and the Afrasian Imagination*. New York: Columbia University Press.

Descartes, René. 1996. *Meditations on First Philosophy: With Selections from the Objections and Replies*. Cambridge: Cambridge University Press.

Detmers, Ines. 2011. "New India? New Metropolis? Reading Aravind Adiga's *The White Tiger* as a 'Condition-of-India Novel.'" *Journal of Postcolonial Writing* 47(5): 535–45.

Devi, Mahasweta. 1995. *Imaginary Maps*. Translated by Gayatri Chakravorty Spivak. New York: Routledge.

Dionne, Craig. 2006. *Rogues and Early Modern Culture*. Ann Arbor: University of Michigan Press.

Dirks, Nicholas B. 2006. *The Scandal of Empire: India and the Creation of Imperial Britain*. Cambridge, MA: Harvard University Press.

Dixon, Conrad. 1980. "Lascars: The Forgotten Seamen." In *Working Men Who Got Wet*, edited by R. Ommer and G. Pantma. St. Johns: Maritime History Group, Memorial University of Newfoundland.

Doron, Assa and Robin Jeffrey. 2018. *Waste of a Nation: Garbage and Growth in India*. Cambridge, MA: Harvard University Press.

Doshi, Vidhi. 2016. "Coal India Accused of Bulldozing Human Rights Amid Production Boom," *Guardian*, July 13, 2016.

Dunn, Peter N. 1990. "Spanish Picaresque Form as a Problem of Genre." In "Genre Studies in Hispanic Literature," special issue, *Dispositio* 15(39): 1–15.

Edney, Matthew. 1997. *Mapping an Empire: The Geographical Construction of British India, 1765–1843*. Chicago: University of Chicago Press.

Elliot, Jane, and Gillian Harkins. 2013. "Introduction: Genres of Neoliberalism." *Social Text Online*, no. 115: 1–18. http://socialtextjournal.org.

Engel-Ledeboer, M. S. J., and H. Engel. 1964. *Carolus Linnaeus: Systema Naturae 1735*. Leiden: Brill.

Esty, Joshua D. 1999. "Excremental Postcolonialism." *Contemporary Literature* 40(1): 22–59.

Ewald, Janet J. 2000. "Crossers of the Sea: Slaves, Freedmen, and Other Migrants in the Northwestern Indian Ocean, c. 1750–1914." *American Historical Review* 105(1): 69–92.

Fanon, Franz. 1995. *The Wretched of the Earth*. New York: Grove Press.

Federici, Sylvia. 2004. *Caliban and the Witch: Women, the Body, and Primitive Accumulation*. Brooklyn: Autonomedia.

Fernandes, Walter. 2012. "Land, Environmental Degradation and Conflicts in Northeastern India." In *Agriculture and a Changing Environment in Northeastern India*, edited by Sumi Krishna. London: Routledge.

Ferreira da Silva, Denise. 2007. *Toward a Global Idea of Race*. Minneapolis: University of Minnesota Press.

Fisher, Michael H. 1991. *Indirect Rule in India: Residents and the Residency System, 1764–1858*. Delhi: Oxford University Press.

Fisher, Michael H. 2006. "Working Across the Seas: Indian Maritime Labourers in India, Britain, and in Between, 1600–1857." *International Review of Social History* 51(S14): 21–45.

Fortin, Jacey, and Lisa Friedman. 2020. "Dakota Access Pipeline to Shut Down Pending Review, Federal Judge Rules." *New York Times*, July 6, 2020.

Fortun, Kim. 2001. *Advocacy after Bhopal: Environmentalism, Disaster, New Global Orders*. Chicago: University of Chicago Press.

Foster, John Bellamy. 2000. *Marx's Ecology: Materialism and Nature*. New York: Monthly Review Press.

Foucault, Michel. 1991. *Discipline and Punish: The Birth of the Prison*. New York: Vintage.

Foucault, Michel. 2010. *The Birth of Biopolitics: Lectures at the Collège de France, 1978–1979*. New York: Picador.

Frankel, Francine R. 1971. *India's Green Revolution: Economic Gains and Political Costs*. Princeton: Princeton University Press.

Frohock, W. M. 1967. "The 'Picaresque' in France Before *Gil Blas*." In "The Classical Line: Essays in Honor of Henry Peyre," special issue, *Yale French Studies*, no. 38: 222–29.

Frykman, N., C. Anderson, L. Heerma van Voss, and M. Rediker. 2013. "Mutiny and Maritime Radicalism in the Age of Revolution: An Introduction." *International Review of Social History* 58(S21): 1–14.

Gadgil, Madhav, and Ramachandra Guha. 1989. "State Forestry and Social Conflict in British India." *Past and Present* 123(1): 41–77.

Gajarawala, Toral. 2009. "The Last and the First." *Economic and Political Weekly* 44(50): 21–23.

Galeano, Eduardo. 1997. *The Open Veins of Latin America: Five Centuries of the Pillage of a Continent*. New York: Monthly Review Press.

Ganzeer. 2016. *The Solar Grid*. Graphic novel series. www.thesolargrid.net.

Gee, E. R. 1940. "History of Coal Mining in India." *F.G.S. Geological Survey of India* 6(3): 313–18.

Ghosh, Amitav. 1992. "Petro-Fictions." *Incendiary Circumstances: A Chronicle of the Turmoil of Our Times*, 138–51. New York: Houghton Mifflin.

Ghosh, Amitav. 1993. "Lessons From the 12th Century." Interview with Gretchen Lushsinger. *Newsweek*, December 13, 1993.

Ghosh, Amitav. 2002a. Correspondence with Dipesh Chakrabarty. https://www.amitavghosh.com.

Ghosh, Amitav. 2002b. *The Glass Palace*. New York: Random House.

Ghosh, Amitav. 2005a. *The Hungry Tide*. New York: Houghton Mifflin.

Ghosh, Amitav. 2005b. "Petrofiction." In *Incendiary Circumstances: A Chronicle of the Turmoil of Our Times*, 138–51. New York: Houghton Mifflin.

Ghosh, Amitav. 2008a. "Of Fanás and Forecastles: The Indian Ocean and Some Lost Languages of the Age of Sail." *Economic and Political Weekly*, June 21, 2008.

Ghosh, Amitav. 2008b. *Sea of Poppies*. New York: Picador.
Ghosh, Amitav. 2011. *River of Smoke*. New York: Picador.
Ghosh, Amitav. 2015a. *Flood of Fire*. New York: Picador.
Ghosh, Amitav. 2015b. "Flood of Fire: Reading and Discussion." Lecture, McNally Jackson Bookstore, New York, September 16, 2015.
Ghosh, Amitav. 2015c. "The Great Derangement: Fiction, History, and Politics in the Age of Global Warming." Lecture, Berlin Family Lectures, University of Chicago, Chicago, September 29, 2015.
Ghosh, Amitav. 2016. *The Great Derangement: Climate Change and the Unthinkable*. Chicago: University of Chicago Press.
Gilman, Stephen. 1966. "The Death of Lazarillo de Tormes." *PMLA* 81(3): 149–66.
Gilroy, Paul. 1993. *The Black Atlantic: Modernity and Double Consciousness*. Cambridge, MA: Harvard University Press.
Goh, Robbie B. H. "The Overseas Indian and the Political Economy of the Body in Aravind Adiga's The *White Tiger* and Amitav Ghosh's *The Hungry Tide*." *Journal of Commonwealth Literature* 47(3): 341–56.
Goldsmith, Oliver. 1770. *The Deserted Village*. Project Gutenberg. www.gutenberg.org.
Gómez-Barris, Macarena. 2017. *The Extractive Zone: Social Ecologies and Decolonial Perspectives*. Durham, NC: Duke University Press.
Greenblatt, Stephen. 2012. "Invisible Bullets: Renaissance Authority and Its Subversion, *Henry IV* and *Henry V*." In *Political Shakespeare: Essays in Cultural Materialism*, 2nd ed., edited by J. Dollimore and A. Sinfeld, 18–47. Manchester: Manchester University Press.
Grove, Richard H. 1996. *Green Imperialism: Colonial Expansion, Tropical Island Edens and the Origins of Environmentalism, 1600–1860*. Cambridge: Cambridge University Press.
Guardian. 2015. "Dutch Appeals Court Says Shell May Be Held Liable for Oil Spills in Nigeria." December 18, 2015.
Guha, Ramachandra. 1983. "Colonialism, Capitalism and Deforestation." *Social Scientist* 11(4): 61–64.
Guha, Ramachandra. 1989. *The Unquiet Woods: Ecological Change and Peasant Resistance in the Himalayas*. New Delhi: Oxford University Press.
Guha, Ramachandra. 1990. "An Early Environmental Debate: The Making of the 1878 Forest Act." *Indian Economic and Social History Review* 27(1): 65–84.
Guha, Ramachandra. 2002. "Environmentalist of the Poor." *Economic and Political Weekly* 37(3): 204–7.
Guha, Ramachandra. 2008. *India after Gandhi: The History of the World's Largest Democracy*. New York: Harper.
Guha, Ramachandra, and Juan Martinez Alier. 1997. *Varieties of Environmentalism: Essays North and South*. New York: Routledge.
Guha, Ranajit. 1988a. "The Prose of Counter-Insurgency." In *Selected Subaltern Studies*, edited by Gayatri Chakravorty Spivak and Ranajit Guha, 45–88. New York: Oxford University Press.
Guha, Ranajit. 1988b. "On Some Aspects of the Historiography of Colonial India." In *Selected Subaltern Studies*, edited by Gayatri Chakravorty Spivak and Ranajit Guha, 37–44. New York: Oxford University Press.
Guha, Ranajit. 1996. *A Rule of Property for Bengal: An Essay on the Idea of Permanent Settlement*. Durham, NC: Duke University Press.

Guilhamon, Lise. 2011. "Global Languages in the Time of the Opium Wars: The Lost Idioms of Amitav Ghosh's Sea of Poppies." *Commonwealth* 34(1): 67.
Guillén, Claudio. 1971. *Literature as System: Essays Toward the Theory of Literary History*. Princeton, NJ: Princeton University Press.
Guillén, Claudio. 1987. *The Anatomies of Roguery: The Origins and the Nature of Picaresque Literature*. New York: Garland.
Gupta, Akhil. 1998. *Postcolonial Developments: Agriculture in the Making of Modern India*. Durham, NC: Duke University Press.
Gupta, Akhil. 2015. "An Anthropology of Electricity from the Global South." *Cultural Anthropology* 30(4): 555–68.
Guru, Gopal. 2015. "They Always Speak with their Eyes Cast Down: Dalits on the Margin of Indian Democracy." In "Indian Politics under Modi," special issue, *Social Text Online*, February 27, 2015. http://socialtextjournal.org.
Han, Stephanie. 2013. "Amitav Ghosh's Sea of Poppies: Speaking Weird English." *The Explicator* 71(4): 298–301.
Haraway, Donna. 2016. *Staying with the Trouble: Making Kin in the Chthulucene*. Durham, NC: Duke University Press.
Harrison, Mark. 1999. *Climates and Constitutions: Health, Race, Environment and British Imperialism in India, 1600–1850*. New Delhi: Oxford University Press.
Harvey, David. 2001. "Globalization and the 'Spatial Fix.'" *Geographische Revue* 2: 23–30.
Harvey, David. 2005. *The New Imperialism*. New York: Oxford University Press.
Harvey, David. 2007. *A Brief History of Neoliberalism*. New York: Oxford University Press.
Harvey, David. 2011. "The Future of the Commons." *Radical History Review* 2011(109): 101–7.
Hatmaker, Susan. 2017. "Coal Ash." In *Fueling Culture: 101 Words for Energy and Environment*, edited by. Imre Szeman, Jennifer Wenzel, and Patricia Yaeger. New York: Fordham University Press.
Hemalatha, Karthikeyan. 2019. "'Our Livelihood Depends on This Land': A Solar Park in Gujarat Is Hurting a Pastoral Community." *Scroll*, August 6, 2019.
Hensley, Nathan K., and Philip Steer. 2018. "Signatures of the Carboniferous: The Literary Forms of Coal." *Ecological Form: System and Aesthetics in the Age of Empire*. New York: Fordham University Press.
Hitchcock, Peter. 2000. "They Must be Represented? Problems in Theory of Working-Class Representation." *PMLA* 115: 20–32.
Hitchcock, Peter. 2003. "The Genre of Postcoloniality." *New Literary History* 42(2): 299–330.
Hitchcock, Peter. 2016. "Energy Bars." *Reviews in Cultural Theory* 6(3): 22–24.
Hofmeyr, Isabel. 2007. "The Black Atlantic Meets the Indian Ocean: Forging New Paradigms of Transnationalism for the Global South Literary and Cultural Perspectives." *Social Dynamics*, 33(2): 3–32.
Hofmeyr, Isabel. 2010. "Universalizing the Indian Ocean." *PMLA* 125(3): 721–29.
Hofmeyr, Isabel. 2012. "The Complicating Sea: The Indian Ocean as Method." *Comparative Studies of South Asia, Africa and the Middle East* 32(3): 584–90.
Hofmeyr, Isabel. 2019. "Provisional Notes on Hydrocolonialism." *English Language Notes* 57(1): 11–20.
Howe, Cymene. 2019. *Ecologics: Wind and Power in the Anthropocene*. Durham, NC: Duke University Press.
Huber, Frauke, and Uwe H., dirs. 2009. Martin *White Gold: Killing Seeds*.

Huggan, Graham. 1995. "Decolonizing the Map." In *The Postcolonial Studies Reader*, edited by Bill Ashcroft and Gareth Griffiths, 407–11. London: Routledge.
Jaffer, Aaron. 2013. " 'Lord of the Forecastle': Serangs, Tindals, and Lascar Mutiny, c. 1780–1860." *International Review of Social History* 58(21): 153–75.
James, C. L. R. 1953. *Mariners, Renegades and Castaways: The Story of Herman Melville and the World We Live In*. Hanover, NH: Dartmouth College Press.
Jameson, Frederic. 1982. *The Political Unconscious: Narrative as a Socially Symbolic Act*. Ithaca, NY: Cornell University Press.
Joseph, Manu. 2012. "In Search of the Indian in Indian English Literature." *New York Times* January 18, 2012.
Joshi, Gaurav, and Komali Yennetti. 2010. "Community Solar Energy Initiatives in India: A Pathway for Addressing Energy Poverty and Sustainability?" In "Energy Poverty Varieties," edited by Komali Yennetti, Oleg Golubchikov, Roberto Lamberts, special issue, *Energy & Buildings* 210: 1–14.
Kalyan, Rohan. 2014. "The Magicians' Ghetto: Moving Slums and Everyday Life in a Postcolonial City." *Theory, Culture & Society* 31(1): 49–73.
Kerr, Ian J. 2006. "On the Move: Circulating Labor in Pre-Colonial, Colonial, and Post-Colonial India." *International Review of Social History* 51(S14): 85–109.
Khan, Sami Ahmad. 2016. "Others in India's Other Futures." *Science Fiction Studies* 43(3): 479–95.
Kincaid, Jamaica. 1996. "The Flowers of Empire." *Harper's Magazine* (April): 28–31.
Kinney, Arthur F. 1973. *Rogues, Vagabonds, & Sturdy Beggars: A New Gallery of Tudor and Early Stuart Rogue Literature Exposing the Lives, Times, and Cozening Tricks of the Elizabethan Underworld*. Barre, MA: Imprint Society.
Klein, Naomi. 2015. *This Changes Everything: Capitalism vs. the Climate*. New York: Simon and Schuster.
Kooria, Mahmood. 2012. "Between the Walls of Archives and Horizons of Imagination: An Interview with Amitav Ghosh." *Itinerario* 36(3): 7–18.
Koven, Seth. 2006. "Introduction: Eros and Altruism in Victorian London." In *Slumming: Sexual and Social Politics in Victorian London*, 1–22. Princeton, NJ: Princeton University Press.
Kumar, Ankit. 2015. "Cultures of Lights." *Geoforum* 65: 59–68. doi:10.1016/j.geoforum.2015.07.012.
Kumar, Rajiv. 1981a. "Nationalisation by Default: The Case of Coal in India, Part I." *Economic and Political Weekly* 16(17): 757–68.
Kumar, Rajiv. 1981b. "Nationalisation by Default: The Case of Coal in India, Part II." *Economic and Political Weekly* 16(18): 824–30.
Larsen, Victoria Tietze. 2009. "Nicholas B. Dirks, *The Scandal of Empire: India and the Creation of Imperial Britain*." Review. *International Journal of the Classical Tradition* 16(1): 145–48.
Lauret, Sabine. 2011. "Re-mapping the Indian Ocean in Amitav Ghosh's: *Sea of Poppies*." *Commonwealth Essays and Studies* 34(1): 55–65.
Lazarus, Neil. 2011. *The Postcolonial Unconscious*. Cambridge: Cambridge University Press.
Le Guin, Ursula. 2020. *The Carrier Bag Theory of Fiction*. London: Ignota Books.
LeMenager, Stephanie. 2014. *Living Oil: Petroleum Culture in the American Century*. New York: Oxford University Press.
Levine, Caroline. 2015. *Forms: Whole, Rhythm, Hierarchy, Network*. Princeton, NJ: Princeton University Press.

Linebaugh, Peter, and Marcus Rediker. 2012. *The Many-Headed Hydra: Sailors, Slaves, Commoners, and the Hidden History of the Revolutionary Atlantic*. Boston: Beacon Press.
Lionnet, Francoise. 1993. "Créolité in the Indian Ocean: Two Models of Cultural Diversity." *Yale French Studies* 82(1): 101–12.
Locke, John. 2002. *The Second Treatise of Government and A Letter Concerning Toleration*. New York: Dover Thrift.
Lopéz, Alfred. 2007. "Introduction: The (Post) Global South." *The Global South* 1(1): 1–11.
Lowe, Lisa. 1996. *Immigrant Acts: On Asian American Cultural Politics*. Durham: Duke University Press, 1996.
Lowe, Lisa. 2015a. "History Hesitant." *Social Text* 33(4): 85–107.
Lowe, Lisa. 2015b. *The Intimacies of Four Continents*. Durham, NC: Duke University Press.
Ludden, David. 1999. *Agrarian History of South Asia*. Cambridge: Cambridge University Press.
Lukács, Georg. 1974. *The Theory of the Novel*. Cambridge, MA: Massachusetts Institute of Technology Press.
Lyell, Charles. 1997. *The Principles of Geography*. London: Penguin Classics.
Mahlstedt, Andrew. 2013. "Animal's Eyes: Spectacular Invisibility and the Terms of Recognition in Indra Sinha's *Animal's People*." *Mosaic* 46(3): 59–74.
Maillol, J. M., M.-K. Seguin, O. P. Gupta, H. M. Akhauri, and N. Sen. 2003. "Electrical Resistivity Tomography Survey for Delineating Uncharted Mine Galleries in West Bengal, India." *Geophysical Prospecting* 47(2): 103–16.
Maiorino, Giancarlo. 2003. *At the Margins of the Renaissance: Lazarillo de Tormes and the Picaresque Art of Survival*. University Park: Pennsylvania State University Press.
Malm, Andreas. 2016a. *Fossil Capital: The Rise of Steam Power and the Roots of Global Warming*. New York: Verso.
Malm, Andreas. 2016b. "Who Lit This Fire? Approaching the History of the Fossil Economy." *Critical Historical Studies* 3(2): 215–48.
Malm, Andreas. 2018. *The Progress of this Storm: Nature and Society in a Warming World*. New York: Verso.
Mandel, Ernest. 1999. *Late Capitalism*. New York: Verso.
Mann, Charles. 2015. "Coal or Solar? The Energy India Picks May Decide Earth's Fate." *Wired* Dec 2015. https://www.wired.com/2015/11/climate-change-in-india.
Marx, Karl. 1973. *Grundrisse*. New York: Vintage.
Marx, Karl. 1978. "On Imperialism in India." In *Marx-Engels Reader*, edited by Robert C. Tucker, 653–64. New York: W. W. Norton, 1978.
Marx, Karl. 1981. *Capital Volume III*. Translated by David Fernbach. New York: Penguin.
Marx, Karl. 1990. *Capital Volume I*. New York: Penguin.
Marx, Karl. 1992. *Capital Volume II*. New York: Penguin.
Marx, Karl, and Frederick Engels. 1968. *On Colonialism*. Moscow: Progress Publishers.
Mbembe, Achille. 2013. "Necropolitics." *Public Culture* 15(1): 11–40.
McKittrick, Katherine, ed. 2015. *Sylvia Wynter: On Being Human as Praxis*. Durham, NC: Duke University Press.
McPherson, Kenneth. 1993. *The Indian Ocean: A History of People and the Sea*. Delhi: Oxford University Press.

Metcalf, Barbara D., and Thomas R. Metcalf. 2002. *A Concise History of India*. Cambridge: Cambridge University Press.
Metcalf, Thomas R. 2007. *Imperial Connections: India and the Indian Ocean Arena, 1860–1920*. Berkeley: University of California Press.
Mill, John Stuart. 1990. *The Collected Works of John Stuart Mill: XXX, Writings on India*. Edited by John M. Robson, Martin Moir, and Zawahir Moir. London: Routledge.
Mill, John Stuart. 2002. *On Liberty*. New York: Dover Thrift.
Miller, Stuart. 1967. *The Picaresque Novel*. Cleveland, OH: Case Western Reserve University Press.
Mishan, Ligaya. 2008. "Poisoned." Review. *New York Times*, March 9, 2008.
Mishra, Pankaj. 2006. "The Myth of the New India." *New York Times*, July 6, 2006.
Mitchell, Timothy. 2011. *Carbon Democracy: Political Power in the Age of Oil*. New York: Verso.
Mitra, Subrata K. 2011. *Politics in India: Structure, Process and Policy*. London: Routledge.
Mohapatra, Himansu S. 2013. "Babu Fiction in Disguise: Reading Aravind Adiga's *The White Tiger*." In *Writing India Anew*, edited by Krishna Sen and Rituparna Roy, 129–44. Amsterdam: Amsterdam University Press.
Mookerjea, Sourayan. 2018. "Accumulated Violence, or the Wars of Exploitation: Notes Toward a Post-Western Marxism." *Mediations* 32(1): 95–114.
Moore, Jason W. 2003. "Ecology & Imperialism." Review. *Monthly Review* 55(2): 58–62.
Moore, Jason W. 2015. *Capitalism in the Web of Life: Ecology and the Accumulation of Capital*. New York: Verso Books.
Moore, Jason W. 2016. *Anthropocene or Capitalocene?: Nature, History, and the Crisis of Capitalism*. Edited by Jason W. Moore. Oakland, CA: PM Press.
Moore, Jason W. 2017. "The Capitalocene, Part I: On the Nature and Origins of Our Ecological Crisis." *The Journal of Peasant Studies* 44(3): 594–630.
Moretti, Franco. 2000. *The Way of the World: The Bildungsroman in European Culture*. New York: Verso.
Morton, Timothy. 2013. *Hyperobjects: Philosophy and Ecology after the End of the World*. Minneapolis: University of Minnesota Press.
Moynagh, Maureen. 2011. "Human Rights, Child-Soldier Narratives, and the Problem of Form." *Research in African Literatures* 42(4): 39–59.
Mukherjee, Janam. 2015. *Hungry Bengal: War, Famine and the End of Empire*. New York: Oxford University Press.
Mukherjee, Meenakshi. 2000. *The Perishable Empire: Essays on Indian Writing in English*. London: Oxford University Press.
Mukherjee, Pablo Upamanyu. 2006. "Surfing the Second Waves: Amitav Ghosh's Tide Country." *New Formations: A Journal of Culture/Theory/Politics*, no. 59: 144–57.
Mukherjee, Pablo Upamanyu. 2010. *Postcolonial Environments: Nature, Culture and the Contemporary Indian Novel in English*. New York: Palgrave.
Mukherjee, Radhakamal. 1916. *The Foundations of Indian Economics*. London: Longmans Green.
Neeson, J. M. 1996. *Commoners: Common Right, Enclosure and Social Change in England, 1700–1820*. London: Cambridge University Press.
Nehru, Jawaharwal. 2004. *The Discovery of India*. New York: Penguin.
Nehru, Jawaharwal. 2007. "Tryst with Destiny." *Guardian*. April 30, 2007.

Nixon, Rob. 2011. *Slow Violence and the Environmentalism of the Poor*. Cambridge: Harvard University Press.
Nixon, Rob. 2012. "Neoliberalism, Genre, and 'The Tragedy of the Commons.'" *PMLA* 127(3): 593–99.
Nussbaum, Felicity, ed. 2003. *The Global Eighteenth Century*. Baltimore: Johns Hopkins University Press.
Oskarsson, Patrik, and Siddarth Sarren. 2019. "Adivasiness as Caste Expression and Land Rights Claim-Making in Central-Eastern India." *Journal of Contemporary Asia* 50(5): 831–47.
Owen, David Edward. 1934. *British Opium Policy in China and India*. New Haven, CT: Yale University Press.
Parenti, Christian. 2011. *Tropic of Chaos: Climate Change and the New Geography of Violence*. New York: Nation Books.
Patel, Raj, and Jason W. Moore. 2017. *A History of the World in Seven Cheap Things*. Berkeley: University of California Press.
Patnaik, Utsa, and Sam Moyo. 2009. "Origins of the Food Crisis in India and Developing Countries." *Monthly Review* 61(3).
Patnaik, Utsa, and Sam Moyo. 2011. *The Agrarian Question in the Neoliberal Era: Primitive Accumulation and the Peasantry*. Oxford: Fahamu.
Patterson, Orlando. 1985. *Slavery and Social Death: A Comparative Study*. Cambridge: Harvard University Press.
Pattullo, Henry. 1772. *An Essay upon the Cultivation of the Lands, and Improvements of the Revenues of Bengal*. London: T. Becket and P. A. de Hondt.
Pearson, Michael. 2003. *The Indian Ocean*. London: Routledge.
Perera, Sonali. 2014. *No Country: Working Class Writing in the Age of Globalization*. New York: Columbia University Press.
Povinelli, Elizabeth A. 2016. *Geontologies: A Requiem to Late Liberalism*. Durham, NC: Duke University Press.
Powys Whyte, Kyle. 2019. "Kyle Powys White." February 28, 2019. In *Cultures of Energy*, hosted by Dominic Boyer and Cymene Howe. Episode 166. http://culturesofenergy.com/166-kyle-powys-whyte.
Prakash, Gyan. 1990a. *Bonded Histories: Genealogies of Labor Servitude in Colonial India*. Cambridge: Cambridge University Press.
Prakash, Gyan. 1990b. "Writing Post-Orientalist Histories of the Third World: Perspectives from Indian Historiography." *Comparative Studies in Society and History* 32.2 (1990): 383–408.
Prakash, Gyan. 1992. "Postcolonial Criticism and Indian Historiography." *Social Text*, no. 31/32: 8–19.
Prashad, Vijay. 2001. "The Technology of Sanitation in Colonial Delhi." *Modern Asian Studies*. 35(1): 113–55.
Prashad, Vijay. 2007. *The Darker Nations*. New York: The New Press.
Rawson, Michael. 2010. *Eden on the Charles: The Making of Boston*. Cambridge: Harvard University Press.
Reddy, Sheela. 2008. "The Ghazipur and Patna Opium Factories Together Produced the Wealth of Britain." Interview with Amitav Ghosh. *Outlook*, May 26, 2008. https://magazine.outlookindia.com.
Reno, Josh. 2015. "Waste and Waste Management." *Annual Review of Anthropology* 44: 557–72.

Reno, Josh. 2018. "What Is Waste?" *Worldwide Waste: Journal of Interdisciplinary Studies* 1(1): 1–10.
Retamar, Roberto Fernanez. 1989. *Caliban and Other Essays*. Minneapolis: University of Minnesota Press.
Reynolds, Bryan. 2002. *Becoming Criminal: Transversal Performance and Cultural Dissidence in Early Modern England*. Baltimore: Johns Hopkins University Press.
Richards, John F. 1981. "The Indian Empire and Peasant Production of Opium in the Nineteenth Century." *Modern Asian Studies* 15(1): 59–82.
Richards, John F. 2002. "Opium and the British Indian Empire: The Royal Commission of 1895." *Modern Asian Studies* 36(2): 375–420.
Rickel, Jennifer. 2012. " 'The Poor Remain': A Posthumanist Rethinking of Literary Humanitarianism in Indra Sinha's *Animal's People*." *Ariel* 43(1): 87–108.
Rico, Francisco. 1984. *The Spanish Picaresque Novel and the Point of View*. Cambridge: Cambridge University Press.
Rico, Francisco. 2006. "*Lazarillo de Tormes*." In *The Novel: Volume II, Forms and Themes*, edited by Franco Moretti, 146–51. Princeton: Princeton University Press.
Ricouer, Paul. 1984. *Time and Narrative, Volume I*. Chicago: University of Chicago Press.
Robbins, Bruce. 2006. "A Portrait of the Artist as a Social Climber." In *The Novel: Volume II, Forms and Themes*, edited by Franco Moretti, 409–35. Princeton: Princeton University Press.
Robbins, Bruce. 2007. *Upward Mobility and the Common Good: Toward a Literary History of the Welfare State*. Princeton: Princeton University Press.
Robins, Nick. 2004. "The World's First Multinational." *New Statesman* 133(4718/4719): 31–33.
Robins, Nick. 2006. "Licensed to Loot." *Ecologist* 36(10): 52–55.
Robins, Nick. 2012. "The Corporation That Changed the World: How the East India Company Shaped the Modern Multinational." *Asian Affairs* 43(1): 12–26.
Rodriguez-Luis, Julio. 1979. "The Modal Approach to the Picaresque." *Comparative Literature* 31(1): 32–46.
Rose, Lionel. 1988. *Rogues and Vagabonds: Vagrant Underworld in Britain, 1815–1985*. New York: Routledge.
Rousseau, Jean-Jacques. 2003. *On the Social Contract*. New York: Dover Thrift.
Roy, Anjali Gera. 2012. "Ordinary People on the Move: Subaltern Cosmopolitanisms in Amitav Ghosh's Writings." *Asiatic* 6(1): 32–46.
Roy, Arundhati. 1999. *The Cost of Living*. New York: Modern Library.
Roy, Arundhati. 2011. *Walking with the Comrades*. New York: Penguin.
Roy, Arundhati. 2017. *The Doctor and the Saint: Caste, Race, and Annihilation of Caste*. New York: Penguin.
Roy, Binayak. 2014. "Exploring the Orient from Within: Amitav Ghosh's *River of Smoke*." *Postcolonial Text* 9(1): 1–21.
Roy, Tirthankar. 2008. "Sardars, Jobbers, Kanganies: The Labour Contractor and Indian Economic History." *Modern Asian Studies* 42(5): 971–98.
Royal Commission on Opium. 1894. "Minutes of Evidence Taken Before the Royal Commission on Opium 29th January to 22nd February 1894." London: Eyre and Spottiswoode.
Rukeyser, Muriel. 2018. *The Book of the Dead*. Morgantown: West Virginia University Press.

Rumore, Micheal Angelo. 2015. "Provincializing Humanism: Reflections on the World of Matter." *Social Text*, no. 122. https://socialtextjournal.org.

Rumore, Micheal Angelo. 2021a. "Petro-Cosmopolitics: Oil and the Indian Ocean in Amitav Ghosh's *The Circle of Reason*." In *Oil Fictions: World Literature and our Contemporary Petrosphere*, edited by Stacey Balkan and Swaralipi Nandi. University Park: Penn State University Press.

Rumore, Micheal Angelo. 2021b. "Toward the Black Indian Ocean: Race and the Human Project in the Afro-Asian Imagination," PhD diss., City University of New York.

Rushdie, Salman. 1981. *Midnight's Children*. New York: Random House.

Sahgal, Nayantara. 2007. "The Ink Is Soiled." *Outlook India,* March 5, 2007.

Said, Edward. 1983. *The World, the Text, and the Critic*. Cambridge: Harvard University Press.

Sanyal, Kalyan. 2007. *Rethinking Capitalist Development: Primitive Accumulation, Governmentality and Postcolonial Capitalism*. New Delhi: Routledge.

Sardi, Sebastian. 2018. *Black Diamond*. https://www.sebastiansardi.com/fwp_port folio/black-diamond.

Sassen, Saskia. 2005. "The Global City: Introducing a Concept." *Brown Journal of World Affairs* 11(2): 27–43.

Scheer, Herman. 2002. "Exploiting Solar Resources: The New Economic and Political Freedom." *The Solar Economy: Renewable Energy for a Sustainable Global Future*, 62–89. London: Earthscan.

Schiebinger, Londa, and Claudia Swan. 2005. *Colonial Botany: Science, Commerce, and Politics in the Early Modern World*. Philadelphia: University of Pennsylvania Press.

Schwarz, Roberto. 2013. "Objective Form: Reflections on the Dialectic of Roguery." *Literary Materialisms*, edited by Mathias Nilges and Emilio Sauri. New York: Palgrave Macmillan. doi: 10.1057/9781137339959_11.

Sen, Krishna and Rituparna Roy. 2013. "Introduction." In *Writing India Anew*, edited by Krishna Sen and Rituparna Roy, 9–26. Amsterdam: Amsterdam University Press.

Sengupta, Vishnupriya. 2009. "Of 'Other' Histories and Identities: Partition Novel from the Indian Subcontinent." *Social Semiotics* 19(4): 499–513.

Sethi, Manpreet. 2006. "Land Reform in India: Issues and Challenges." In *Promised Land: Competing Visions of Agrarian Reform*, edited by Peter Rosset, Raj Patel, and Michael Courville, 73–92. Oakland, CA: Food First Books.

Shakespeare, William. 2015. *The Tempest*. In *The Norton Shakespeare*, edited by Stephen Greenblatt, Walter Cohen, Suzanne Gossett, Jean E. Howard, Katharine Eisaman Maus, and Gordon McMullen, 3205–266. New York: W. W. Norton.

Shamsie, Kamila. 2015. "Beyond the Clouds." Review. *Guardian*, September 15, 2007.

Sharpe, Henry. 1919. *Selections from Educational Records: 1781–1839*. Calcutta: Bureau of Education.

Sharpe, Jenny. 1995. "Figures of Colonial Resistance." In *The Postcolonial Studies Reader*, edited by Bill Ashcroft and Gareth Griffiths, 99–103. London: Routledge.

Shidore, Sarang, and Joshua W. Busby. 2019. "What Explains India's Embrace of Solar? State-led Energy Transition in a Developmental Polity." *Energy Policy* 129: 1179–89.

Shipley, George. 1982. "The Critic as Witness for the Prosecution: Resting the Case Against Lázaro de Tormes." *PMLA* 97(2): 179–94.

Shiva, Vandana. 2005. *Earth Democracy: Justice, Sustainability and Peace.* Cambridge: South End Press.

Shutzer, Matthew. 2021. "Subterranean Properties: India's Political Ecology of Coal." *Comparative Studies in Society and History* 63(2): 400–432.

Siegel, Benjamin Robert. 2018. *Hungry Nation: Food, Famine, and the Making of Modern India* Cambridge: Cambridge University Press.

Simmons, Colin. 1976. "Recruiting and Organizing and Industrial Labour Force in Colonial India: The Case of the Coal Mining Industry." *Indian Economic and Social History Review* 8(4): 464–65.

Singh, Omendra Kumar. 2012. "Reinventing Caste: Indian Diaspora in Amitav Ghosh's *Sea of Poppies.*" *Asiatic* 6(1): 47–62.

Sinha, Indra. 2007. *Animal's People.* New York: Simon & Schuster.

Sinha, Indra. 2009. "Bhopal/25 Years of Poison." *Guardian*, December 3, 2009.

Slaughter, Joseph. 2006. "Enabling Fictions and Novel Subjects: The *Bildungsroman* and International Rights Law." *PMLA* 121(5): 1405–23.

Slaughter, Joseph. 2007. *Human Rights, Inc.: The World Novel, Narrative Form, and International Law.* New York: Fordham University Press.

Smith, Neil. 1984. *Uneven Development: Nature, Capital, and the Production of Space.* Athens: University of Georgia Press.

Snell, Heather. 2008. "Assessing the Limitations of Laughter in Indra Sinha's *Animal's People.*" *Postcolonial Text* 4(4): 1–15.

Soja, Edward. 2011. *Postmodern Geographies: The Reassertion of Space in Critical Social Theory.* 2nd Ed. New York: Verso.

Solnit, Rebecca. 2009. *A Paradise Built in Hell.* New York: Penguin Books.

Spence, Mark David. 2000. *Dispossessing the Wilderness: Indian Removal and the Making of the National Parks.* New York: Oxford University Press.

Spivak, Gayatri Chakravorty. 1988. "Can the Subaltern Speak?" In *Marxism and the Interpretation of Culture*, edited by Cary Nelson and Lawrence Grossberg, 271–312. Chicago: University of Illinois Press.

Spivak, Gayatri Chakravorty. 1999. *A Critique of Postcolonial Reason: Toward a History of the Vanishing Present.* Cambridge, MA: Harvard University Press.

Spivak, Gayatri Chakravorty. 2003. *Death of a Discipline.* New York: Columbia University Press.

Spivak, Gayatri Chakravorty. 2010. *Nationalism and the Imagination.* New York: Seagull Books.

Spivak, Gayatri Chakravorty. 2018. "How Do We Write Now?" *PMLA* 133(1): 166–70.

Stehlin, John G. 2018. *Cyclescapes of The Unequal City: Bicycle Infrastructure and Uneven Development.* Minneapolis: University of Minnesota Press.

Stoler, Laura Ann. 2002. *Carnal Knowledge and Imperial Power: Race and the Intimate in Colonial Rule.* Berkeley: University of California Press.

Stoler, Laura Ann. 2006. "On Degrees of Imperial Sovereignty." *Public Culture* 18(1): 125–45.

Stoler, Laura Ann. 2013. *Imperial Debris: On Ruins and Ruination.* Durham, NC: Duke University Press.

Stone, Robert. 1998. *Picaresque Continuities: Transformations of Genre from the Golden Age to Goethezeit.* New Orleans: University Press of the South.

Streeby, Shelley. 2018. *Imagining the Future of Climate Change: World-making Through Science Fiction and Activism.* Oakland: University of California Press.

Subrahmanyam, Sanjay. 2008. "Diary: Another Booker Flop." Review. *London Review of Books* 30(21): 42–43. https://www.lrb.co.uk/the-paper/v30/n21/sanjay-subrahmanyam/diary.
Suleri, Sara. 1992. *The Rhetoric of English India*. Chicago: University of Chicago Press.
Szeman, Imre. 2001. "Who's Afraid of National Allegory?" *The South Atlantic Quarterly* 100(3): 803–27.
Szeman, Imre. 2016. *After Oil*. Morgantown: West Virginia University Press.
Szeman, Imre. 2017. "Conjectures on World Energy Literature: Or, What Is Petroculture?" *Journal of Postcolonial Writing* 53(3): 277–88.
Szeman, Imre. 2021. "Afterward." In *Oil Fictions: World Literature and our Contemporary Petrosphere*, edited by Stacey Balkan and Swaralipi Nandi. University Park: Penn State University Press.
Szeman, Imre, and Dominic Boyer, eds. 2017. *Energy Humanities: An Anthology*. Baltimore: Johns Hopkins University Press.
Tagore, Rabindranath. 1918. *Nationalism*. London: Macmillan. Project Gutenberg.
Tagore, Rabindranath. 1925. "Cult of the Charkh." *The Swaraj Foundation*. https://www.swaraj.org/articles-and-books.
Tangia, Rahul, and Samantha Gross. 2019. "Coal in India: Adjusting to Transition." The Brookings Institute, paper 7, March 2019, www.brookings.edu/wp-content/uploads/2019/03/fp_20190731_coal_in_india.pdf.
Tarr, Courtney. 1927. "Literary and Artistic Unity in the *Lazarillo de Tormes*." *PMLA* 42(2): 404–21.
Taylor, Jesse Oak. 2013. "Powers of Zero: Aggregation, Negation, and the Dimensions of Scale in Indra Sinha's *Animal's People*." *Literature and Medicine* 31(2): 177–98.
Thiel, Stephanie. 2011. "Global Anomie and India: A Conceptual Approach." *Indian Journal of Asian Affairs* 24(1): 17–34.
Thompson, E. P. 1963. *The Making of the English Working Class*. New York: Vintage.
Thompson, E. P. 1971. "The Moral Economy of the English Crowd in the Eighteenth Century." *Past & Present*, no. 50: 76–136.
Thompson, E. P. 1993. *Customs in Common: Studies in Traditional Popular Culture*. New York: The New Press.
Trocki, Carl. A. 1999. *Opium, Empire, and the Global Political Economy: A Study of the Asian Opium Trade*. London: Routledge.
Tsing, Anna Lowenhaupt. 2015. *The Mushroom at the End of the World: On the Possibility of Life in Capitalist Ruins*. Princeton: Princeton University Press.
Vallette, Jim. 1999. "Larry Summers's War Against the Earth." Counterpunch.org, June 15, 1999.
Vardy, Alan. 2003. *John Clare: Politics and Poetry*. New York: Palgrave Macmillan.
Varma, Rashmi. 2004. "Provincializing the Global City: From Bombay to Mumbai." *Social Text* 22(4): 65–89.
Varma, Rashmi. 2012. *The Postcolonial City and Its Subjects*. New York: Routledge.
Vergès, Francoise. 2003. "Writing on Water: Peripheries, Flows, Capital, and Struggles in the Indian Ocean." *positions* 11(1): 241–57.
Vergès, Francoise. 2017. "The Racial Capitalocene." Blog post. Verso Books. August 30, 2017. https://www.versobooks.com/blogs/3376-racial-capitalocene.
Verma, Gita. 2003. *Slumming India*. New Delhi: Penguin Books.
Viswanathan, Gauri. 1992. *Masks of Conquest: Literary Study and British Rule in India*. New York: Columbia University Press.

Vital, Anthony. 2008. "Towards an African Ecocriticism: Postcolonialism, Ecology and 'Life & Times of Michael K.'" *Research in African Literatures* 39(1): 87–106.
Voyles, Traci Brynne. 2015. *Wastelanding: Legacies of Uranium Mining in Navajo Country.* Minneapolis: University of Minnesota Press.
Walcott, Derek. 1987. "The Sea is History." In *Collected Poems, 1948–1984*, 345–61. New York: Farrar, Strauss, and Giroux.
Wallerstein, Immanuel. 1988. "The Bourgeois(ie) as Concept and Reality." *New Left Review* 167: 91–106.
Walton, John K. & David Seddon. 1994. *Free Markets and Food Riots: The Politics of Global Adjustment.* Cambridge: Wiley-Blackwell.
Weheliye, Alexander P. 2014. *Habeas Viscus: Racializing Assemblages, Biopolitics, and Black Feminist Theories of the Human.* Durham, NC: Duke University Press.
Wenzel, Jennifer. 2016. "Taking Stock of Energy Humanities." *Reviews in Cultural Theory* 6(3): 30–34.
Whitburn, Christine J. 1974. *Knaves and Swindlers: Essays on the Picaresque Novel in Europe.* London: Oxford University Press.
Whyte, Kyle P. 2018. "Indigenous Science (Fiction) for the Anthropocene: Ancestral Dystopias and Fantasies of Climate Change Crises." *Environment & Planning E: Nature and Space* 1(1–2): 224–42.
Wicks, Ulrich. 1974. "The Nature of the Picaresque: A Modal Approach." *PMLA* 89(2): 240–49.
Wicks, Ulrich. 1989. *Picaresque Narrative, Picaresque Fictions: A Theory and Research Guide.* New York: Greenwood.
Williams, Evan Calder. 2011. *Combined and Uneven Apocalypse: Luciferian Marxism.* Ropley: Zero Books.
Williams, Raymond. 1973. *The Country and the City.* New York: Oxford University Press.
Williams, Raymond. 1977. *Marxism and Literature.* New York: Oxford University Press.
Williams, Raymond. 2006. *Culture and Materialism: Selected Essays.* New York: Verso, 2006.
Wilson, Sheena. 2018. "Energy Imaginaries: Feminist and Decolonial Futures." In "Materialism and the Critique of Energy," edited by Brent Ryan Bellamy and Jeff Diamanti, special issue, *Meditations* 31(2): 377–412.
Wise, A. C. 2017. *Sunvault: Stories of Solarpunk and Eco-Speculation.* Edited by Pheobe Wagner and Brontë Christopher Wieland. Nashville, TN: Upper Rubber Boot Books.
Wolpert, Stanley. 1977. *A New History of India.* 8th Ed. Oxford: Oxford University Press.
Woodbridge, Linda. 2001. *Vagrancy, Homelessness, and English Renaissance Literature.* Chicago: University of Illinois Press.
Wynter, Sylvia. 1971."Novel and History, Plot and Plantation." *Savacou*, no. 5: 95–102.
Wynter, Sylvia. 2003. "Unsettling the Coloniality of Being/Power/Truth/Freedom: Towards the Human, after Man, Its Overrepresentation—An Argument." *CR: The New Centennial Review* 3(3): 257–337.
Yaeger, Patricia. 2011. "Literature in the Ages of Wood, Tallow, Coal, Whale Oil, Gasoline, Atomic Power, and Other Energy Sources." *PMLA* 126(2): 305–10.
Yang, Anand A. 1998. *Bazaar India: Markets, Society, and the Colonial State in Bihar.* Berkeley: University of California Press.

Yates, Michelle. 2011. "The Human-As-Waste, the Labor Theory of Value and Disposability in Contemporary Capitalism." *Antipode* 43(5): 1679–95.
Yenneti, Komali, and Rosie Day. 2015. "Procedural (In)justice in the Implementation of Solar Energy: The Case of Charanaka Solar Park, Gujarat, India." *Energy Policy* 86: 664–73.
Yenneti, Komali, and Rosie Day. 2016. "Distributional Justice in Solar Energy Implementation in India: The Case of Charanka Solar Park." *Journal of Rural Studies* 46: 35–46.
Yusoff, Katheryn. 2018. *A Billion Black Anthropocenes or None*. Minneapolis: University of Minnesota Press.
Zakaria, Fareed. 2006. "India Rising." *Newsweek*, March 6, 2006.

Index

Page numbers in italics refer to figures.

Abani, Chris, 1, 3, 10, 17, 20
abjection, 100
accumulation by dispossession, 9–10
Adiga, Aravind, 3
   See also The White Tiger
adventure tropes, 7, 48
aesthetics, 58, 78–81, 132
age of coal, 108–14
age of flowers, 51, 61–65, 68, 108, 146
agriculture, 26–28, 78, 89
   See also the cotton belt; land enclosure; poppy cultivation; *Sea of Poppies* (Ghosh)
Ahmed, Siraj, 64
Ahuja, Ravi, 71
Alaimo, Stacy, 77–78, 96–97, 167n32, 171n11
Alarcón, Daniel, 17
Al-Dabbagh, Abdullah, 165n3
Alexander, Meena, 49
Aliers, Juan, 45, 143
Alter, Robert, 7–8, 16, 48
alterity, 10, 21
Ambedkar, B. R., 119
Amrith, Sunil, 22, 37, 44–45, 53, 61–62
Anand, Mulk Raj, 24, 33, 113, 119
Animal's People (Sinha)
  overviews, 30–31, 85–86
  autobiographical narration parody, 91–92
  Coatesville, Pennsylvania, 86–87
  developmentalism critiques, 19, 86–93
  economic dimensions, 8, 16, 78–79
  energopolitics, 97, 106
  as environmental picaresque, 99–102
  first-person narration, 18
  genre, 103–4
  global flows, 96
  Green Revolution critique, 85
  heterotopias, 95–96
  historical contexts, 78–79
  human figurations, 31
  imperial liberalism, 92, 101–2
  labor, 95
  versus *Lazarillo de Tormes,* 85, 90–91, 100, 103–6
  memento mori tropes: aborted fetuses, 101–2; dispossession, 90; graves, 21, 84–85; late capitalist, 21, 30–31, 79, 87; *pícaro* figures, 91; postcolonial, 84–85, 93–96
  music leitmotif, 102–4
  necropolitical imaginary, 85
  neoliberal Arcadianism, 101
  pesticide disaster, 79, 85
  pícaro/rogue figures, 79, 85, 89–91, 93, 96, 98, 100–1, 103–4, 106
  the picturesque, 83–86, 93
  political resistance, 102–3
  politics of global toxicity, 86, 102–4
  as postcolonial picaresque, 90, 104, 106
  as rogue tale, 6

Animal's People (continued)
  slow violence, 18–19
  socioeconomic critiques, 104
  structure, 88
  temporality, 91, 99–101
  transcorporeality, 32, 86
  Union Carbide, 79, 85, 102
  uplift ideology critiques, 88, 93
Anthropocene, 9, 33, 45, 98, 108–9
anthropolitics, 98
AP. *See Animal's People* (Sinha)
Aravamudan, Srinivas, 18
Asia, 142
autobiography, 7, 23, 67, 91–93
Azuela, Mariano, 142

Bacon, Francis, 59
Bakhtin, Mikhail, 17, 19, 47
  See also chronotopes
Barbieri, Giovanni Francesco
  (Guercino), 79–80, *81*
Barney, Darin, 34
Barrell, Jonathan, 83, 170n3
Bataille, George, 157
bauxite industry, 122, 142
Bayman, Anna, 14
Bay of Bengal, 22, 37, 38
beautification programs, 119
Bengal, 28, 42–43, 65
Bennett, Jane, 41
Bhopal, 78–79, 81
  See also Animal's People (Sinha)
Bihar
  coal industry, 107
  displacement, 28–29
  forced opium production, 65
  land enclosure, 63
  land tenure legislation, 66
  migrant labor, 29
  poppy fields, 5, 22
  See also Sea of Poppies (Ghosh)
Bildung, 24, 39–40, 73, 116
Bildungsroman, 16, 21, 115, 121
biopolitics, 98, 123, 129
Blake (Delaney), 7, 67, 72
Boetzkes, Amanda, 125, 128, 154
Bonneuil, Christophe, 41, 151
The Book of the Dead (Rukeyser), 96
Bose, Sugata, 23, 47, 53–54

Boyer, Dominic
  anthropolitics, 98
  energologic, 115
  energopolitics, 97, 106–7, 123
  energy history, 108
  energy transition, 157
  hyper-subjects, 77, 96
  social awareness of fossil fuels,
    122
  solar power, 158
British rule of the Indian subcontinent
  coal dependence, 109
  corruption, 64
  cotton extraction, 22
  education policies, 37
  land tenure, 39, 168n4
  military dominance, 168n4
  opium's roles in, 38, 61–62, 65,
    168n2
  taxation (*diwani*), 62
  See also East India Company (EIC)
Bt cotton, 77–78, 89
Burke, Edmund, 39, 83
Burton, Antoinette, 47
Buscón, Él (Francisco de Quevedo),
  6–7, 17–18, 90
Bush, George W., 91

Cáceres, Berta, 141
capital accumulation, 41–42
capitalism
  corporate, 22
  European rise, 6
  extractive, 1–3
  fossil, 116
  global inequality, 88–89, 92
  plantation, 42–43
  See also late capitalism
Capitalocene, 41–42
carbon culture, 122
carbon democracy, 114, 172n9
carbon fiction, 117, 130, 136–37,
  173n19
  See also The White Tiger (Adiga)
carbon imaginary, 98, 117, 119, 129
  See also energopolitics
carbon picaresque, 106, 108–9, 118,
  138

Carson, Rachel, 94
Carter, Marina, 74–75
Caveat for Common Cursitors Vulgarly Called Vagabonds, A (Harman), 16
Cerro de Pasco Resources, 141
Chakrabarty, Dipesh
  aesthetics and hygiene, 132
  capital accumulation and environmental damage, 42
  climate change, 167n27
  colonialist rhetoric, 120–21
  philosophical anthropology, 163
  planetarity, 35, 141, 147
  provincialism, 61, 76
  waste, 126
Chambers, Iain, 57
Chamoiseau, Patrick, 17, 171n12
Chandler, Frank Wadleigh, 7, 25
Charanka Solar Park, 145–48, 155–60, 163
Chatterjee, Partha, 37–38, 131
Cheah, Pheng, 45
cheap labor, 59–61, 97, 117
cheap nature
  enabling ideologies, 97
  human-nonhuman categorical flattening, 129
  humans as, 43, 168n6
  Ibis Trilogy (Ghosh), 29–30, 40–41, 44, 48
  Moore, Jason W., 29, 40–42, 168n6
  Plantationocene, 9, 42, 58, 129
  plantations, 42–43
  Sea of Poppies (Ghosh), 58
Chowdhury, Shoveon, 160
chronotopes, 17, 47, 53–58
City of Clowns (Alarcón), 17
Clare, John, 64
Clean India initiative, 5, 26
coal
  C21 use increases, 152
  and cultural production, 114
  imaginaries, 119–20, 122
  as property, 112
  slum ecologies, 129–35
  as vibrant matter, 136
  See also coal industry

"Coal" (Lorde), 130
Coal India Limited (CIL), 111–12
coal industry, Indian
  British Empire's dependence, 109
  contemporary use of, 150
  developmentalism, 108
  Dhanbad, 107
  East India Company involvement, 107–8
  ecological damage, 110–11, 121
  extraction processes, 110–11
  labor, 107–9, 111, 115, 117
  land seizures, 112
  national dependence, 121–22
  nationalization, 110–12
  Raniganj mine, 121–22
  state-building, 120–21
  See also The White Tiger (Adiga)
Coatesville, Pennsylvania, 86–87
Cohen, G. A., 166n16
Cohen, Margaret, 47, 54–55
Coleridge, Samuel Taylor, 13, 83
collective resistance, 139–40
colonialist rhetorics, 120–21
colonial knowledge systems, 69–70
colonial logics, 37–38
the commons, 147, 167n29
commons enclosure
  developmentalism, 157, 159
  energy transition considerations, 145
  England, 12
  India, 4, 9, 34, 142, 146
  justice for, 157
  producing rogues, 11–15
  South America, 141
  See also land enclosure
The Competent Authority (Chowdhury), 160
conservation efforts, 143–44
Constable, John, 79
constitutive limits, 136
conversos, 18, 167n24
Coolie (Anand), 24, 119
coolies, 40
Coolitude writing, 74–75
Cornwallis, Charles, 39, 63, 66
Cornwallis Code, 63, 66
cosmopolitanism, 55, 169n16

cotton, 22, 77–78, 89
the cotton belt
  destruction of, 77–78
  extractivism, 3–4
  farmer suicide crisis, 28, 89, 95, 122
counter-insurgency genre, 14–15
country-city dichotomies, 119
criminal class, 13
Cross, Jamie, 35, 148, 154–55

Al-Dabbagh, Abdullah, 165n3
da Silva, Denise Ferreira, 10, 118, 172n15
Davies, Thom, 121
Davis, Mike, 32, 130
Dawson, Ashley, 122, 167n23, 173n1
Debaise, Didier, 97
Dekker, Thomas, 14
Delaney, Martin, 7, 67, 72
Delhi, 120–21, 131
De Quincey, Thomas
  British rule, 169n14
  colonialist rhetoric, 120
  opium dreams, 50
  opium trade, 62–63
  Orientalism, 72–73, 132
Desai, Gaurav, 55
Descartes, René, 59
The Deserted Village (Goldsmith), 64, 84
developmentalism
  agricultural impacts, 89
  Animal's People (Sinha), 19, 86–93
  coal industry, 108
  fossil capitalism, 116
  global toxicity, 88
  Indian rhetorics, 79–80
  liberty, 93
  negative impacts, 88–89
  popular support, 89
  See also Green Revolution; improvement
developmental temporality, 15
Devi, Mahasweta, 3, 34
Dhanbad, 107, 119, 121–22, 125
Dickens, Charles, 70

Dionne, Craig, 14–15
Dirks, Nicholas, 39
displacement
  Bihar, 28–29
  Indigenous communities, 146–47
  itinerancy, 4, 114–15, 167n22
  new India, 26
  Partition, 27–28
  pícaro figures, 8, 165n10
  works addressing, 3–4
  See also Sea of Poppies (Ghosh)
Dongria Kondh (Indigenous people), 34, 142–43
Doron, Assa, 32, 124
Dunn, Peter, 11
Dutch Royal Shell, 141

East India Company (EIC)
  Bengal damage, 29
  coal industry involvement, 107–8
  Cornwallis Code, 63, 66
  dissolution, 39, 64
  educational policy, 37
  famine roles, 63–64
  opium monopoly, 39, 66
  poppy program, 65
ecological imperialism, 68
econopoetics, 87, 100
ecosystem people, 45
Edney, Matthew, 168n4
Él Buscón (Francisco de Quevedo), 6–7, 17–18, 90
the Emergency, 5, 165n7
enclosure. *See* commons enclosure; land enclosure
energologics, 115
energopolitics, 97, 106–7, 118, 123, 154
energy
  culture inseparability, 34, 114
  grids, 158–60
  markets, 158
  as methodology, 137
  sources and ideologies, 151
  unconscious, 122
  See also coal; Energy Humanities; energy transition; solar power
Energy Humanities
  electrical grids, 158

energy-culture inseparability, 34
energy histories, 108, 122
energy unconscious, 122
interpretive methods, 135
invisibility tropes, 119, 137
limits, 137
petrofiction, 172n11
reading energy, 119, 165n5
structural absences, 20, 117, 136
Energy Transfer Partners, 140, 173n2
energy transition
  extractivist ethos, 160
  Indigenous knowledge, 157
  Petrocultures Research Group principles, 162–63
  political economy, 145–46, 149, 157–58
  solar power, 150–52
  unjust, 149
Enjoy Poverty (documentary), 126
Enlightenment language, 59
Enlightenment Orientalism, 18
environmentalism of the poor, 143–44
Equiano, Olaudah, 7
erasures of labor. *See* labor erasures
"Et in Arcadia Ego" (Guercino), 79–80, *81*
"Et in Arcadia Ego" (Poussin), 31, 79, *80*, 93
evolutionary psychology, 139–40
extraction, 99, 139, 144, 153
  See also coal; mining industry; opium trade
extractive capitalism, 1–3
  See also coal industry
extractive zones, 21, 32, 89, 99, 116–17

famines, 28, 63–64
farmer suicide crisis, 28, 89, 95, 122
Federici, Silvia, 17
FF. *See Flood of Fire* (Ghosh)
first-person narration, 7, 16, 18
Flood of Fire (Ghosh)
  colonial *Bildung* critique, 39–40

East India Company, 67
  labor, 75–76
  Opium Wars, 67, 76
  sepoys, 67, 75–76
  uplift narrative critique, 67
flowers, age of, 51, 61–65, 68, 108, 146
flowers of empire, 68
Forest of Flowers (Saro-Wiwa), 3
fossil capitalism, 116
  See also coal industry
fossil fuels, 118, 122
  See also coal
fossil subjects, 123–24
Foucault, Michel, 98, 173n18
free market ideology, 89
free trade, 91
Fressoz, Jean-Baptiste, 41, 151

Gainsborough, Thomas, 13, 93
Gandhi, Indira, 5, 110, 165n7, 178
Gandhi, Mohandas, 119, 159
Ganzeer, 160–62
genre, 23, 104
  See also the picaresque; the postcolonial picaresque
geoengineering, 155
geontopower, 97–99, 129
Ghosh, Amitav
  age of flowers, 146
  agriculture, 28
  C19 Indian history, 52
  climate change, 126–27
  development programs, 171n6
  The Glass Palace, 2
  The Great Derangement, 126–27, 171n6
  The Hungry Tide, 2
  magical realism critiques, 4, 49
  modernity, 17, 115
  petrofiction, 161, 172n11
  sailing ships, 47–48
  See also Flood of Fire; Ibis Trilogy; River of Smoke; Sea of Poppies
Gilroy, Paul, 9
girmitiyas, 73–75
The Glass Palace (Ghosh), 2, 29, 46
globalization of form, 23–25

Global South, 20, 54, 167n25
global subjects, 124
global toxicity
  aesthetic logic, 78–81
  Animal's People (Sinha), 86, 102–4
  developmentalism, 88
  politics, 31, 78, 86, 88, 91
Goldsmith, Oliver, 64, 84
Gómez-Barris, Macarena, 21, 34, 116, 136, 139, 173n19
  See also extractive zones
governmentality, 131, 173n18
GP. See The Glass Palace (Ghosh)
GraceLand (Abani), 1, 3, 10, 17, 20
The Great Derangement (Ghosh), 126–27, 171n6
Green, Robert, 16
Greenblatt, Stephen, 6
Green Revolution
  overview, 77
  Animal's People (Sinha), 85
  damage done, 3–4, 89, 106
  driving ideologies, 31, 85
greenwashing, 109, 145
Guercino (Giovanni Francesco Barbieri), 79–80, *81*
Guha, Ramachandra, 34, 45, 143
Guha, Ranajit, 14, 30, 44, 61
Guillén, Claudio, 7, 16, 21, 91–92, 95
Gujarat, 146, 151, 153
Gupta, Ankhil, 159

habitability, 147
half-outsiders, *pícaros* as, 6–7, 21, 96
Hall, Stuart, 9
Haraway, Donna
  the Anthropocene, 9
  imagining anew, 136
  Plantationocene, 42
  sky-gazing Anthropos, 5–6, 41, 77
  thought, 159
  vibrant materiality, 41
Hard Times (Dickens), 70
Harman, Thomas, 16
Harvey, David, 78
Hastings, Warren, 39, 66
Hitchcock, Peter, 23, 104, 136
Hofmeyr, Isabel, 55, 169nn15–16

Homo Modernus, 118, 123, 128–29, 172n15
Honduras, 141
Howe, Cymene, 144–45, 163
HT. See The Hungry Tide (Ghosh)
Huggan, Graham, 24
The Hungry Tide (Ghosh), 2–3
Huxley, Aldous, 120
hyper-subjects, 77, 96–99

Ibis Trilogy (Ghosh)
  overviews, 29, 76
  age of flowers, 61–65, 68, 108, 146
  cheap nature, 29–30, 40–41, 44, 48, 58
  chronotopes, 55–57
  colonial knowledge systems, 69
  coolie figures, 40
  cosmopolitanism, 55
  East India Company commentary, 39–40
  as environmental picaresque, 45–53
  extractive capitalism's *longue durée*, 3
  farmer crisis, 4
  historico-material sensibility, 46
  indenture theme, 73–74
  Indian Ocean re-mapping, 53–56
  labor, 44, 58
  language, 46–47, 75
  lascars, 38, 70–71
  mutiny tropes, 72–73
  nonlinearity, 53
  opium trade, 5, 38, 44, 63
  perspective, 49
  plantation economies, 42
  poppy cultivation, 38–39
  satire of popular opium narratives, 49–50
  as speculative fiction, 76
  structure, 22–23
  vibrant materiality, 41
  See also Flood of Fire; River of Smoke; Sea of Poppies
Imaginary Maps (Devi), 3, 34
imperial botany, 59

imperial liberalism
　Animal's People (Sinha), 92, 101–2
　consumerism, 127
　enabling ideologies, 59–60
　India post-independence, 78
　necropolitics, 129
　The White Tiger (Adiga), 138
　wilderness logics, 144
improvement
　colonial schemes, 30, 43
　Linnaeus's taxonomy enabling, 59
　literary depictions, 4–5
　Lockean, 11, 30, 59–60, 92, 139
　Sea of Poppies (Ghosh), 4
　solar power, 146
　See also developmentalism
indentured labor, 73–75
India
　commons enclosures, 4, 9, 34, 142, 146
　Delhi, 120–21, 131
　developmentalist rhetoric, 79–80
　displaced persons, 26
　economic liberalization, 172n8
　environmental tyranny resistance, 34–35
　fossil economy overview, 2
　Gujarat, 146, 151, 153
　imperial liberalism, 78
　independence movement, 121
　mass urbanization, 27
　Nationalist politics, 119
　new, 5, 27–28, 78, 93, 95, 112, 121
　peasant resistance to corporations, 142
　political hegemony methods, 37
　raiyati system, 26, 66–67, 167n29
　slum ecologies, 32
　See also agriculture; Bihar; British rule of the Indian subcontinent; coal industry, Indian; solar power industry, Indian
Indian Ocean
　Bay of Bengal, 22, 37
　colonial knowledge systems, 69–70
　Ghosh's remapping, 53–57
　imaginaries, 45, 47, 53, 74, 76
　indentured labor, 73–75

lascars, 38, 43, 70–73, 168n3, 169n22
slave trade, 29, 73–74
See also opium trade; *Sea of Poppies* (Ghosh)
Indian Ocean Studies
　Amrith, Sunil, 22, 37, 44–45, 53, 61–62
　archives, 53
　Bose, Sugata, 23, 47, 53–54
　circulation, 38, 71
　colonial-era communities, 44
　Desai, Gaurav, 55
　the Global South, 54
　histories, 45, 54
　Hofmeyr, Isabel, 55, 169nn15–16
　identity, 10
　methodologies, 45, 54
　Rumore, Micheal, 45
　terraqueous ontology of space, 54
　trade, 48
India Shining, 26, 32, 121, 135
Indigenous communities
　collective resistance, 139–44
　displacement, 146–47
　Dongria Kondh, 34, 142–43
　as inhuman, 26
　Maldhari, 140, 146–48, 156, 163
　solar industry resistance, 144, 148
　sovereignty, 156
the inhuman
　overview, 125
　colonial ontologies, 124
　epistemes creating, 30–31, 70
　versus *Homo Modernus,* 118
　Indigenous communities, 26
　labor, 79, 81, 129
　racism, 109, 132
　reification as fungible, 10, 43
　subjects of late liberalism, 98–99
　voyeurism, 83
　The White Tiger (Adiga), 117, 127–29
intimacy, 74
invisibility
　labor, 80–81, 95, 117
　tropes, 119, 137
　waste management, 125
itinerancy, 4, 114–15, 167n22

James, C. L. R., 38
Jameson, Frederic, 122
Janu, C. K, 35
Jeffrey, Robin, 32, 124
jester figures, 17
Jharkhand, 112
John, Joya, 15
Joshi, Ruchir, 160

Kalamb, Krishna, 95, 171n8
Kant, Immanuel, 83
Kerr, Ian, 72
Kincaid, Jamaica, 59, 68
Knight, Richard Payne, 83–84
Kumar, Rajiv, 110–12

labor
  as abstraction, 70
  Animal's People (Sinha), 95
  artistic representations, 31, 79–80, *81*, 93
  cheap, 59–61, 97, 117
  circulation, 71–72
  coal industry, 107–9, 111, 115, 117
  colonial, 88
  Flood of Fire (Ghosh), 75–76
  forced poppy cultivation, 64–65
  Ibis Trilogy (Ghosh), 44, 58
  indentured, 73–75
  inhuman, 79, 81, 129
  invisibility, 80–81, 95, 117
  itinerant, 114–15
  Lockean, 70
  Marxist, 70, 116
  migrant, 29
  peasant, 81, 83–84, 91
  petrol-dominant economies, 114
  petroleum industry, 115
  the picturesque, 31, 79–80, *81*, 83–85, 93
  poppy cultivation, 38, 168n2
  shared topographies, 23–24
  soldiers, 75–76
  The White Tiger (Adiga), 116–17, 126–28
  See also labor erasures
labor erasures
  aesthetic, 79–80, 95

Animal's People (Sinha), 95
  greenwashing, 109
  the picturesque, 83–85, 91, 93
  Williams, Raymond, 79
laborers as waste, 116
Lagos, 1, 165n1
land, 12, 66, 68, 147
  See also land enclosure
land enclosure
  Bihar, 63
  and conceptions of citizen-subjects, 12–13
  criminalization of poverty, 9
  economic models sanctioning, 9
  effects of, 12–13, 64, 166n14
  Indigenous resistance, 139
  Lockean, 12, 166nn15–16
  the new picaresque, 23
  rogues, 11–14
  Sea of Poppies (Ghosh), 55
  solar power industry, 140, 144, 146–48, 156
  See also commons enclosure
landscape aesthetics, 170n3
  See also the picturesque
lascars, 38, 43, 70–73, 168n3, 169n22
The Last Jet-Engine Laugh (Joshi), 160
late capitalism
  Animal's People (Sinha), 21, 30–31, 79, 87
  definition, 165n6
  postmodern geographies, 95–96
Latin America, 141–42
Latour, Bruno, 97
La Via Campesina, 142, 173n7
Lazarillo de Tormes
  overviews, 1, 18
  abjection, 100
  absence of self-realization, 16
  versus *Animal's People* (Sinha), 85, 90–91, 100, 103–6
  economic critiques, 100
  popularization of the picaresque, 165n3
  rivers, 58
  third man figures, 19

titular *pícaro*, 6, 17–18
vagabond defense, 16
wanderings, 48
Le Guin, Ursula, 166n13
Levins, Richard, 97
Lewontin, Richard, 97
Linebaugh, Peter, 12, 17
Linnaeus, Carl
  influence on imperialism, 59–60, 67–68, 128
  monoculture influence, 30
  Plantation aesthetics, 58
  taxonomy of humans, 60
  taxonomy of plants, 2, 59–60
Lin Zexu, 57, 169n17
literary humanitarianism, 90
Locke, John
  improvement of self and property, 11, 30, 59–60, 92, 139
  labor, 70
  land as capital, 12
  land enclosure arguments, 12, 166nn15–16
  social contracts, 92
Lorde, Audre, 130
Lorrain, Claude, 79
Los de Abajo (Azuela), 142
Lowe, Lisa
  autobiography, 7, 67
  colonial labor, 88, 91
  coolies, 40
  ethnic *Bildungsroman*, 115
  imperialism, 59–60
  intimacy, 74

Macaulay, T. B., 37, 61
Maiorino, Giancarlo, 8, 10, 21, 100, 167n24
Maldhari people, 140, 146–48, 156, 163
Malm, Andreas, 41, 118, 137, 168n8, 171nn1–2
manifest destiny, 173n10
Mann, Charles, 144
maritime tropes taxonomy, 55
Martens, Renzo, 126
Marx, Karl, 40–41, 70, 116
masquerade tropes, 48–49

Mbembe, Achille, 97, 123, 129
Melville, Herman, 56, 71–72
memento mori, 79, 83–84, 93, 95
  See also Animal's People (Sinha)
methyl isocyanate (MIC), 78–79
Midnight's Children (Rushdie), 4, 18, 27–28, 105, 167n30
Mill, John Stuart, 30, 43, 59, 92
Miller, Stuart, 16
mini-grid economy, 159–160
mining industry, 110, 122, 142, 171n3
  See also coal industry
Mistry, Rohinton, 90
Mitchell, Timothy, 114, 172n9
Modi, Narendra, 5, 89, 109, 112, 119–20, 151–53
Monsanto, 77–78, 89, 94
Moore, Jason W., 29, 40–42, 128, 168n6
Morton, Timothy, 77
Mother India (film), 114
Moynagh, Maureen, 104
Muir, John, 143
Mukerjee, Janam, 28
Mukherjee, Pablo
  on *Animal's People,* 103–4, 126
  corporate capitalism, 22
  politics of global toxicity, 31, 78, 86, 88, 91
  postcolonial environments, 19, 23–25
  See also postcolonial picturesque
Muniz, Vik, 126
mutiny tropes, 72–73

Naipaul, V. S., 85, 90
nationalism versus cosmopolitanism, 169n16
necropolitics, 123, 129
necropower, 97, 125
Neeson, J. M., 166n14
Nehru, Jawaharlal, 108, 119, 152
neoliberalism, 139–40, 173n1
new India, 5, 27–28, 78, 93, 95, 112, 121
  See also India Shining

the Niger Delta, 1–2, 141
Nixon, Rob
  on *Animal's People,* 30, 85, 99–100
  economic dimensions of the picaresque, 8
  environmental picaresque, 99–100
  petromodernity, 137
  slow violence, 18–19, 45
nonhuman matter, 41, 129, 172n17
  See also the inhuman
nonlife, 98–99

oil. *See* petroleum
opium addiction, 51–52
opium factories, 50, 169n13
opium trade
  British empire's dependence, 38, 61–62, 65, 168n2
  coal dependence, 109
  East India Company monopoly, 39, 66
  economic genocide, 63–64
  economic histories, 61–62
  famine, 63–64
  forced production, 65
  histories of, 44
  Ibis Trilogy (Ghosh), 5, 38, 44, 49–50, 63
  land requirements, 63
  plantations, 38
  poppy cultivation, 38, 43, 64–65, 168n2
  Royal Opium Commission, 38, 44, 168n2
  tax revenues, 66–67
  See also Sea of Poppies (Ghosh)
Opium Wars, 57, 66–67, 76
Orwell, George, 85

Panchayat Raj system, 156, 159
participatory justice, 157
Partition, 27–28
Patel, Raj, 128
Perera, Sonali, 24
pesticides, 94
  See also Union Carbide
Petrocultures Research Group (PRC), 162

petrofiction, 117, 161, 172n11
petroleum
  GraceLand (Abani), 1, 3
  labor, 115
  refuse, 124
  The White Tiger (Adiga), 120, 124, 137
phenomenology of passage, 49
the picaresque
  Bildung subversion, 24
  carbon, 106, 108–9, 118, 138
  economic dimensions, 8, 10, 100
  econopoetics, 87, 100
  environmental, 99–102
  episodic structures, 91
  first-person perspective, 7, 16
  genealogy, 165n3
  itinerancy trope, 4
  land enclosure, 23
  maritime novels, 56
  new, 22–24
  nonteleological mode, 15, 23–24, 118, 160
  prior scholarship, 25
  pseudo-autobiography, 23
  realist novels, 119
  versus rogue literature generally, 16
  rupture with prior traditions, 7
  satire, 13, 18, 22, 87
  slow violence representation, 45
  socioeconomic critique, 104
  Spanish conventions, 8
  subaltern representation, 22–23
  temporalities, 15, 24, 100
  viral metaphors, 11
  wandering and adventure tropes, 7
  See also pícaro figures; the postcolonial picaresque; rogues
pícaro figures
  Animal's People (Sinha), 79, 85, 89–91, 93, 96, 98, 100–1, 103–4, 106
  antagonists to bourgeois protagonists, 15
  displacement trope, 8, 165n10
  jesters, 17

postcolonial, 4–5, 8
versus rogues, 8
Sea of Poppies (Ghosh), 45–46, 58, 70
socio-political parodies, 16
as third man figures, 17
upward mobility narrative resistance, 21
The White Tiger (Adiga), 10, 113, 118, 134
See also rogues
the picturesque, 31, 79–80, *81*, 83–86, 93
planetarity, 35, 141, 147
plantation aesthetics, 58
plantation capitalism, 42–43
Plantationocene, 9, 42, 58, 129
See also cheap nature
political hegemony methods, 37–38
politics of global toxicity, 31, 78, 86, 88, 91
Pope, Carl, 143
poppy cultivation, 38, 43, 64–65, 168n2
the postcolonial picaresque
extractive capitalism, 1–2
pícaro figures, 4
predecessors, 1, 165n3
rogues, 5, 20–21, 90
postcolonial picturesque, 81, 83–85
the postcolony, 19–20
Poussin, Nicholas, 31, 79, *80,* 93
poverty criminalization, 9, 14
Povinelli, Elizabeth, 86, 97–99, 136, 168n8
Prakash, Gyan, 26, 63, 65–66, 68
Prashad, Vijay, 92
Price, Uvedale, 83

Quevedo, Francisco de, 6

Rao, P. V. Narasinha, 150
Rediker, Marcus, 12, 17
Reno, Josh, 128, 130
Richards, John, 168n2
Richards, John F., 61–62, 64
River of Smoke (Ghosh)
botanical imperialism, 67–69

colonial dispossession, 9
colonial knowledge systems, 69–70
colonial peasants and commodity crops, 42–43
demand for change, 76
dictionaries, 70
gardens, 68–69
language, 58
medica materia, 67, 69–70
onto-epistemological violence, 30
painters, 67–69, 170n21
setting, 46
rivers, 57–58
Robbins, Bruce, 10
rogue literature, 11, 16, 25
See also the picaresque
rogues
overview, 6
aesthetic roots, 6–7, 11
alterity, 10, 21
versus bourgeois mythology, 15–16
as bourgeois subjects, 15
as commoners, 12
conditions enabling the emergence of, 11–14, 166n19
cony-catching pamphlets, 6, 11, 13–14, 16, 135, 166n17
criminalization, 14
discursive function, 15
English novels, 14
half-outsiders, 6–7, 21, 96
versus liberal heroes, 101
versus *pícaro* figures, 8
postcolonial, 5, 20–21, 90
Shakespearean, 17
transversality, 10–11
types of, 16
See also pícaro figures
Rousseau, Jean-Jacques, 59, 92–93
Roy, Arundhati
bauxite industry critiques, 122
corporate capitalism, 89
The Cost of Living, 119
false encounters, 14
Indigenous rights, 142
Walking with the Comrades, 3

Royal Opium Commission, 38, 44, 168n2
RS. See River of Smoke (Ghosh)
Rukeyser, Muriel, 96
Rumore, Micheal, 45
Rushdie, Salman, 4, 18, 27–28, 105, 167n30

sacrificial zones, 21, 26, 87, 125
Sardar Sarovar dam, 115, 172n10
Sardi, Sebastian, 121
Saro-Wiwa, Ken, 2–3, 141
Sassen, Saskia, 1
Scheer, Herman, 148–49, 158–60
the sea chronotopes, 57–59
The Sea is History (Walcott), 57
Sea of Poppies (Ghosh)
  overview, 43–44
  Bildung parodies, 73
  bodies, 49–51
  cheap nature, 58
  chronotopes, 56, 58
  displacement, 26, 46, 52–53, 55, 165n10
  East India Company, 64
  improvement, 4
  indentured labor, 73–75
  Indian Ocean, 55
  land enclosure, 55
  language, 56
  lascars, 71–73
  masquerade tropes, 48–49
  mutinies, 73
  opium production and trade, 50, 62, 63, 66
  perspective, 49
  pícaro/rogue figures, 45–46, 58, 70
  poppy farmers, 64–65
  as rogue tale, 46, 51
  sailing ships and movement, 48–49
  setting, 46–47
  structure, 71
  trade networks, 55
SELCO, 160
Sethi, Manpreet, 27
Shiva, Vandana, 3–4, 9, 63, 122

Sierra Club, 143–44
Singh, Manmohan, 5, 95, 112, 121, 149
Sinha, Indra. *See Animal's People*
Sioux Community, 140–41
Slaughter, Joseph, 90, 115–16
slow violence, 18–19, 45, 112–13, 137
  See also Union Carbide
Slumdog Millionaire (film), 115–16
slums
  contributing factors, 27
  liberal voyeurism, 126, 131
  solar industry producing, 148
  The White Tiger (Adiga), 5, 24, 124, 130–33, 138
Smith, Adam, 11, 39, 44, 63–64
social contracts, 59–60, 92–93
Soja, Edward, 95–96
The Solar Grid (Ganzeer), 160–62
Solar India, 149–50
solarity, 149, 159
solar lamps, 154
solar power, 150–55, 158–60
solar power industry, Indian, 140, 144–48, 155–60, 163
soldiers, 75–76
Solnit, Rebecca, 173n1
SP. See Sea of Poppies (Ghosh)
special economic zones (SEZ), 145–46
speculative analytical methodology, 136–37, 173n19
Spivak, Gayatri Chakravorty, 10, 22, 167n25
steam engines, 151
Stoler, Ann Laura, 21
Streeby, Shelley, 140, 163
the subaltern, 10–11
the subjunctive, 163
the sublime, 83
suicide economies, 4, 122
Summers, Larry, 61, 88, 91–92
sustainability and resource imperialism, 144–45
Swachh Bharat, 5, 26
Szeman, Imre, 34, 108, 122, 136, 157

Tagore, Rabindranath, 119
Tata Steel, 3, 120, 140, 144–45
The Tempest (Shakespeare), 17
terraqueous ontology of space, 54
Texaco (Chamoiseau), 171n12
Thermocene, 108, 138
third man figures, 17, 19
Thompson, E. P., 166n20
Torabully, Khal, 74–75
toxic bodies, 77–78, 171n11
transcorporeality, 32, 96–97, 167n32
transversality, 10–11
Trocki, Carl, 44, 61–62, 109
Tsing, Anna, 9, 130, 172n17
Turner, Frederick Jackson, 173n10

Union Carbide
　development campaign, 79–80, 82
　pesticide factory disaster, 78–79, 81, 88
　protests, 102
　tunnel collapse, 96–97, 99
　See also Animal's People (Sinha)
Unquiet Woods (Guha), 34
Untouchable (Anand), 33, 113, 119
urban-rural relationships, 9

vagabonds, 13
Vardy, Alan, 79
Vedanta Resources, 3, 19, 34, 122, 129, 142–43, 173n9
Velázquez, Diego, 13
Vergès, François, 42
vibrant materiality, 41
Village Minstrel (Clare), 64
Volcan, 141
voyeurism, 126

Walcott, Derek, 57
Walking with the Comrades (Roy), 3
Wallerstein, Immanuel, 15, 21–22
Wark, Mackenzie, 138
waste
　colonialism, 125
　laborers as, 116
　management, 125–26
　nonhuman, 129–35
　and the outside, 126
　peasant land, 146
　taxonomies, 128–29
　The White Tiger (Adiga), 32–33, 112, 116, 124, 137
Waste Land (documentary), 126
wastelanding, 33, 116, 167n33
waterside chronotopes, 47
Weheliye, Alexander, 10, 31
Wenzel, Jennifer, 137
Whitehead, Alfred North, 97
The White Tiger (Adiga)
　overview, 118
　as carbon fiction, 33–34, 114, 117, 120, 123–24, 136–37
　as carbon picaresque, 106, 108–9, 118, 138
　coal, 120, 123–24, 137
　energy source logics, 115
　imperial liberalism, 138
　infrastructural imaginary critiques, 131
　the inhuman, 117, 127–29
　labor, 116–17, 126–28
　laboring bodies, 126
　labor invisibility, 117
　literary criticism of, 120–21
　new India critiques, 112, 121, 135
　petrol, 120, 124, 137
　picaresque tropes, 118, 133–35
　pícaro/rogue figures, 10, 113, 118, 134
　political critiques, 114, 118
　sites of extraction and production, 20
　versus *Slumdog Millionaire*, 115–16
　slums, 5, 24, 124, 130–33, 138
　urban environments, 27, 132–33
　waste, 32–33, 112, 116, 124, 137
　zamindars, 110
Whyte, Kyle Powys, 144, 159
Williams, Raymond, 9, 23, 79, 95, 104

Wilson, Sheena, 158
Woodbridge, Linda, 14
Wordsworth, William, 13, 83–84, 160n4
world literature, 24–25
world-making, 140, 148, 163
WT. See The White Tiger (Adiga)
Wynter, Silvia, 10, 31, 41, 77, 98, 172n16

Yaeger, Patricia, 122
Yellowstone National Park, 143–44
Yusoff, Kathryn, 98–99, 128–30

zamindari system, 26, 63–66, 110, 167n29, 171n3
zones of exception, 21–22
zones of exclusion, 116–18
zones of extraction, 21, 116

www.ingramcontent.com/pod-product-compliance
Lightning Source LLC
Chambersburg PA
CBHW070804230426
43665CB00017B/2478